declassified

declassified

A Low-Key Guide to
the High-Strung World
of Classical Music

ARIANNA WARSAW-FAN RAUCH

G. P. PUTNAM'S SONS
NEW YORK

PUTNAM
— EST. 1838 —

G. P. Putnam's Sons
Publishers Since 1838
an imprint of Penguin Random House LLC
penguinrandomhouse.com

Library of Congress Cataloging-in-Publication Data
Names: Warsaw-Fan Rauch, Arianna, author.
Title: Declassified: a low-key guide to the high-strung world of classical music / Arianna Warsaw-Fan Rauch.
Description: New York: G. P. Putnam's Sons, 2022. |
Includes bibliographical references and index.
Identifiers: LCCN 2022019089 (print) | LCCN 2022019090 (ebook) |
ISBN 9780593331460 (hardcover) | ISBN 9780593331477 (ebook)
Subjects: LCSH: Music appreciation. | Music—Humor. | Warsaw-Fan Rauch, Arianna.
Classification: LCC MT90 .R27 2022 (print) | LCC MT90 (ebook) |
DDC 781.1/7—dc23/eng/20220418
LC record available at https://lccn.loc.gov/2022019089
LC ebook record available at https://lccn.loc.gov/2022019090

Printed in the United States of America
1st Printing

BOOK DESIGN BY KRISTIN DEL ROSARIO

TO MY FAMILY:

My parents,
who gave me everything,
who taught me most of what I know,
and who still let me roast them in these pages.

My sister,
who's given and taught me just as much—
and who always believes in me so loudly I have to listen.

My husband,
who can't sing to save his life
but who's nevertheless the most beautiful song in mine.

My kids,
who inspired this book and sometimes even let me write it.

CONTENTS

introduction

There's a story my parents like to tell—about how I became a violinist. It starts off with me, when I was two and a half, losing my voice because I wouldn't stop singing the Queen of the Night's bombshell second aria in Mozart's *The Magic Flute*.[1]

Who could have guessed that the notoriously strenuous number—which vaults and arpeggiates and somersaults around and above the standard limits of the soprano range in a breathtaking display of power, technique, and virtuosity—would prove unhealthy for the vocal cords of a two-year-old?

My parents took me to the doctor, who diagnosed me with nodules. He also said, famously, "You've *got* to find a way to shut that kid up." So my parents brought me home, sat me down, and asked if I wanted to play the piano. They knew I loved music—and they had two pianos already, for my dad.

---

1 The original title is *Die Zauberflöte*. (Which is just "the magic flute" in German.)

But I said no. I wanted to play the violin.

The rest of the story is just a sigh, which somehow manages to say *she was always such a pain in the ass* while also encapsulating and claiming credit for the whole of my training and career: my two degrees from Juilliard, my competition wins and concert tours, my album, the time I mangled the concertmaster solo in John Adams's *The Death of Klinghoffer* while Adams himself was conducting. All of it, according to this sigh, was foretold the minute my parents trusted their collective gut and caved to the demands of their imperious toddler.

All of it, that is, until I quit the violin and walked away from music just a few years into my professional career. No one saw *that* coming. Except possibly Carol, my high school counselor.

Anyway, it's a tidy little ball of yarn, isn't it? It has all the things you look for in a story: adversity, kismet, stubborn toddlers, throat nodules.

But it's also bullshit.

First off, it makes some pretty questionable leaps. For instance, it takes great liberties with the definition of the word "singing." And it hinges on the flawed premise that, when I said I wanted to play the violin, I actually knew what I was talking about. Plus, the whole point of the story—the thing that lends it significance—is that *this* was when I decided to become a violinist.

It wasn't, though. It was when I started taking *lessons*. But I took ballet lessons, too—and ski lessons, and tennis lessons, and golf lessons. And if you'd asked me, at the age of two, what I actually wanted *to be* when I grew up, I would have said "the next Picabo Street" on Tuesday, and "the prima ballerina of American Ballet Theatre" on Wednesday, and "James Bond" all the other days of the week.

So when *did* I pledge my heart, my soul, and all of my waking hours to classical music? I was seven. And it was because of a boy. But we'll get to that later.

What Is "Classical Music," Anyway?

When I was a kid, there was no classical music. There was just *music*—Bach, Mozart, Brahms, Beethoven. And it was everywhere in our house, at all times of the day and often at night because my mom never wanted our dogs to feel lonely.

My dad was a concert pianist who eventually began teaching at Phillips Academy, a boarding school in Andover, Massachusetts. When he wasn't giving piano lessons, teaching music theory courses, practicing on his Steinway (or his Bechstein), or, later, coaching me and my sister, a cellist, through our practice sessions, he could be found in front of his old Quad electrostatic speakers, buried in a score.

My parents acquired a rescue dog toward the end of my high school career: Hogan was his name. He was quite literally starving when he came to us—and his fear of going hungry never left him. The way Hogan was about eating—the way he'd devour three bowls of chicken and oatmeal and dog food and then snatch a whole wheel of brie from the kitchen counter—and then scavenge through the laundry bin and scarf up nine socks—never any pairs—was the way my dad used to be about music. (He still loves it, by the way. It's just that he plays a lot of golf these days, too.)

My mom, an English teacher, was our family's token nonmusician. She did play the French horn in school, though—and she's always loved Bach and Brahms and the other Austro-German greats. For years she also threatened to haunt the rest of us unless we agreed to perform Tchaikovsky's Piano Trio at her funeral.[2] (Now she just wants us to smuggle her ashes onto this one South Pacific military reserve so that we can scatter her, at sunset, into her favorite bit of ocean.)

She and my dad used to teach a course called Words and Music at Andover. Together they would analyze operas and teach musical texts like Joyce's "The Dead." They'd explicate compositions inspired by works of literature—like Mendelssohn's *A Midsummer Night's Dream* and Prokofiev's *Romeo and Juliet*. They'd also embarrass their teenage daughters by likening musical climaxes to orgasms and insisting that John Dowland's "Come Again" was explicitly sexual both in text and in compositional form. (They were right, though. It is.)

I was surrounded by this music from the very beginning—and some of you, I know, are already concluding that that's why I love it. You're thinking to yourselves that classical music is an acquired taste. Like caviar. But you're wrong.

First off, caviar is disgusting.

I've been trying to force my palate to tolerate it for well over a decade—because I've always seen myself, in my mind's eye, as the kind of suave, sophisticated person who eats the stuff. But there's no getting around the fact that it's revolting. It tastes like fishy snot blisters that explode onto your tongue when you bite into them. Classical music doesn't.

Second, classical music isn't an *actual* genre. I'm still going to call it that sometimes, in this book—but it's really just a collection of

---

2 Tchaikovsky's Piano Trio in A minor, Op. 50, is one of the longer, more challenging pieces in the trio repertoire, which is largely why my mom picked it. That and the fact that its gorgeously tragic sonorities often lead to melodramatic sobbing, even in the least emotional of settings.

music from another time. Lots of times, as we'll cover in chapter 1. Yes, it's still old, but so what? Old things can be amazing. Do you like cake? Are you telling me that if a royal chef from the court of Versailles traveled through time to offer you one of his cakes, you'd turn your back on it because Hostess also makes Ho Hos? Why not just eat the Versailles cake *and* the Ho Hos? That's what I'd do. And what I did, metaphorically speaking.

Operas and symphonies may have been my family's bread and butter, but we listened to all kinds of music. Pop music for cleaning; Ella Fitzgerald and Louis Armstrong for celebrating; and those bleak, muted, unforgivably depressing folk songs my mom used to force on us in order to contextualize human suffering (or possibly just give us a taste of it). And the only thing that separated these various sounds—at the beginning, at least—was whether or not I liked them. Bach? Absolutely. Bon Jovi? Yes, please. Simon and Garfunkel? *Hell* no. The point is: when I lost my voice singing that Queen of the Night aria, I had no notion that the music I was listening to was *niche* music.

And, indeed, it wasn't. In the Western world, "classical music" was the *only* music that was written for fifteen centuries, and during those centuries it fulfilled every societal need from dirge to dance music to concert piece.[3] The "classical" bit is a construct.

This is important to understand, because what it means is that this music was composed for *people*—not aficionados. There was no secret or special education that was required back in Mozart's time in order to enjoy it. You are every bit as qualified as the people who were sitting front and center at the premiere of Beethoven's Fifth.

---

3 Folk music was also a thing, but it came through the oral tradition. Which some people like to distinguish from the written tradition by throwing around the term "art music." I am not one of these people.

But you've been told, by society's subtle and not-so-subtle cues, that classical music is stuffy and boring and intellectual—and Not for You. Well, I'm here to tell you that nothing could be further from the truth.

Do you remember the Little Bear books, when Little Bear goes to Mother Bear and says, "I'm cold—I want something to put on"—so Mother Bear makes him a hat and he's happy for two seconds and then he comes back and says, again, "I'm cold—I want something to put on"—so Mother Bear makes him a coat and he's happy again, but then he comes back and says—*again*—"I'm cold—I want something to put on"—and so Mother Bear makes him some boots . . . until eventually Little Bear realizes that his *own* fur coat—the one he's had all along—is warmer than any hat or coat or boots he could wear; that he is, in fact, enough, just as he is? My goal for this book is to equip you with all the things you *don't* need in order to enjoy this music so that you can step out into the world of listening fully confident in the knowledge that you, in your own pelt, are enough.

Because you are. Really.

The problem, if there is a problem, is that you're too much. Too stimulated. Too busy. Too educated in society's perceptions of the classical industry.

This book will help to get you away from all that. Think of it as a couples retreat, but where your partner is a misunderstood amorphous collection of music instead of a misunderstood amorphous collection of needs and insecurities—and where your therapist rambles on in a continuous, opinionated monologue without ever pausing to listen to how you feel about anything. Sound good? I'm glad.

Together we'll cover:

· The seven major periods of the classical not-genre—and how to find the ones you like

- Common stereotypes of the industry—from type-A violinists to the rowdy, bald, brass-playing fraternity brothers of the orchestra

- When to clap (and when not to) during a live performance

- How to decipher the obnoxiously complicated and sterile titles you will encounter

Plus: the top classical music needle drops in movies (from *Raging Bull* to *The Shawshank Redemption* to *The Silence of the Lambs*), the craziest superstitions in the classical canon (like Beethoven's haunted hair and the famous Curse of the Ninth Symphony), and the must-listen short lists—because we're talking about a thousand years' worth of music and not all of it was created equal.

I'll also offer a bit of context (it's helpful to understand the trends and pop culture references that surround any composition, whether it was written last year or four centuries ago); lots of titillating anecdotes; a backstage tour of the industry; and a whole bunch of random tangents that will make you say "Huh?"

Basically, you'll leave these pages with enough expertise to join the ranks of those insufferable connoisseurs who've been scaring you away from this music for all these years—only, you won't join their ranks, because you'll know better.

A true gentleman, as my dad likes to say, is someone who *can* play the accordion, but doesn't.

But What If I Just Don't Care About Classical Music?

So maybe it wasn't the insufferable connoisseurs who were scaring you off. Maybe your life is just full. Or you're still honeymooning with all the amazing streaming services at your disposal. But here are three reasons to carve out some time for classical music:

REASON NO. 1: IT MATTERS

Everyone knows it's a critical time for civil rights, democracy, and public health. These things matter. But so does Art. Not only does it remind us of our ability, as people, to create beauty in spite of life's chaos and strife, it pushes us to look beyond our basic needs and instincts, many of which *cause*, through the fear they engender, the conflicts of our modern society. It also offers a ground for connectivity—a kind of meeting place—that's set apart from these conflicts.

Just as critically, Art can be its own form of protest, empowering the voiceless and enabling change. The classical repertoire contains pieces that were composed to inspire camaraderie, to rebel against injustices, and to champion the downtrodden. Of course, many of the great classical works have also been used to support and glorify existing power structures—to elevate one group above the rest. Think of what's happening now: the entire repertoire is seen as a collection of anthems for (white) privilege, exemption, and entitlement.

I'd like to see these pieces used, instead, as anthems of unification. I'd like to tear down the walls of elitism and privilege that have kept the industry so isolated and misunderstood and whitewashed. Because this music deserves it. Because *you* deserve it. And because nothing—not respect, not the protection of the law, not education, not music—should be reserved for one small group that sets itself above the rest.

REASON NO. 2: THE INSIDE JOKES

In *The Spy Who Loved Me*, the villain Karl Stromberg indecorously drops his female assistant into a shark tank. He executes the feat from the comfort of his gilded dining room, where he observes her fluid struggle through a blue-tinged window as the strains of Bach's third orchestral suite echo over the sound system. The woman's graceful kicks are no match for the shark's aggressive poking at her crotch (in the seventies, sharks could still get away with that kind of thing) and soon she is left dead and dressless, as we always knew she would be, floating tragically in her underwear. The window into the aquarium is replaced by Botticelli's *The Birth of Venus*—a must for any neoclassical subaqueous residence—and the scene is over.

What's funny about all this, beyond the obvious hilarity of a person being eaten by a shark, is that the second movement of Bach's third orchestral suite, which continues serenely throughout the scene, is known popularly as "Air on the G-string."[4]

REASON NO. 3: IT'S BEAUTIFUL MUSIC

A few years before I gave up the violin, I was in Montréal, attending a concert at the Place des Arts. By this time, I'd come a long way from blowing out my vocal cords with Mozart arias—in good ways and bad. I'd graduated from Juilliard, I was performing in prestigious halls and concert series, I lived in a beautiful apartment, and I had a rock of an engagement ring that blinded my audiences whenever I played.

But despite this glossy facade, all was not well. The ring felt less like a meaningful symbol of love than a to-do notification that had been flashing at me for over three years; the apartment felt like a pretty place I just happened to be house-sitting; the concerts I was getting were good enough to validate and fuel my ambition but not

---

4 A "g-string," for those of you who don't know, can be either the lowest string on a violin or a less comfortable version of a thong.

good enough, yet, to satiate it—which made it difficult for me to enjoy performances given by other people. Particularly by other violinists. *Particularly* by other violinists who were my infuriatingly-more-successful-than-me then-fiancé (to be henceforth known, in this book, as Golden Violin Boy—or GVB).

I was in the audience because I had to be, and I was miserable about it. The speeches—which always have to be given twice in Montréal, once in French and then again in English—weren't helping.[5]

Instead of listening to them, I was wallowing in my thoughts, which were increasingly bitter and unflattering. *Why wasn't I on that stage? Hadn't I also won Juilliard's concerto competition? Hadn't I also served as concertmaster of the Juilliard Orchestra and performed on the school's coveted Stradivarius and Guarneri del Gesù violins? Why was everyone so obsessed with GVB?*

"Blah, blah, the importance of the arts," the speaker on the stage was saying. "Blah, blah, transcending biology . . . Blah, blah, the generous support of Mr. and Mrs. Blah."

When the man finally left the podium, he was replaced by another speaker: a tall woman with the style and carriage of a Francophone but the smile of an Anglophone. She was representing the bank that was sponsoring that night's concert. She knew nothing about classical music, she said, and rarely listened to it. But she had a story she wanted to share.

She'd been in the car with her five-year-old daughter when it had occurred to her to turn the radio to a classical station. They never listened to classical music, so she was curious to see how her daughter would react.

---

5 Half the population pretends not to understand English—or is too offended by it to derive any meaning from its sounds—and the other half is the same way about French.

"Do you know what kind of music this is?" she asked after a few minutes.

Her daughter nodded.

"You do?" The woman was surprised. "What kind of music is it, then?"

"It's beautiful music," her daughter said.

That story chastened me. It forced me to confront the fact that something in my life was terribly wrong. Something apart from the fact that I seemed unable to feel happy for the man I supposedly loved. I'd forgotten what this music had sounded like to me as a kid—back when it wasn't "classical" music, but simply a part (my *favorite* part) of the rich tapestry of sounds that had defined my childhood. I'd forgotten that it wasn't only a way to succeed—a thing I was good at. It was a thing that I loved.

And That's Why I Wrote This Book

That's the one key truth that's buried at the heart of my parents' "why I'm a violinist" story. (A truth that's wrapped in lies that are wrapped in truths, making it a kind of turducken where the duck layer is actually tempeh.) I love this music. I loved it when I was blowing out my vocal cords at the age of two and I loved it that night in Montréal, at the age of twenty-four. Even if I needed a slap in the face from a five-year-old girl to remind me of it.

And *after* that slap in the face, it occurred to me that I was in the same boat as a lot of other people. Just as I'd allowed my professional frustrations to tarnish and define *my* relationship with this music, plenty of would-be listeners were letting the genre's unappealing stigmas and cultural baggage define *their* relationship with this music. We were both letting our toxic associations with the industry ruin this font of sublimity and eloquence and beauty—of soul-bursting sounds that encapsulate our shared human experience. And that struck me as both tragic and stupid.

It was my desire to avoid this tragic stupidity that led me, ultimately, to write this book.

I wanted everyone to hear this music the way that little French Canadian girl heard it. The way *I* heard it once—and the way I hear it now, again. In other words, I want people to hear this music for what it *is*: beautiful music.

declassified

Chapter 1

classical music isn't a thing

A Very Biased Overview of 1,400 Years of Music

When I was a toddler, I risked all kinds of hearing loss so that I could lie under my father's piano, listening to him play Bach's Goldberg Variations. This was before I'd seen *The Silence of the Lambs*.

It was also before I discovered the Queen of the Night, before I developed those throat nodules, and before I started violin lessons. It was back when I was a bit like that little girl from Montréal—when Bach was just "beautiful music," and my ears were little more than enthusiastic sponges.

Bach was my favorite composer for much of my childhood. His pieces were filled with mysterious puzzles and dark, echoing caverns and those dazzling blades of sunlight that pierce through the clouds on gray days. All things that fascinated me.

There was also something about his music—its puzzle-like quality, perhaps—that challenged me to create my own. So one day, a few years into my musical studies (when I was five or six), I sat down with a pad of manuscript paper and one of those tiny golf pencils that are always lying around my parents' house, determined to compose the world's greatest piece for violin. I scratched away for what felt like hours—experimenting with different combinations of notes, tearing off pages and dramatically crumpling them up, crossing things out and rewriting until I reached perfection. When I'd crafted a whole phrase, I brought it to my dad. Some of my note-heads were on backward, I knew, but the music, I was sure, was incredible.

And I was right. It was incredible. It just wasn't original. It was the first two measures of Bach's G-Minor Violin Sonata.

Vivaldi was another one of my favorites at that age. I didn't love *everything* of his—I didn't care for "Spring" or "Summer" or anything you'd hear in a commercial for cat food—but his double cello concerto, his aria "Vedrò con mio diletto," and his "Winter" all shared a clarity of sound, a rhythmic drive, and a sometimes-dark intensity that drew me to them. I loved Vitali, too. And Corelli.

Baroque music—we'll get to what that is in a bit—was my jam.

Do you know what wasn't my jam? Medieval music. I hated Medieval music.

The thing is, though, that for years I didn't *know* I hated it. Or rather: I didn't know Medieval music was a thing that existed. All I knew was that once every so often, a sparse, skeletal-sounding piece—the musical equivalent of *SNL*'s Debbie Downer—would issue from those Quad speakers and suddenly the sky would turn black and all the plants in our house would wilt and all the joy in my tiny child-heart would instantly shrivel up. Then the piece would end and everything would go back to normal.

I'd never heard of Baroque music, either. I knew that I loved Bach and Vivaldi and Vitali and Corelli, but I didn't understand that there was a link between these composers—that they all belonged to the same group. It wasn't until later, when I was eightish, and my mom put up a poster in our bathroom outlining the six different periods of classical music[1]—that I made the connection. That bathroom was where everything started to come together in my mind—where I realized that nearly all of the music I hated came from one single era. And when I realized this, I was *pissed* no one had told me sooner—because with that one word—"Medieval"—I could have spared myself hours of torment.

Which is why we're covering compositional periods here, in chapter 1.

Classical Music Isn't a Thing

My kid was a much cuter toddler than I was. He had to be—because feeding him was a pain in the ass. He wouldn't eat anything that was green. It didn't matter whether it was an avocado or a slice of kiwi or the last of the pistachio macarons that Dadda brought home for Valentine's Day. If it was tinted or flecked with anything from celadon to emerald, he fed it to the trash can monster before anyone could get it within smelling distance of his face.

To him, the logic was clear: he'd tried a green food once before and hadn't liked it—so it stood to reason that he'd find all other green foods equally objectionable.

Most people approach classical music in a similar way. They've heard snippets of it in movies and commercials and elevators—snippets, mind you, that are often chosen to support whatever stereotype said movie, commercial, or elevator is trying to promote—and they think they know how they feel about the entire body of work. But just as kale tastes nothing like Granny Smith apples, which taste

---

1 It was six back then, but now it's seven. The compositional period I was born into expired with the dawn of the twenty-first century.

nothing like pistachio macarons, Mozart sounds nothing like Shostakovich, which sounds nothing like Wagner. (Who, by the way, was a giant asshole.)[2]

Classical music, as most people think of it, isn't a real thing. As I said in the intro, it's really just centuries of (all sorts of) music shoved into one hodgepodge of a genre. It encompasses hundreds of contrasting musical styles. Sometimes I say things like "classical music is beautiful" or "I love classical music" (turn back, like, three pages), but I find plenty of "classical" pieces truly unbearable. For instance: everything that came out of the Medieval period.

People seem to expect this kind of picking and choosing when it comes to other genres. You can like Beyoncé without liking Justin Bieber. And most people, I believe, like the Beatles without liking Nickelback. But ironically, the differences between Beyoncé and Bieber or the Beatles and Nickelback are far less drastic than the harmonic and rhythmic differences between Monteverdi and late Schoenberg or Debussy and Bach. (And I'm not even mentioning— yet—the differences between quartets and operas or piano sonatas and symphonies—*or* the differences created by the musicians who actually perform these works.)

The point is: you don't have to like *all* classical music in order to be allowed to listen to some of it.

My dream for you, insofar as this book is concerned, is not for you to be able to say, at the end of it, "I like classical music"—but for you to be able to say, rather, "I like *Beethoven*." Or "I like Rach- maninoff." Or "I appreciate the impeccable proportions and lyricism of Haydn and Mozart, but I prefer these attributes in the edgier,

---

2 But this is a topic for another book. One that I will write someday when I'm ready to feel angry for a whole year.

quirkier, more harmonically dissonant context of, say, Prokofiev during his neoclassical phase."

Only, please don't actually say that unless you're speaking to someone who already hates you.

Compositional Periods

There are, in fact, two "classical musics."

I know. First I said there *was* no classical music and now I'm saying there are two. Just bear with me for a minute.

At first, there really was no classical music. But then, *people*— people who are dead, so we can't yell at them—came in and started labeling things.

Classical Music the Genre,[3] in its broadest definition, encompasses most of the Western music composed between AD 500 and 1900-ish, as well as all of that music composed after 1900-ish that stems from the same tradition (i.e., not pop, not jazz, not folk). Most people, though, when they speak of "classical music," mean Western music composed between 1600 and 1900, plus the music of a handful of composers after that stretch.

Then there's the Classical *period*, which lies *within* the frame of the larger genre, spanning from approximately 1730 to 1820.[4] Both the Classical period and the classical genre are labels invented by later generations (the composers of this period, like Mozart and Haydn, for example, didn't think of themselves as "classical"

---

3 As I said, there is no real genre here, but I'm going to stick with this word because that's how most people think of it.

4 People argue about the exact dates—1750–1830 is another popular window—but it's all approximate, so I've chosen to agree with Wikipedia.

composers)—but the Classical period is the more useful label, for reasons I will explain below.

Composers, like pop artists and bands, have their own unique sounds. These can even shift—and often do—over the course of a composer's life. But there are also larger, universal musical styles and aesthetic trends that flourish during each era—and in the classical world we mark these trends, as they apply to *music*, with compositional periods.

The trends of these eras aren't isolated. They're a reflection and a part of society's broader mood swings—like fashion, speech, artistic movements, and so on. One of my early violin teachers, a strict but likable Polish woman whose only weakness was for red wine, used to have me study the contemporary art and architecture of whichever compositions she assigned me. It was a welcome break from the usual drill work she demanded—and a great excuse to stare at period clothes and naked bodies.[5] But it was also fascinating to see how Bach's compositions echoed the formality of his seventeenth-century surroundings; how Mozart's works reflected the balance, proportion, and relative restraint seen in the architecture and artwork of the late 1700s; and how, over the course of the next two centuries, composers and artists moved herdlike toward expressivity and romanticism and then on to the abstract and nontraditional.

While there are still significant differences between the styles of individual composers within each time frame, the broader trends serve as helpful guidelines for anyone looking to determine or expand upon their listening preferences. If you like Mozart's general sound, you may also like the sounds of Haydn and Beethoven

---

5 I was eleven, an age when curiosity outstripped access.

(during the latter's early and middle periods in particular)—or if you like Bach, the logical next step for you would be to sample Handel and Vivaldi—and so on and so forth. It's possible that these stylistic preferences even carry across artistic mediums: that those who appreciate the pensiveness and majesty of Caspar David Friedrich's landscapes might gravitate toward Brahms, while fans of Monet might enjoy the glimmering scintillation of Debussy. Either way, a basic overview of these periods and stylistic movements is key to navigating the genre.

The seven basic periods that constitute the classical genre are: Medieval, Renaissance, Baroque,* Classical,* Romantic,* 20th-Century, and Contemporary.

The three periods I've starred (Baroque, Classical, and Romantic) make up what is known as the "Common Practice Period." This contains most of the household names of the repertoire—your Tchaikovskys, your Mozarts, your Beethovens, and what have you. But in fact, the word "common" here has nothing to do with popularity or renown. The "common" in "Common Practice Period" refers to the standardized (shared) *practices* adhered to by the composers of these eras—and more specifically, to the sound that we define as *tonal*.

The periods after the Common Practice Period (20th-Century and Contemporary) are of equal importance to the repertoire and include many names you're likely to recognize—like Stravinsky, Prokofiev, and Hans Zimmer. The Medieval and Renaissance periods, on the other hand, while crucial in laying the groundwork for the music that followed, are generally considered fringe territory.

As for what all these periods *sound like* . . .

The best way to find out is to listen to them, preferably with a scotch. As much as I'd like to spare you the agony that is Medieval music, I don't want you to take my word for it that it's awful. Some of you may well love it—and it's your reaction that's important.[6]

So here are some listening lists—one per compositional period—along with some quick facts and biased descriptions. Please keep in mind that: (*a*) all of the pieces listed below contain a wide range of characters and sounds, so what you hear at the beginning won't necessarily resemble what you'll be hearing half a minute or several minutes into the music, and (*b*) these lists, along with the others you'll find in this book, were my equivalent of *Sophie's Choice*. If you don't make use of them, my sacrifices will have been for nothing.

THE MEDIEVAL PERIOD

TIME FRAME: AD 500–1400 (liberally) or 1150–1400 (popularly, if "popular" is a word that can be applied here)

NOTABLE COMPOSERS: Hildegard von Bingen (1098–1179), Léonin (1150-ish–1200-ish), Pérotin (1155-ish–1205-ish), Guillaume de Machaut (1300–1377)

> * Hildegard von Bingen was a woman. Enjoy the gender diversity; you won't get another taste of it for a while.

WHAT IT SOUNDS LIKE: Misery. Despair. Oppression. The Medieval period, as you've probably learned from history classes and/or computer games involving armored trolls and buxom elves, was a dark time. Its music was dark, too. This may be because it reflects the darkness of the environment from which it stemmed, but I would not be at all surprised to learn that it was, in fact, the *cause* of

---

6 I look forward to our spirited Twitter/Instagram debates.

this darkness. Some of the pieces from this era are actually kind of cool, but the vast majority sound like the musical embodiment of the bubonic plague.

Early music was modal rather than tonal, meaning that it was based on alternative scales that predate our modern concept of harmony. They were a bit like prototypes of the scales we use now: eerie, children's-toy prototypes with wonky, soulless eyes and chillingly proportioned bodies. One of the more popular modes of the time was the Dorian mode: the single most depressing thing mankind has ever invented. I can't explain *why* this particular selection of notes is so upsetting, but if you've ever been in a very cheerful mood and then been confronted with the song "Scarborough Fair" and suddenly found yourself looking for some rope to wrap around a ceiling joist in the barn you don't have, you already know what I'm talking about. That is what the Dorian mode does to people. Which is why I always avoid music from the Medieval period—and Simon and Garfunkel—at all costs.

This period also encompasses Gregorian chant, an early form of liturgical music developed by the Roman Catholic Church. It's kind of like the primordial ooze of classical music. You've probably heard it before—if nowhere else then in that scene in *Monty Python and the Holy Grail* where the monks process by, droning in unison and hitting their faces periodically with planks of wood. Incidentally, this is exactly how I would react if I had to spend my days singing Gregorian chant.

WHAT IT MIGHT SOUND LIKE TO SOMEONE WHO HATES IT LESS THAN I DO: Catacombs. Dark soulfulness. A lone tree stripped of its leaves. The search for reason. Or, perhaps, acceptance of the human condition—of the darkness of winter—of cold and hunger and pain.

WHAT IT SOUNDS LIKE, LITERALLY:

- "Ave Maria, O auctrix vite"—Hildegard von Bingen

- "Nunc aperuit nobis"—Hildegard von Bingen

- "Je vivroie liement"—Guillaume de Machaut (BEWARE THE DORIAN MODE)

- "Beata viscera"—Pérotin

- "Viderunt omnes"—Pérotin[7]

- If you want to listen to Gregorian chant, just look up "Gregorian chant." It literally all sounds the same.

THE RENAISSANCE PERIOD

TIME FRAME: 1400–1600

NOTABLE COMPOSERS: Guillaume Dufay (1397–1474), Josquin de Prez (1450/55–1521), Thomas Tallis (1505–1585), Giovanni Pierluigi da Palestrina (1525–1594), William Byrd (1539/40–1623), John Dowland (1563–1626), Claudio Monteverdi (1567–1643)[8]

WHAT IT SOUNDS LIKE: A field trip to Medieval Times. It's no wonder that Medieval-themed places use Renaissance-inspired music for their shows; no one would come if they used real Medieval

---

7 Okay, so I do kind of like this one.

8 I hate it when composers straddle compositional periods. Monteverdi is a bridge composer, but for my ears, he belongs here.

scores. Or, at least, no one would come *back* because they'd all have killed themselves on the way home.

A lot of Renaissance music evokes court jesters and jig-like dances, neither of which I generally enjoy, but what I do like about this period are its songs and choral works. My hatred of the preceding era makes the celestial-sounding sonorities of Thomas Tallis all the more uplifting; his music sounds, to me, like the first rays of hope after a full millennium of utter wretchedness—like the first green buds emerging from the branches, or pushing up through the frozen earth. I'm not an expert on Western religion, but if I had to make a guess based purely on shifts in the musical landscape, I'd say that at some point between the Medieval and Renaissance eras, religious officials started focusing a *bit* less on Hell and eternal damnation and a bit more on Heaven and salvation. It should be noted, however, that this period still contains plenty of pieces written in the Dorian mode for those of you looking to jump-start your instant and lasting depressions.

Interestingly, many of the songs—and by this I mean compositions for single voice and accompaniment[9]—from this era are much closer to pop songs in terms of structure, length, and harmonic simplicity than the compositions of the next few centuries. This is probably why Sting recorded an album of sixteenth-century songs with lutenist Edin Karamazov back in 2006. Commercially, the album didn't do as well as some of his others, but his performance of John Dowland's "Come Again" (the same song my parents used against me as a weapon of embarrassment in their Words and Music class) did convince me that he deserves his status as a sex icon. So at

---

9   All the other kinds of compositions in the classical genre are called "pieces."

least I don't have to waste time arguing with people about that anymore.

**SOME LESS DEPRESSING SONORITIES TO OVERWRITE THE MEM-
ORY OF THE LAST PERIOD:**

- "Ne irascaris, Domine"—William Byrd

- "Come Again"—John Dowland

- "J'ai mis mon cuer"—Guillaume Dufay (this is the only court-
jester-sounding one I've included)

- "Zefiro torna"—Claudio Monteverdi

- "Missa Papae Marcelli"—Giovanni Pierluigi da Palestrina

- "If Ye Love Me"—Thomas Tallis[10]

THE BAROQUE PERIOD

TIME FRAME: 1600–1750

NOTABLE COMPOSERS: Jean-Baptiste Lully (1632–1687), Arcangelo Corelli (1653–1713), Henry Purcell (1659–1695), Johann Sebastian Bach (1685–1750),[11] George Frideric Handel (1685–1759),
Domenico Scarlatti (1685–1757), Antonio Vivaldi (1678–1741)

---

10 This is my favorite on the list.

11 Whenever people refer to "Bach," they always mean *this* Bach. But because several of his
   kids (he somehow managed to have twenty of them while composing his well-
   over-a-thousand pieces) went on to follow in his musical footsteps, other Bachs like Carl

WHAT IT SOUNDS LIKE: Solemnity. Or genius. Or power. You know when you're wearing a cape because the Archbishop of Canterbury is about to anoint you sovereign of the United Kingdom of Great Britain and Northern Ireland and the other realms and territories that come with it? Or when you're an iconically named cannibalistic mastermind in the midst of chewing off a prison guard's face to an ironically placid score? Like that.

Baroque music has a reputation for being formal (hence its ceremonial uses) and for being cerebral (hence its associations with evil geniuses). Musicians complain about these associations, but there are actually good reasons for them. Much of this music *was* composed explicitly for religious or ceremonial use—in fact, Handel's "Zadok the Priest," which he wrote (along with three other coronation anthems) for the coronation of King George II, has been performed at every British monarch's coronation since. Formal court dances were also a major source of inspiration for many composers. And it's important, too, to consider that this period overlapped with the Age of Enlightenment and the Scientific Revolution. Composers were participants in the larger cultural mindsets of their respective times, so it follows that these works contain a certain amount of intellectual exploration.

By the height of the Baroque period, there were standardized compositional techniques and principles (like counterpoint: the combining of two or more separate, active voices according to a specific set of harmonic rules)—and composers were eager to test and expand upon them. This is another element that can sometimes give this music a mathematical, almost geometric feel. Bach's music,

---

Philipp Emmanuel Bach and Johann Christian Bach pop up from time to time as well. Their music is nice and all, but their dad's is better.

which even features things like hidden codes and fractals, is particularly known for its structural complexity.

What so many of my colleagues object to, I believe (and I object to it, too, for the record), is when Baroque music is *reduced* to its anatomical virtuosity. It's not that it isn't sometimes formal—or that it isn't sometimes like a brainy puzzle. (That was one of the things that drew me to it, remember, when I was a kid.) It's just that "formal" and "cerebral" are not the best or most accurate adjectives to describe this music.

The Baroque period is where those buds of hope and faith that emerged during the Renaissance period blossom into a musical spring. Precision and structural perfection are not the objectives of this music, but rather by-products of a higher aim: to create something magnificent and grand—like a cathedral built of notes instead of stone, in the name of faith or whichever unknowable flicker of transcendence human beings seem to feel and grasp at.

Consider Handel's "Zadok the Priest." The music begins as a gentle rippling—hushed and reverent yet glimmering with anticipation. A single line emerges, too unchanging to be called a melody but compelling nonetheless, through its nobility. It rises unstoppably like the dawn, growing in intensity and resolve until the rippling underneath can no longer be restrained—and the music swells, in one unified surge, into a divine and immaculate pronouncement. The listener cannot help but feel awed and humbled by its power—its sublimity—and has no choice but to submit.

"Zadok the Priest" is still a relevant coronation anthem not because of its history, but because of the impact of Handel's music. It's so effective, in fact, at inspiring this sense of awe and humility in those who hear it that the Union of European Football Associations uses an adaptation of it for its Champions League anthem. UEFA could have chosen from any number of popular songs ("We Are the

Champions," for instance)—or commissioned works in any number of styles—but as they were making their choice in 1992, it was a coronation anthem that Handel had written over two centuries earlier that spoke to them—that *still* speaks to millions of fans (like my FC Bayern Munich–obsessed husband) every year.

GIVE ME GENIUS VILLAINS AND CATHEDRALS MADE OF NOTES:[12]

· Goldberg Variations, BWV 988—Johann Sebastian Bach

· *St. John Passion*, BWV 245—Johann Sebastian Bach

· Violin Sonata No. 1 in G Minor, BWV 1001
—Johann Sebastian Bach

· *The Well-Tempered Clavier*, BWV 846–893
—Johann Sebastian Bach

· Concerto grosso in G Minor, Op. 6, no. 8, "Christmas Concerto"
—Arcangelo Corelli

· *Water Music*, Suite No. 1 in F Major, HWV 348
—George Frideric Handel

· "Zadok the Priest," HWV 258—George Frideric Handel

· Piano Sonata in B Minor, K. 27—Domenico Scarlatti

· Concerto for Two Cellos in G Minor, RV 531—Antonio Vivaldi

· "Vedrò con mio diletto," from the opera *Giustino*—Antonio Vivaldi

---

12 The order here is alphabetical by composer—because we absolutely have to start with Bach—but the later lists will be mainly chronological.

THE CLASSICAL PERIOD

TIME FRAME: 1730–1820

NOTABLE COMPOSERS: Joseph Haydn (1732–1809), Wolfgang Amadeus Mozart (1756–1791), Ludwig van Beethoven (1770–1827)[13]

WHAT IT SOUNDS LIKE: Money. At least, that's what Hollywood and Madison Avenue want you to think. Together with Baroque music, Classical music is often used to denote fussy refinement.

But it's only on the surface that it embodies the things that Hollywood wants it to—that it's inherently restrained by rules and conventions (like counterpoint—though a more lilting and melodic version of it than the kind found in the Baroque period). If you give it a few earnest moments of listening, you'll find that there are layers here— of suppressed ecstasy and pathos, of soulful penetration, of bubbling joy and seething rage. And it's the tension between these disparate sides, between exterior and interior, that lends this music its power.

It can also be pretty slapstick. Modern audiences don't always have the contextual awareness, or feel they have the permission, to recognize musical jokes when they occur, but the audiences of the day were more at ease when it came to this type of music.[14] In *The Marriage of Figaro*, for example, Mozart openly mocks the con-

---

13 There is some debate as to whether Beethoven is a Classical or a Romantic composer. Given that he's Beethoven, he should really just have a category all to himself. But then we'd have to give Mozart one, too—and Bach—and then the others would feel left out. I like him better here, as a late Classical/bridge composer, than in the Romantic period. Also because there are way too many Romantic composers and a man like Beethoven deserves more real estate.

14 This isn't a criticism of today's listeners. Back then people just didn't have other forms of quality entertainment like *Succession* or *Halo: Fireteam Raven*.

temptible Count Almaviva by scoring his arias with comical hiccup-like blips and plodding, exaggeratedly simple melodies. He even hints at the character's sexual ineptitude by giving his phrases early and abruptly thunderous climaxes. In *Don Giovanni*, he simultaneously mocks and lauds himself by quoting one of his other *Marriage of Figaro* arias, scoring it as the background music for Giovanni's supper, which prompts Leporello (Giovanni's cheeky but loyal servant) to complain that he's sick of hearing *Figaro* wherever he goes.

And this is to say nothing of Mozart's scatological works, which we'll get to later.

There were other funny composers, too. At the end of Haydn's Opus 33, no. 2 quartet (entitled "The Joke"), Haydn uses surprise pauses, unnatural breaks, and misleading cadences to trick the audience into clapping too early—and then too late. And in the second movement, he writes in a number of tasteless slides, creating a goopy, drunken effect that flies in the face of the period's aesthetic. Or any kind of aesthetic, really.

The great composers of the era adhered to the period's signature grace and lyricism, but they never left it at that. They always incorporated something funnier—or something more profound.

SHOW ME THE MONEY:[15]

- Piano Concerto No. 21 in C Major, K. 467
  —Wolfgang Amadeus Mozart

- Piano Quartet No. 1 in G Minor, K. 478
  —Wolfgang Amadeus Mozart

---

15 Mozart first—because he's Mozart—then chronological. (Beethoven is my personal favorite, but his music conforms less to the style at hand. Haydn is wonderful, too, but the competition here is ferocious.)

- *Le nozze di Figaro* (*The Marriage of Figaro*)
  —Wolfgang Amadeus Mozart

- Clarinet Quintet in A Major, K. 581
  —Wolfgang Amadeus Mozart

- Cello Concerto No. 1 in C Major, Hob. VIIb:1—Joseph Haydn

- String Quartet in E-flat Major, Op. 33, no. 2, "The Joke"
  —Joseph Haydn

- Piano Concerto No. 3 in C Minor, Op. 37
  —Ludwig van Beethoven[16]

- Symphony No. 3 in E-flat Major, Op. 55, "Eroica"
  —Ludwig van Beethoven

- String Quartet No. 10 in E-flat Major, Op. 74, "Harp"
  —Ludwig van Beethoven

- Piano Trio in B-flat Major, Op. 97, "Archduke"
  —Ludwig van Beethoven

THE ROMANTIC PERIOD

TIME FRAME: 1820–1915

NOTABLE COMPOSERS: Franz Schubert (1797–1828), Felix Mendelssohn (1809–1847), Frédéric Chopin (1810–1849), Robert

---

16 As mentioned, Beethoven is a "bridge" composer—and a unique one at that. His later music (which I'm withholding for now) truly departs from the style of the Classical era, but even these works tilt, in varying degrees, in a Romantic direction.

Schumann (1810–1856), Richard Wagner (1813–1883), Giuseppe Verdi (1813–1901), Clara Schumann (1819–1896), Johannes Brahms (1833–1897), Pyotr Ilyich Tchaikovsky (1840–1893), Antonín Dvořák (1841–1904), Edvard Grieg (1843–1907), Giacomo Puccini (1858–1924), Gustav Mahler (1860–1911), Richard Strauss[17] (1864–1949), Amy Beach (1867–1944), Sergei Rachmaninoff (1873–1943), Samuel Coleridge-Taylor (1875–1912)

WHAT IT SOUNDS LIKE: Feelings. Sometimes the breathtaking and transformative kind that capture exactly what it's like to love or grieve or wonder. And sometimes the hyperdramatic, berserk kind that offer you a terrifying glimpse into what used to go on inside your pathologically jealous ex-boyfriend's head whenever you got a text from anyone with a penis who wasn't your dad.

The Romantic period is an era of *more*. Its pieces are longer, louder, and more intense—with sweeping gestures, a juicier range of harmonies, and generally larger, more diverse ensembles (which create richer, fuller sounds). This period also has more composers of note, many of whom I was forced, most painfully, to exclude from the list above.

Technically, music from this period is called "Romantic music." I have trouble referring to it as such, though, because it makes me sound like I'm in the year 2001, trying to sell a five-hundred-track CD set of the world's most romantic songs on the Home Shopping Network.

Music from this era isn't exactly "romantic" in the candle-lined-hot-tub sense of the word, although if you want to listen to it in the

---

17 This is not the guy who wrote all the waltzes. His name was *Johann* Strauss. The second. (Johann Strauss the first was also a composer. Because otherwise things would have been way too straightforward.)

hot tub, be my guest. This kind of romanticism is more connected to the Sturm und Drang movement—and the ideals of the French Revolution—and whatever it was in the water that made people like Edgar Allan Poe and Lord Byron fall in love with their cousins.

Some of it—particularly in the early period—is still restrained, tempering expressivity and luxuriousness with structural discipline. Some of the later music, however, gives me the feeling that I've been looped into a very long and exhausting public therapy session marked by a series of undeniably profound revelations—but *also* by a good amount of complaining and weeping and airing out of confessions I might have chosen to spare myself, had I been given the choice.

Which is the point, I suppose; this was all part of the gradual loosening (or unraveling, depending on your view) of structure and discipline that took place as the period progressed, when elements like form and proportion became secondary to self-expression.

This period contains—undoubtedly—some of the most accessibly stimulating music the genre has to offer, and the increased emotional fluidity is what tons of people love about it. I just sometimes find it a *bit* annoying that when I throw a two-hour tantrum it's "immature," but when Mahler does it, everyone hails him as an innovative genius simply because he had the foresight to write his out in score form.

LET'S HEAR THIS NOT-ROMANTIC ROMANTIC MUSIC:[18]

· Impromptu in G-flat Major, Op. 90, no. 3 (D. 899, no. 3) —Franz Schubert

· Ballade No. 1 in G Minor, Op. 23—Frédéric Chopin

---

18 The order here is chronological.

- Piano Trio No. 2 in C Minor, Op. 66—Felix Mendelssohn

- Piano Trio in G Minor, Op. 17—Clara Schumann

- Cello Concerto in A Minor, Op. 129—Robert Schumann

- Piano Quintet in F Minor, Op. 34—Johannes Brahms

- Violin Concerto in D Major, Op. 35—Pyotr Ilyich Tchaikovsky

- *Parsifal*—Richard Wagner[19]

- Piano Trio No. 4 in E Minor, Op. 90, B. 166, "Dumky"
  —Antonín Dvořák

- Ballade in A Minor for Orchestra, Op. 33
  —Samuel Coleridge-Taylor

- *Ein Heldenleben*, Op. 40—Richard Strauss

- Piano Concerto in C-sharp Minor, Op. 45—Amy Beach

- Symphony No. 4 in G Major—Gustav Mahler

- Piano Concerto No. 2 in C Minor, Op. 18—Sergei Rachmaninoff

THE 20TH-CENTURY PERIOD

TIME FRAME: Really?

NOTABLE COMPOSERS—EARLIER: Claude Debussy (1862–1918),
Jean Sibelius (1865–1957), Arnold Schoenberg—*early period* (1874–
1951), Charles Ives (1874–1954), Maurice Ravel (1875–1937), Béla

---

19 Who, again, was an asshole.

Bartók (1881–1945), Igor Stravinsky (1882–1971), Anton Webern (1883–1945), Alban Berg (1885–1935), Florence Price (1887–1953), Sergei Prokofiev (1891–1953), Lili Boulanger (1893–1918), Paul Hindemith (1895–1963), Erich Wolfgang Korngold (1897–1957), Dmitri Shostakovich (1906–1975)

NOTABLE COMPOSERS—LATER: Aaron Copland (1900–1990), Olivier Messiaen (1908–1992), Elliott Carter (1908–2012), Samuel Barber (1910–1981), John Cage (1912–1992), Witold Lutosławski (1913–1994), Benjamin Britten (1913–1976), George Walker (1922–2018), György Ligeti (1923–2006), Pierre Boulez (1925–2016), Tōru Takemitsu (1930–1996), Coleridge-Taylor Perkinson (1932–2004)

WHAT IT SOUNDS LIKE: Sometimes it sounds like Romantic music; and sometimes it sounds like someone ran a piece from the Classical era through a weird *Addams Family* filter. Sometimes it sounds jarring and percussive in an engaging, thrilling kind of way; and sometimes it sounds like Aunt Hilda's cat is walking on your piano.

This period has no unified sound or set of aesthetics. It, like the larger classical genre, is the aggregate of many different styles and movements (including serialism, neoclassicism, minimalism, and modernism). What can be said about the era as a whole, though, is that it illustrates a gradual trend away from traditional scales and foot-tapping rhythms, and shows, instead, a mass migration toward new or unorthodox methods of composition.

Twentieth-century music tends to experiment with the abstract and nontraditional: to bring in new techniques and sometimes extramusical elements, to challenge the usual harmonies we expect, and to keep us slightly off-balance through its use of the irregular. It features composers like Samuel Barber and the young Arnold

Schoenberg, whose music is both harmonious and emotive, along-side composers like Pierre Boulez and the *mature* Arnold Schoenberg, who utilized something called the "twelve-tone" technique: a strict method of composition that blurs the lines between music and mathematics and adheres to an entirely different musical aesthetic.

Then there are guys like Stravinsky, Prokofiev, and Hindemith, whose works push against traditional tonalities while also experimenting with compositional motifs and techniques from the Classical and Baroque eras. And there are also composers like Steve Reich, Karlheinz Stockhausen, and John Cage, who often turned out pieces that were as much concept as content. Stockhausen's *Helikopter-Streichquartett* was written for string quartet and four helicopters.[20] And John Cage's *4'33"* consists only of musicians (or anyone, I suppose) walking onto the stage, sitting silently for four minutes and thirty-three seconds, and walking out. The music is the sound of the audience's reaction.

Certain old-school classical music fans avoid music from the twentieth century—just as some fans of Leonardo da Vinci and Renoir avoid the Tate Modern and MoMA—but there are many people who find its diversity, perspective, and intellectual richness more provocative than the products of the earlier periods. Some of my favorite pieces come from this era, as do many of my least favorite pieces.

I should also tell you a bit about Impressionism, which is a

---

20 As it happens, I once performed a highly stylized version of Stockhausen's *Helikopter-Streichquartett* in Juilliard's black box theater. The space does not accommodate four helicopters, but their effect was simulated by clever lighting and enormous fans that kept threatening to blow the music off our stands. The missing element of danger was provided by our eighteenth-century dominatrix costumes, which were highly flammable. The number of wires and octopus plugs surrounding our skirts necessitated an "I'm on fire" protocol and several stripping drills, which never came into play, but served, nevertheless, to give our performances a lively kick.

stylistic movement that began in France in the later part of the nine-teenth century and stretched into the early twentieth. Its placement here is debatable, but its tonal ambiguity makes it an even poorer fit for the Romantic period, which, as you'll remember, makes up one-third of the Common Practice Period—a period that was united by its shared tonality.

Claude Debussy and Maurice Ravel are the big names here, al-though many see Gabriel Fauré as the father of the style. (Ravel even studied with him. Debussy didn't, but he *is* buried in the same cem-etery.)

The aesthetic trends of this style are essentially the same as those of the Impressionist painters: the idea is to depict mood, as well as visual phenomena like sunlight on water. Here you'll find music that's evocative rather than decisive, effective rather than structur-ally resolute—closer to liquid mercury in substance than the often-sinewy material of the Romantics. There are sudden, sparkling bursts of color and shimmering textures, and occasional dips into the modes of the Medieval and Renaissance periods.[21] It's very French in sound, but even my father—who blames everything on the French (despite the fact that his only real complaint is that their food gives him indigestion)—cannot deny that this is some of the most electrifying music the repertoire has to offer.

Interestingly, Debussy did not approve of the term "Impressionism"—or the "imbeciles" who labeled him as one of its practitioners. Unfor-tunately for him, though, he *is* the quintessential Impressionist composer according to our contemporary definition of the term, and there's not much that he can do about it now that he's buried in the Cimetière de Passy. (With Fauré.)

---

21 Though thankfully not much of the Dorian mode.

JUST TELL ME WHAT TO PUT IN MY SPOTIFY PLAYLIST:[22]

· String Quartet in G Minor, Op. 10—Claude Debussy

· *Prélude à l'après-midi d'un faune*, L. 86—Claude Debussy

· Piano Trio in A Minor—Maurice Ravel

· *La Valse*—Maurice Ravel

· *The Rite of Spring* (*Le sacre du printemps*)—Igor Stravinsky

· *Clairières dans le ciel*—Lili Boulanger

· Symphony No. 1 in D Major, Op. 25, "Classical Symphony" —Sergei Prokofiev

· Piano Quintet in E Major, Op. 15—Erich Wolfgang Korngold

· *The Miraculous Mandarin* Suite, Op. 19, Sz. 73—Béla Bartók

· Viola Concerto—William Walton

· Violin Concerto—Alban Berg

· *Quartet for the End of Time* (*Quatuor pour la fin du temps*) —Olivier Messiaen

· String Quartet No. 8 in C Minor, Op. 110—Dmitri Shostakovich

· *Lamentations: Black/Folk Song Suite for Solo Cello* —Coleridge-Taylor Perkinson

· *Quatrain II*—Tōru Takemitsu

· *Helikopter-Streichquartett*—Karlheinz Stockhausen

---

22 This is also in chronological order—to highlight the gradual move away from tonality.

THE CONTEMPORARY PERIOD

TIME FRAME: If you're a composer and you're alive, this is you.

NOTABLE COMPOSERS, DIVIDED BY GENERATION (BECAUSE BIRTH DATES/PREDICTED DEATH DATES ARE AWKWARD):

- *Silent Generation:* John Corigliano, Philip Glass, Meredith Monk, Arvo Pärt, Steve Reich, Ellen Taaffe Zwilich

- *Boomers:* John Adams, John Luther Adams, Thomas Adès, Eleanor Alberga, George Benjamin, Unsuk Chin, Tan Dun, Michael Gordon, Jennifer Higdon, Aaron Jay Kernis, David Lang, Kaija Saariaho, Julia Wolfe, Hans Zimmer

- *Gen X:* Andy Akiho, Marcos Balter, Raven Chacon, Gabriela Lena Frank, Jake Heggie, John Mackey, Missy Mazzoli, Andrew Norman, Paola Prestini, Sarah Kirkland Snider, Christopher Theofanidis, Eric Whitacre

- *Millennial:* Timo Andres, Courtney Bryan, Reena Esmail, Jessie Montgomery, Nico Muhly, Gity Razaz, Ellen Reid, Caroline Shaw, Carlos Simon

- *Gen Z:* TBD

One of the cool things about listening to new music is that you get to play an active role in history. It's like watching *The Masked Singer* live so that you can vote—instead of waiting, as I do, until after the results are announced because you can't bear to take part in the squelching of any of these very-well-off celebrities' temporary dreams. The flip side of this is that Time has yet to make its edits to the field. Plenty of Classical and Baroque composers who were popular back in the day have been largely forgotten in the centuries since. These are just a few of the wonderful composers who live among us. I can say with confidence that their music deserves to be heard, but it would take a very talented prognosticator to say which of today's composers will be equated, in the future, to the names I've listed in the previous sections. And the only thing I've ever been good at predicting is how my sister's relationships will play out.[23]

WHAT IT SOUNDS LIKE: Twentieth-century music. As I mentioned earlier, Contemporary music is really an extension of the 20th-Century period. There was no magical shift that occurred at the millennium (despite what Y2K doomsday preppers predicted), apart from the expiration of the descriptor "twentieth century." And because a lot of these composers have very selfishly sprawled out across both time periods, many of the works we consider "contemporary" were, in fact, composed in the twentieth century.

The two trends I want to mention are these:

First, the lines between the various sound worlds are blurring. Some of this music sounds closer to pop or jazz than what most people think of as "classical." Second (and this is partly because of the line-blurring), while much of today's classical music *is* atonal and experimental, the last few decades have seen a number of composers move back toward tonality, reversing the trend of the 20th-Century period.

Many contemporary composers employ a wide range of styles—often even within the same piece of music. John Corigliano's score for *The Red Violin* is relatively homogenous and tonal, but his Symphony No. 3, entitled "Circus Maximus," spans from pronounced harmonic clashes to something I can only describe as honky-tonk to

---

23 She loves it.

suspended zero-gravity, zero-tonality soundscapes to, as you might have guessed, circus music. One of the central movements, "Channel Surfing," mimics the effect its title promises by jumping abruptly through a series of contrasting musical segments.

John Adams is another fan of the stylistic patchwork quilt. The opening of his opera *The Death of Klinghoffer* utilizes sonorities one might hear in a musical by Sondheim, while the opera's big concertmaster solo—the one I accidentally rewrote in a performance, once, while Adams was conducting—was inspired by Schoenberg's earlier German Romantic works. And there's another moment in the opera when the music shifts into a vapid, hollow, pop-like sound, which Adams picked to highlight the stupidity of a particular character. (Kind of a burn for the pop genre.) Adams calls his music "post-style," which I like. And not only because I'm hoping to get off his shit list.

Caroline Shaw is an example of a younger composer who's taken up the "post-style" mantle. Her *Partita for 8 Voices*, which is one of the coolest pieces I've heard, visits practically every sound world an ensemble of eight vocalists *can* visit, including (among other things): spoken-word poetry, a twangy kind of folk music, a stunning Tallisesque chorale, futuristic spaceship noises, Medieval tropes, and something that sounds, to me, like the calls of highly musical marine animals. You should really just listen to it.

LET'S GET TO THE VOTING BIT:[24]

- *Cantus in Memoriam of Benjamin Britten*—Arvo Pärt

- Violin Concerto No. 1—Philip Glass

- *The Death of Klinghoffer*—John Adams

---

24 Are you getting tired of my telling you that the order is chronological?

- Air for Violin and Piano—Aaron Jay Kernis

- *Sept Papillons*—Kaija Saariaho

- *Sleep*—Eric Whitacre

- *Water Passion After St. Matthew*—Tan Dun

- Symphony No. 3, "Circus Maximus"—John Corigliano

- *The Little Match Girl Passion*—David Lang

- *Oceanic Verses*—Paola Prestini

- *Hilos*—Gabriela Lena Frank

- *Partita for 8 Voices*—Caroline Shaw

- Cello Concerto—Unsuk Chin

- *Portrait of a Queen*—Carlos Simon

- *Cadenza for the Once Young*—Gity Razaz

- Violin Concerto No. 2, "Narcissus"—Eleanor Alberga

- "Peace"—Jessie Montgomery

"Für Elise"

I had a lot of music boxes growing up. Practically every significant adult in my childhood gave me a music box at one point or another. One of these boxes had a little ballerina who popped up when you opened the lid, spinning rigidly in place to Beethoven's "Für Elise."

To this day, that piece still sounds tinny to me—and I always expect it to go all wobbly and flat and then taper down to a stop halfway through the fourth bar.

I must have heard "Für Elise" well over 4,067,582 times by now. And I still think it sounded better as a music box jingle than a concert piece. I can't say it's a *bad* piece; I have no idea whether or not it is—because I've heard it so many goddamn times, in so many contexts, played by so many bad pianists, that I can no longer assess it without prejudice. But I suspect that it's not a particularly good example of Beethoven's work—because Beethoven himself chose not to publish it. It was found among his belongings after his death, along with a revised version that he also did not publish.

It's unfortunate, therefore, that it's become the poster child for the entire genre.

Whatever else you take away from this chapter—whether you retain the dates of the Baroque period[25]—or the definition of the word "counterpoint"[26]—I hope you'll remember that classical music comprises *a lot of* different sounds and that it's okay (even helpful) for you to discriminate between them.

I hate Medieval music. Beethoven wasn't a fan of "Für Elise." Tchaikovsky, as we'll touch on later, thought Brahms was "untalented" and "mediocre." And there was a teacher at Juilliard who refused to teach any music that was written after the year 1900.[27]

You're allowed to dislike some of this music, too—as long as you don't let it stop you from finding the pieces you *like*.

---

25 They're 1600–1750.

26 The combining of two or more separate, active voices according to a specific set of harmonic rules.

27 Once, when he was judging end-of-year juries (performances given by each student for a panel of teachers who make comments and assign grades), he was confronted by Hindemith's cello sonata from the year 1923. The only comment he left was a giant question mark.

Chapter 2

talent isn't a thing, either

Okay, Fine, So It's a Thing,
but It's Less of a Thing Than You Think

I spent a year learning "Twinkle, Twinkle, Little Star." *A year.*[1]

And before this period of staggering musical development was even possible, I had to learn how to *hold* a violin—and how to stand with it—which I did using an empty tissue box taped to a ruler and the round insert of a pizza box with feet drawn on it.

My bow was made not out of wood but out of stackable markers. Remember those? With the colorful caps that fit onto both ends? I'm not sure they were even meant for stacking, actually. They certainly weren't meant for *staying* stacked. I still remember scrambling across the hideous linoleum tiles of my parents' kitchen floor several times each practice session to collect them whenever they broke apart. I also remember *remembering* scrambling across that hideous linoleum tile floor thirteen years later, when I was scrambling across a different floor because I'd just broken my *real* bow—a bow that had been made in the early 1900s by London's W. E. Hill & Sons, for which

---

1 Granted, I was at an age where I'd just learned how to touch my index finger to my thumb, but still.

my parents had paid seven thousand dollars. Of course, my first thought on that occasion was *every* profanity ever—but after calming down a bit I realized I probably should have seen it coming.

After the tissue box, I graduated to a bright orange factory-made violin. It was essentially a toy—and the sound it made was like a fork on a plate, with a chipmunk voice filter over it. (Or like me, when I was two and a half, singing Mozart arias.) The stack of markers was replaced by a more structurally sound plastic bow that was decorated with colorful tape—so that I could see where the top, middle, and bottom portions of it were without having to do any math.

Then came my year of "Twinkle," which was hardly inspiring, but was far less oppressive and soul-crushing than practicing would eventually become. (That is, the "Twinkle" period wasn't oppressive and soul-crushing *for me*; it was likely both those things for my dad, who used to sit through all my practice sessions.)

Every step, every motion, was laid out for me. None of it was intuitive. *Keep your fingers curved, let your arm lead your shifts, don't pick your sister's nose with your bow.* After my muscles had absorbed these motions and I could finally play with some semblance of grace and dexterity, things started to feel more natural. Quite natural, in fact. I'd hear a beautiful phrase in a recording and I'd play it back, with the same inflections. Then I'd try it a different way—and then another different way—and another—until I found a way that felt like me. I didn't really *practice* during this stage of my life; I just reveled in the music, in the thrill of creating sound.

Then one day, when I'd "outgrown" my teacher,[2] I was handed over to a new one, who told me I was doing everything wrong. The

---

2 In total, I've had seven private teachers during my study, which is on the high side of what's normal for professional players. These teacher-student relationships are generally monogamous, but during my master's program I had two at the same time.

wrist on my left hand was too far in; my thumb, which was double-jointed, was sticking too far out; my fingers were hitting the strings at the wrong angle. Everything became awkward and uncomfortable again—everything was reduced, once more, to a science.

All of this is why my mother, when bored, scours the darkest corners of the internet for local newspaper articles about individuals who are supposedly so talented that they're able to ascend, effortlessly, to the heights of virtuosity—and sends them to me. Well, this and the fact that watching me spiral into exasperated madness is her sport, her play: the thing she does for laughs because sitcoms and comedians and all the things that make normal people laugh just don't do it for her.

Hey, Ars: Have you heard about the man from Ogallala, Nebraska, who found a rusty old trumpet in his attic and was playing the solo from Bach's Brandenburg Concerto No. 2 a week later?[3] And *here's* a guy who ate ten platefuls of Tater Tots at the university cafeteria one morning, spent the next three days on the toilet, and was so dehydrated on the fourth day that he collapsed onto the piano bench in front of the piano he just *happened* to have but had never used before, only to find that he could play the entirety of Liszt's "La campanella" from memory—even though he still has no idea who Liszt is.[4]

---

3 Bach's six "Brandenburg Concertos" are some of his most cherished, exquisite works, and the second of these strikes fear into the hearts of even the bravest of trumpet players. A trumpeter friend of mine in the Boston Symphony Orchestra says that playing it is like trying to sing a perfect falsetto first thing in the morning while squeezing your temples with your palms for twenty minutes straight.

4 Franz Liszt is considered one of the greatest pianists of all time and is known for the virtuosic piano compositions he left behind. His "La campanella" is one of the most obnoxiously difficult of these.

Every time I hear the words "natural player," I pull out a fistful of my hair.

I once had a cabdriver who, upon seeing my violin, launched into a monologue about how lucky I was to be "gifted"—and to have a job that was "fun all the time." *He'd* tried the violin once, too, you see, but holding the instrument had been painful and uncomfortable, which he'd just assumed, for some reason, was *not* the way playing the violin was supposed to feel.

I remember wanting to show him my peeling fingertips and the lump on the index finger of my bow hand and the pus that was leaking and clotting from my neck at the spot where my chin rest chafed against it. I wanted to tell him about the pressure of performing— about my irrational but nevertheless consuming fear of vomiting onstage and the intense, cranky self-loathing that set in whenever my finger landed a fraction of a millimeter shy of or past where I'd trained it to. I didn't, though. Instead I gave him a 20 percent tip, because I knew, on some level, that I *was* lucky (as is anyone who can afford to whine about things like job satisfaction)—and that there were plenty of musicians who hadn't spiraled into such dark, self-pitying depths who would have agreed with his assessment.

I'm not saying, by the way, that natural attributes don't play a role. Even I, with my year spent on "Twinkle," seem to have some inherent agility, coordination, or neurological inclination that renders me slightly more adept at music-making than my husband, Stephan, who's very gifted in the field of law but whose German anthem sounds just like his French anthem (and not because he's German and thinks they should be one and the same).[5] But there is

---

5 Stephan has given me his blessing to write whatever I want about him as long as I tell you that his name is pronounced *SHTEH*-fon, with the emphasis on the first syllable—as opposed to "ste-FON" like the *SNL* character. More on *SHTEH*-fon later.

still no definition of the word "natural" that encompasses what I went through to play the violin.

The Un-naturals

Now, some of you may be thinking to yourself, "Well, I hate to be rude, but is it possible that the issue here is that you just aren't talented *enough*?"

That's a question I can't really answer without ice cream, but I *can* tell you that my answer doesn't matter. You can ask any of the world's most famous classical musicians, and all but possibly one liar[6] will confirm that playing an instrument at a professional level requires endless amounts of slogging away, constant maintenance, and an extremely high tolerance for frustration and physical discomfort. No one sounds good right away. The difference between a talented and an untalented violinist, at the beginning, is not a difference of good or bad; it's the difference of whether you'd sacrifice your firstborn or only your favorite aunt in order to make the noise stop.

To go any further, we have to get into what the word "talent" actually means. Which is tricky because the *Oxford English Dictionary* offers seven definitions, and the first of these is "a denomination of weight, used by the Assyrians, Babylonians, Greeks, Romans, and other ancient nations" as currency. When referred to in regard to music, though, I believe it usually means aptitude—plus inclination—plus something almost metaphysical, like divine right. But the main thing is that talent speaks to *potential*, not accomplishment.

There's a line about talent that I've heard attributed to David

---

6 You know who you are.

Soyer, who was a cellist, a Juilliard teacher, and the notoriously blunt author of many of my favorite classical music quotes. Supposedly, after listening to a prospective student play an entire concerto, he looked the kid straight in the eye and said, "Either you didn't practice or you have no talent." This kick in the nuts highlights an important truth: a talented person who hasn't put in the time will sound very much like a person who isn't talented. This is because there's so much physical conditioning and muscle control that's needed in order to execute classical compositions at a professional level.

Here's what I mean.

Ten years ago, I was playing Paganini caprices in international competitions.[7] My hands hurt like hell afterward—because Paganini is a dick—but they recovered relatively quickly. If I tried to play a Paganini caprice *now*, unpracticed and out of shape as I am (violinistically speaking), I would end up in the hospital. And not only from imploding with self-directed anger. My level of talent, though—whatever that is—is the same as it's always been. The difference is physical fitness.

This is how I know that my mother's *man from Ogallala* and Tater Tot junkie are lying. Whatever talent was bestowed upon them by lightning strikes or severe indigestion (because, sure—there are wonders of the universe I can't begin to comprehend), it did not come with the kind of musculature that's needed to play two of the hardest classical solos in the repertoire.

Still, I get that "Man's Rusty Attic Find Leads to Carnegie Hall Debut (and Tetanus)" makes a far better headline than "Girl Prac-

---

7   Paganini caprices are horrible, athletic pursuits—like contortionist gymnastics routines crossed with some kind of ancient torture ritual. They are the bane of my existence.

tices Every Day of Life, Makes Incremental Progress"—and I agree that there's something magical and intoxicating about the idea of a person who has Been Chosen. So here are a few *real* examples of astonishing natural talent to keep that inegalitarian magic alive:

W. A. MOZART
(1756–1791)

I know you're all, "Ugh, *everyone knows*—we all *get* it—Mozart was a genius." But you don't. You don't know and you don't get it. And neither do I, for that matter. His genius is so great that it cannot be gotten.

Not only did Mozart compose some of the greatest, most exquisite music *ever*, he did so—apparently—with relative ease.[8] He wrote over six hundred pieces during his short lifetime, and the first of these he composed at the age of five. (I assume, too, that unlike *my* first composition, his was actually original.)

He was also a remarkable pianist and violinist—and when he was six, he began performing at the courts of various European nobles (such as Empress Maria Theresa, King Louis XV, and King George III) with his sister, Nannerl, and father, Leopold. Mozart's letters contain frequent allusions to the dexterity of his composing process, and also, less relevantly, detailed descriptions of his bowel movements.

In one letter, dated April 8, 1781, Mozart refers to a sonata for violin and piano that he planned to perform the following day with a violinist named Brunetti, explaining that he composed the piece

---

8 I said "relative," God damn it. He still had to train like mad.

"last night between 11 and 12." He goes on to write: "So that I can be done, I've only written out the accompaniments for Brunetti and kept my [piano] part in my head." In other words, Brunetti would have a violin part and enough measures of the piano score in front of him to know where to enter, but Mozart would perform *his* entire part (which he'd conceived, remember, over the course of an hour, two days earlier) without ever having seen it on a page.

In another letter to his father, dated December 30, 1780, Mozart writes, "Now I have to go, because I have to write like crazy—everything is already composed—but it still isn't written."

Mozart was either an alien being whose brain reacted extremely well to the earth's atmosphere or the real deal when it comes to musical talent.

NICCOLÒ PAGANINI
(1782–1840)

As I mentioned earlier, Paganini was a dick. I've never met him, of course, but he definitely was one. The proof lies in his 24 Caprices for Solo Violin, and his six violin concertos, all of which he wrote with one goal and one goal only in mind: to show off all the things that *his* fingers could do—like contort and multiply and jump dimensions—that no one else's could. (Everyone has to muscle through them these days, though, because violinists are all competitive egomaniacs who take this sort of thing as a challenge.)[9]

Granted, Paganini raised the bar for the entire field and rewrote what had previously been considered the limits of the instrument's capabilities. But on the other hand, my skin used to tan nicely in the

---

9   Most international competitions make you play two Paganini caprices in the first round.

sunlight before these plagues of the violin repertoire entered my life, and now it freckles and burns if I even so much as pull up the shades.

It might not have been Paganini's fault that he was a dick. Not entirely, at any rate. According to legend, he sold his soul to the devil in exchange for his technique—and it's probably hard to be a nice guy when you don't have a soul. But do you know what else is hard? Playing those damn caprices when you *do* have a soul—and having them smother and strangle that soul, slowly and agonizingly, over hours and hours of practicing in windowless rooms.

I'm not sure Paganini even qualifies as a "natural talent," actually, if the source of his power is, in fact, *super*natural. There's also speculation that he had Marfan syndrome and that his abilities—the length and flexibility of his fingers—came from this. You decide which explanation you prefer.

FELIX MENDELSSOHN
(1809–1847)

Like Mozart, Mendelssohn was a child prodigy. And unlike Paganini, he wasn't a dick. The latter is apparent from his music, which is some of the most joyful I've heard. If you need a character reference, though, I can give you one: Goethe.

Mendelssohn was twelve when his composition tutor, Carl Friedrich Zelter, arranged for him to meet the legendary German poet and polymath, who was deeply impressed by Mendelssohn's abilities and character. During their first meeting—which certainly wasn't their last[10]—Mendelssohn improvised a composition on the spot and performed several fugues by Bach, whose music both he

---

10 They kept in close touch until Goethe's death.

and Goethe worshipped. (Bach's name and music were relatively obscure back then; and in fact, his present-day fame is largely thanks to Mendelssohn, who staged many revivals of his music, including the first performance of the *St. Matthew Passion* since Bach's death.)

Mendelssohn was just thirteen years old when his first piano quartet was published—and two of the works he's best known for, his String Octet and his *A Midsummer Night's Dream Overture* (which are also two of the coolest pieces ever), he wrote at the ages of sixteen and seventeen, respectively. These numbers aren't quite as mind-blowing as Mozart's, but Mendelssohn *is* still one of the greatest and most famous wunderkinds of all time.

FANNY MENDELSSOHN (LATER FANNY HENSEL) (1805–1847)

Felix Mendelssohn's sister Fanny wouldn't make a list of history's most noteworthy composers (it was pretty silly of her to have a vagina if she wanted a career in the 1800s), but her *talent*—her raw potential and capacity for success had she *not* had a vagina—was irrefutable. When she was young and the German language still considered her an "it"—*das Mädchen*—rather than a "she"—*die Frau*—she was believed by many to be the most talented of the Mendelssohn children. Carl Friedrich Zelter, who'd served as Fanny's composition teacher as well as Felix's, was one of the people who subscribed to this belief—early on, at least. Years before introducing Felix Mendelssohn to Goethe, he wrote to the latter that Fanny "could give you something of Sebastian Bach" and went on to describe her as "really something special."

But the Mendelssohn family saw her music-making as an "ornament" rather than a profession—and whether because of societal pressures or inherent reservations about her career, she agreed to prioritize husband-hunting and baby-making over all else. She still composed 460 pieces, though—which is a lot of ornaments.

A few of her works (the song "Italien," for one) appeared in 1827 as part of Felix Mendelssohn's Op. 8 song collection. Which some people view as a sign of Felix's support and other people view as a sign that he was a musical kleptomaniac.

(I don't want to get into it, but to me it's pretty clear that it was a sign of support. First of all, everyone who knows anything about the Mendelssohns knows that Felix and Fanny adored each other. And when Queen Victoria told Felix that "Italien" was one of her favorite songs, he made a point of clarifying that it was Fanny, not he, who'd written it. Moreover, while Felix was less than supportive of the idea of Fanny's professionalism, he was always supportive of her actual *work*, showing her compositions to numerous influential contacts. There's also the fact that Felix did not, in any way, *need* Fanny's music; by 1827, he'd already written his String Octet and his *A Midsummer Night's Dream Overture* and was one of the greatest composers of all time. If you want something to be angry about, be angry about Wagner.)[11]

Inspiritingly (or at least not *dis*piritingly), Fanny's husband—an artist named Wilhelm Hensel—encouraged her to publish her work. And she did, eventually, release a collection of songs after two Berlin publishers approached her, but this wasn't until 1846—one year before her death.

Hearing her music fills me with all kinds of excitement and anguish over what might have been had she been allowed to develop her talent fully. But she did, at least, give notable public performances as a pianist, and she was a highly respected figure

---

11 More on this in that very angry book I'm going to write.

whose views were prized by her brother and many others in the music world.

CLARA WIECK (LATER CLARA SCHUMANN)
(1819–1896)

As far as I know, it wasn't particularly easy to impress Goethe. Even meeting him, I'd guess, wasn't such an easy thing to accomplish. And yet, here we have another twelve-year-old who blew him out of the water the first time she took a seat on his piano bench.

Clara Schumann (as she's generally referred to) was one of the greatest, most renowned pianists of her generation. And her career was well under way by the time she played for Goethe—who pronounced her (if the stories are to be believed) "more power[ful] than six boys put together." He also gave her a bronze medal with his face on it (you can do things like that if you're Goethe), along with the dedication "*Der kunstreichen Clara Wieck*" ("The rich-in-artistry Clara Wieck").

She's often been marginalized as a composer—which is a shame because I find her music lovely—but her pianistic brilliance, as well as the success she enjoyed as a performer during her lifetime, is irrefutable.

Clara soloed with the legendary Leipzig Gewandhausorchester at the age of eleven and went on to perform in all the greatest halls of Europe, for kings and queens and other similarly prominent figures. Her talent *was* extraordinary—she showed a facility and propensity for music from a very early age—but her life was also dictated by an intense regimen of practicing and lessons, which are well documented in her father's writings. (Remember my rants on the importance of physical conditioning.)

Clara had a shinier career than Fanny Mendelssohn's, but she shared Fanny's struggles with traditional gender roles of the time. In an interesting passage from her diary, written during her eventual engagement to Robert Schumann, she writes: "Now I aim to unite the artist and wife as much as possible. That is a difficult task! I can't allow my art to stifle[.] If I did, I would hate myself."

Lucky for her, I guess, that her husband spent his last years locked away in an asylum, thus enabling her to single-handedly support her large family with her concert career.

CAMILLE SAINT-SAËNS
(1835–1921)

The Carnival of the Animals is fun and all,[12] but when I hear Saint-Saëns's music, I don't think to myself, "Holy crap, this man is a genius," as I do when I hear Mozart's or Mendelssohn's. I'm not, in fact, even certain that I *like* Saint-Saëns as a composer. I decided to mention him, though, because (*a*) you might feel differently; and (*b*) I thought those of you who aren't French majors might want to know how to pronounce his name—*sah(n)-saw(s)*; and (*c*) several people I trust describe him as the single most prodigious talent in the history of music.

If I've understood these people correctly, this claim has less to do with his abilities as a composer than it does with the abilities he displayed, early on, as a player. It surprised me to learn this because I'd never heard about his performing career, and I'd read somewhere that his "musical debut" had come at the age of ten. Which had left me unimpressed because I know few players whose "musical debuts" came *after* the age of ten. But then I read that his mother, bless her

---

12 If it doesn't sound familiar to you, you still might know "The Swan," which is a movement from it.

heart, didn't want him to become famous too early, which explains why he waited until he was practically at death's door to make his first public appearance.

It's hard to verify his level of giftedness without any recordings, of course. But he did compose his first piece at the age of three.

ERICH WOLFGANG KORNGOLD
(1897–1957)

Korngold is yet another prodigy, but he's the only one on this list who's won an Oscar—and he's won two, actually—for his film scores. (I'll watch any movie with a Korngold film score, but my favorites are *A Midsummer Night's Dream*—the 1935 version—and *The Adventures of Robin Hood*, from 1938.)

I'm not sure why, but child prodigies from recent centuries always impress me more than child prodigies from centuries past. I think it has to do with Thomas Edison and my willfully ignorant conception that before the invention of the lightbulb, people had very little to do apart from exploring their musical capabilities— whereas immediately following the dawn of electricity, there was suddenly all this *stuff* that distracted them. The problem with Korngold, though, is that I don't know whether he had electricity at home, since the transition from candles was, I gather, a gradual one.

But he was still impressive, I suppose, regardless of whether or not he was distracted by the lightbulbs he may or may not have had in his house. He wrote a ballet, *Der Schneemann* (*The Snowman*)— when he was eleven—which received rave reviews when it was performed at the Vienna Court Opera in 1910. And when he was twelve, Gustav Mahler hailed him as a genius. Richard Strauss also told Korngold's father that there was no need for him to study at a conservatory because he already knew everything they'd be able to teach him at one. He was popularly dubbed "the Mozart of the Twentieth Century," which he wasn't—because there was only one Mozart and he was incomparable—but I do get what they mean.

YO-YO MA
(B. 1955)

In case you're growing weary of all these child prodigies,[13] here's a guy who isn't one. (Whatever his Wikipedia page tries to tell you.) Yo-Yo Ma, for those of you who didn't catch him on *Sesame Street*— or *West Wing*—or *The Simpsons*—or *The Late Show with Stephen Colbert*—is a Very Big Deal. He is to classical music what the Queen is to the United Kingdom. Only younger. And more popular. (I have never heard anyone utter a single word against this man or his playing—which is something I can't honestly say about any other living musician.)[14]

He's often *referred* to as a prodigy because he began performing at the age of four and a half, but there's a recording of him playing at a benefit concert when he was seven—and at that age, he wasn't one. He was still impressive—don't get me wrong—but he wasn't like Sarah Chang, who sounded like a tiny, very solid professional at the age of five.

Grown-up Yo-Yo's technical facility is undoubtedly mind-blowing, but it's still not *the point* of him. Nor is it the reason he's on this list. It's his musicianship, his interpretive abilities, his stage presence, and the energy he radiates whenever he's near a cello.

---

13 Welcome to the club.

14 We're a pretty critical, cranky bunch—probably because we spend so much time locked up alone in practice rooms.

Watching him play is like watching a lamb gambol or a dolphin leap or a sparrow swoop and rocket up toward the clouds. What is natural about his playing is the feeling it creates: that the world—or one small part of it, for one brief moment—is exactly as it was meant to be.

My dad once got to perform a sonata with Yo-Yo Ma. It was the highlight of his piano career.[15] And when our two families had dinner together, my mom got to ask everyone for their views on oral sex—which was the highlight of *her* career in the field of embarrassing her teenage daughters.[16] (I also got to play with Yo-Yo once—in a quartet, for a birthday—because he's friends with one of my teachers, Lynn. But I was playing the viola, not the violin, so it doesn't count. You'll understand why after you read chapter 4.)

Playing with Yo-Yo would be an honor for anyone, but for my dad it was particularly so, as there were few comparably triumphant moments in his music career. He was always an excellent pianist, but he was never solely a performer by trade. He taught, mostly—music theory and piano—and he did some conducting. In recent years, he's transitioned into administrative work.

He was six when he first asked his parents for piano lessons, but they put him off, expecting him to give up on the idea. When he was still asking them three years later, they relented—but they knew little about the industry and were unable to provide the kind of support that serious music careers require. My dad eventually ended up at the Eastman School of Music (one of the most prestigious conser-

---

15 According to me.

16 It's very important to my mom that you know that she "only" brought up oral sex because Richard Kogan, a concert pianist and doctor partly specializing in human sexuality, was also at the dinner. (The embarrassment was real, though.)

vatories in the country), but that wasn't until grad school—and despite the ten-hour practice days he put in there, in a desperate attempt to make up for his slow start, he ultimately realized that it was too late.

Don't go feeling *too* sorry for him, though; he's a very successful man who's often been mistaken for Robert Redford[17] and he excels, infuriatingly, at nearly everything he does. He was captain of the squash team at Phillips Exeter Academy, he graduated from Harvard in three years, his handicap on the golf course is perpetually flirting with scratch, and he skis like an Austrian count who's fallen on hard times and found employment as a ski instructor. His heartache when it comes to the piano is likely a symptom of his pathological need to win at absolutely everything.

Still, a heartache is a heartache, and his was the reason I started playing the violin when I was two, just weeks after I'd first expressed an interest in it. He knew the price of waiting—and he didn't want me to have to pay it, as he had.

He served as my coach in those early days—and also, when my own impetus gave way to more childish whims, the gentle but firm voice of discipline, shepherding me through my practice sessions and pushing me to focus, to work through each challenge. He recorded my lessons and my performances and took notes so that I could analyze my mistakes.

His teachings help me every day, in most things that I do. But there was a cost to this approach, too. He just couldn't see it yet.

---

17 By people who still think he looks the way he did in *The Natural*.

classical music is for snobs

But It's Also for You

My sister was my parents' second failed musical experiment. I use the term "failed" loosely. She is not *herself* a failure—she is a wonderful, intelligent, beautiful, successful, and contributing member of society. And as a cellist she was a wonderful, intelligent, beautiful, successful, and contributing member of the music world—one who attended two of the best conservatories in America and Europe and who did lots of other things that would impress you if you knew about them. What I mean by "failed" is only that she, like me, no longer plays professionally.

Her decision to stop performing (before the age of eighty, when most classical musicians retire) could, perhaps, have been predicted. Whereas it took me until I was twenty-five to admit—to myself and to others—that I didn't absolutely *love* to practice (and even then I had to acknowledge that there were still aspects of it that I found satisfying—or addictive), Marina was clear about this from the start. Sometimes she'd play a few notes before becoming fascinated by the tassels on her rug, and other times she would refuse to sit down on her cello chair in the first place.

She was and still is immune to the strange power our father has always had of making absolutely everyone he meets want his approval,[1] which meant that the persuasive tactics that had always served so effectively to motivate me were useless when it came to her. We would come home from school announcing that so-and-so had invited us over for a playdate or a birthday party, and Dad would say something like, "Well, sure you guys can go—that's what a *normal* kid would do." Then I would cry out in horror and say, "No, Daddy, I don't want to be normal!" Marina would just stare him in the eye and say, "Yup—sounds good to me."

There's a great video of Marina at the age of four, in which she's sitting on her cello chair whimpering, "I don't want to play the cello. I just want to watch a *movie*."

She'd get her wish on the weekends, when our parents would leave—to go grocery shopping or to get their ancient Volvo station wagon fixed.[2] I would always try, diligently, to practice in their absence—as per parental instructions. But inevitably, after half a minute or so, the cello-playing in the next room would stop and I'd hear the patter of little feet coming down the hall—and a few feeble objections later, we'd be sitting on the couch together, remotes in hand, skipping through film after film in a highlights reel of all our favorite spots. Then the sound of car tires on gravel would send us

---

1   One of my earlier boyfriends, a skilled percussionist who's now the principal of a major North American symphony, crumbled under the weight of this the first time I introduced them—announcing, mid-dinner—much to everyone's confusion—that he had just, in the five minutes since we'd all sat down at the table, decided to quit music and apply to Harvard (my parents' alma mater). It did not impress my dad in the way he'd hoped, but that's okay because the symptoms subsided quickly, as did the relationship.

2   That Volvo—my dread of having to be seen in it—is largely why I never got my license.

scampering back to our rooms and we'd jump back into practicing as if we'd been at it all along.

Over the course of our movie-watching—which was considerable, because that Volvo needed fixing *a lot*—we encountered many misrepresentations of classical music, some with relative consistency. These inaccuracies are sometimes annoying (though not as annoying as the horrific faking of *every* actor who has ever attempted to "play" an instrument on camera), but the misrepresentation I want to complain about here is more than that. It's damaging to the industry— and viciously self-perpetuating. It's a PR nightmare that will not end. I am speaking, of course, of the popular adage that classical music is for snobs.

Snobs Love Classical Music

Whenever a TV or film director wants to suggest refinement or stuffiness, a piece of classical music will inevitably be playing in the background of whatever gilded room or formal garden their displaced protagonist has just walked into. Usually, as discussed in chapter 1, it's music from the Classical or Baroque period.

For a few decades in there (the 1980s and '90s were particularly culpable), it was, in fact, nearly always from one of two pieces: Mozart's *Eine kleine Nachtmusik* or Vivaldi's *Four Seasons* (generally "Spring"). When Ace Ventura, pet detective, infiltrates billionaire Ronald Camp's black-tie soiree—or when Vicki Vale enters the museum in Tim Burton's *Batman* just minutes before the Joker arrives to defile it—or when a gloating Lucy Liu bests her young chess opponent in *Charlie's Angels: Full Throttle*—it's *Eine kleine Nachtmusik*. As it is, also—in similar contexts—in *Daddy Day Care*, *There's Something About Mary*, *The Bonfire of the Vanities*, and *Up Close & Personal*.

To name only a few. (Because it's not like Mozart left us over six hundred multi-movement works to choose from, most of which are way better than *Eine kleine Nachtmusik*.)[3]

It's "Spring" from Vivaldi's *Four Seasons*, on the other hand, when Julia Roberts accompanies Richard Gere to his dinner meeting at that fancy restaurant in *Pretty Woman*—and when James Bond meets the villain Maximillian Zorin at a black-tie garden party in *A View to a Kill*—and when King Julien, seated in the first-class cabin of the penguins' makeshift plane in *Madagascar 2*, kicks Melman into coach with the words "It's nothing personal; it's just that we're better than you." (It can also be heard in the snobbiest scenes of *Spy Game*, *The Hangover*, *Pets*, and—since we're at it—*Up Close & Personal*. Again.)

"Spring" is heard in commercials, shows, elevators—always in the most horrible, priggish contexts—to convey a snooty milieu. Whenever I hear it, I immediately break out in hives. So either the movies have truly ruined it for me or Vivaldi was better at capturing the atmosphere of spring than I give him credit for.

Possibly thanks to Google and Spotify, film music directors have begun to realize that the classical repertoire includes more than three pieces and have expanded their snob-scene playlists accordingly.[4] Some examples that spring to mind are: *Kingsman 2*, which uses Tchaikovsky's Serenade for Strings in C Major, Op. 48, for the scene when Eggsy has dinner with the Swedish royal family, and *Bad Moms*, which makes use of Mozart's Piano Quartet in E-flat Major,

---

3 He did.

4 Movies made before the year 1980 also used a wide range of classical pieces (often, even, without mention/implication of snobbery). I can't speak to why this variety went missing for two whole decades, but it's probably linked to whatever aesthetic plague beset the areas of fashion, grooming, car design, and architecture during that same time period.

K. 493, for Christina Applegate's fancy Martha Stewart–catered party.

All of these scenes, among the billions of others I have not listed, underscore the association between classical music and the stuffy, moneyed elite.

Before I explain why this is bullshit—and also why it isn't—I should distinguish between snobs and people with money. There are, of course, plenty of rich people who aren't snobs. Take one of my early benefactors, Paul, an amateur pianist who frequently opens his homes and bank accounts to young, up-and-coming musicians. He has a wine cellar and a membership at the University Club and a place in the Hamptons, but he still drives an absolute-piece-of-crap Volvo that's not quite as bad as my parents' but that still bursts into flames in the middle of I-495 sometimes when the traffic's especially bad. *And* he's been living without a tennis court, which I didn't even know you were allowed to do in the Hamptons. But instead of having one installed—or replacing his car with one that doesn't double as a pizza oven—he bought a Steinway for his favorite performing arts organization when their board members (all of whom probably *do* have tennis courts) didn't want to cough up the cash.

Conversely, there are plenty of people without money who *are* snobs. My roommate while I was at Juilliard was one of the biggest snobs I've met—even though our kitchen counter was the kind that you could peel if you were bored and the only windows in our common area doubled as the wall of our neighbors' living room. All you had to do to bring out his inner Lucille Bluth was to eat a plate of spaghetti Bolognese in front of him—and soon he'd be lecturing you about how spaghetti is *not* the right kind of pasta for a ragù and how salt, in *his* view, is a crutch that's needed only in the absence of true culinary virtuosity. And before long, your presence in the kitchen would no longer stand in the way of his dream of being left alone to read and analyze *Finnegans Wake*.

For the purposes of this chapter, though, this distinction is moot. Anyone with money will be considered a snob (rich people who aren't snobs will forgive me because they're cool like that) and any-one without money who still, for whatever reason, wants to be con-sidered a snob can keep that honorary title but should know that only some of what follows applies to them.

Snobs have, in fact, always been attracted to classical music. They've been making themselves indispensable to the industry's eco-nomic tapestry since the days of Bach and Mozart, when wealthy members of the nobility—kings, princes, archbishops, and what have you—employed musical geniuses the same way they employed cobblers and cooks and couturiers (many of whom were also likely geniuses). The dynamic has evolved slightly since then, but there still isn't a large enough audience base—or enough public funding—to get rid of the snobs altogether.

This is how, in a relatively recent incident called Mahlergate,[5] a whole concert hall of them went full torches-and-pitchforks on a man whose cell phone went off in the middle of a performance of Mahler's Ninth Symphony.

It's also how, a few years back at the Berlin Philharmonic, I ended up getting stuck sitting next to a woman who lost her shit every time anyone clapped between movements.[6]

(It was gross. She kept trying to impress her date by screaming,

---

5 By the two people who called it that.

6 In this case, *movements*, as we will cover later, are segments of a piece.

"No! You're not supposed to clap yet!" at a bunch of people who couldn't hear her.)

Here's what was funny about it:

1. The people who were clapping between movements were politely expressing their enthusiasm for the music. Their applause didn't bother anyone in the hall apart from this woman. This woman's *im*polite expressions of frustration and snobbery, on the other hand, bothered quite a few of the people sitting around her.

2. In going nuts about something that doesn't even bother most performers, she revealed that she was probably far less expert than she was trying to make herself out to be.

3. Imagine having such a fragile equilibrium that this is the sort of thing that unhinges you.

By the way, in case any of this is making you nervous about attending a live performance, don't worry. There's a whole section on concert etiquette in chapter 12 and much of it focuses on when to clap. It also covers when to be a dick about *other* people not knowing when to clap. (Never. You should never be a dick about it.)

Classical Music Is Also for You

The fact that there *are* snobs who listen to classical music does not mean, however, that classical music is *for* snobs. To say that it is is to say that gold and princesses are for ogres—or that all the chocolate that comes into my house is for me. Just because someone *likes* a thing—and happens to be holding that thing hostage—does not mean that that thing is *for* that someone.

In fact, for as long as there have been snobs in the classical music scene, classical musicians have been praying for salvation from them.

Mozart's hatred of his employer the Prince-Archbishop Hieronymus Colloredo was well documented in those letters to his father that did not center around descriptions of his gastrointestinal activity; he often complains in them of how poorly he's treated by the archbishop—and of the archbishop's stinginess—and in one he even writes that he "hate[s] the archbishop to insanity." It's likely that Bach felt similarly about his patron Duke Wilhelm Ernst of Saxe-Weimar, who once imprisoned him for a period of four weeks for the crime of trying to resign.

But musicians often have to swallow their pride and work for people they hate. They need food just like anybody else, and musical instruments require shelter from the elements. I'm lucky to be able to say that the vast majority of my professional contacts have been people I like. But I've still done my fair share of pride-swallowing and ass-kissing. Unfortunately, the story I'd really like to tell you—about this one absolute nightmare of a woman—is off-limits.[7] But I can tell you that I've dealt with plenty of rude and ignorant remarks made by influential patrons—and inappropriate comments and advances made by industry kingmakers and competition judges—and that in most of these instances I've had to be polite and charming—and seemingly *grateful*—so as to avoid losing work and making powerful enemies.

I can also tell you that I once had to eat an entirely raw, uncured jumbo shrimp—even though it was gray and so, *so* rubbery and I'm terrified of germs and bacteria—because it was served to me, after a

---

7 The short of it is that the nightmare-witch *hated* me—and I hated her, but I had to pretend that I didn't—and now she's dead. (I didn't kill her, though. She was just really, really old.)

concert, at the palace-like home of two well-known musical benefactors and I was scared of what would happen if I offended them
(or their private chef). Not really the same as getting thrown in jail
for trying to quit my job, but traumatizing nonetheless.

The good news is that some of the snobs have started dying off,
so there are fewer of them now. This hasn't been overly wonderful
for musicians from a financial standpoint, but it *has* forced the industry to adapt in the hopes of attracting new audiences. (I'm over-
simplifying. Survival is only part of the impetus behind the
changing industry. Many musicians have grown tired of the stag-
nant air surrounding this music and have reached, accordingly, into
their stores of creativity for their own artistic growth and sanity.) As
a result, the classical scene has blossomed into a world of innovation
and experimentation and very trim waistlines. There are young, vibrant, beautiful performers like Sheku Kanneh-Mason, Elena Urioste, Karim Sulayman, J'Nai Bridges, and Yuja Wang—as well as
ensembles like Quatuor Ébène and the hilarious Igudesman &
Joo—who are sweeping through the industry like Marie Kondo
through a walk-in closet, rolling socks and sparking joy with such
dedication that many of the surviving snobs have been converted.[8]

(If *you're* a snob looking to be converted, just google "J'Nai
Bridges, basketball"—or take a look at Karim Sulayman's *I Trust
You*—or listen to Quatuor Ébène's "Someday My Prince Will
Come." If those don't work, then the unapologetic silliness of
Igudesman & Joo's *A Little Nightmare Music*—or the disarming

---

8 I should mention that Yo-Yo Ma has been a proponent of innovation for decades, col-
laborating with artists like Bobby McFerrin, Rosa Passos, and Lil Buck; while Sir James
Galway, another classical legend, has built his popularity around approachable programming, humor, and his wonderful Irishness. But as *Sir James Galway* and *Yo-Yo Ma*, they
are practically industries unto themselves, which separates them, at least insofar as audiences are concerned, from the rest of us.

artlessness and extraordinary musicianship of Elena Urioste and Tom Poster's #UrePosteJukebox Instagram videos—certainly will. Snobs *can*, actually, change. I was a snob back in the day. Or I thought I was, at least. As it turns out, I was just unhappy.)

Here's a story. When I was at Juilliard, I took part in the Gluck Community Service Fellowship Program, which sent students around New York City to play in various facilities—like prisons, schools, and nursing homes.[9] Once, my duo partner, Izia, and I were sent to perform in the psychiatric ward of a hospital.

Going into the experience, I tried my best to embody the kind of calm, enlightened, politically correct attitude that my mother would expect from someone she had raised. But secretly I was terrified. My only associations with psychiatric institutions were the horror movies I'd seen, and at one point, when I turned around to see a wide-eyed face staring at me through the round window in our greenroom, I almost screamed.

Moments later, though, I was greeted by one of the most receptive audiences I'd ever encountered—an audience that was all attentiveness, devoid of any pretense or formality. There was a man who requested the "theme song from *Platoon*," which Izia knew as Barber's *Adagio for Strings*, and as we did our best to reproduce the piece from memory, he sobbed openly in gratitude. There was a woman who was fascinated by our synchronization, challenging us to repeat the beginning of our Mozart duet with our eyes closed and cheering us on throughout the experiment. And there was another woman, with a short pixie cut, who got up and waltzed whenever we played a piece in $\frac{3}{4}$ time.

---

9 This makes me sound very noble and generous, but I actually got paid to be charitable, and I spent all the money on shoes. So nobody should feel compelled to nominate me for sainthood.

These people were not snobs. Some of them weren't even wearing pants. And yet they connected with the music in a way that I have seen few snobs do—and none while sober.

The point is, don't let the snobs push you out. While the classical industry may have been designed with snobs in mind, classical *music* was not. Many former snobs are, like me, converted and ready to welcome you with open arms. And the ones who aren't—the ones who just want things to go back to the way they were when people *enjoyed* getting cell-phone-ring-shamed in front of thousands— don't deserve the beauty these composers gave us—or the thrilling creativity and innovation that my favorite artists are serving up now. It was meant *for you*.

Yes, YOU.

I'll leave you with one final thought:

Mozart once wrote a piece entitled "Leck mich im Arsch." Which translates, roughly, as "Lick Me in the Ass." Not exactly country club music.

conductors are
assholes

And Other Popular Archetypes
of the Classical Music Industry

When I was eleven, my parents sent me away for two months, to a summer music festival for college students, where I had the opportunity of studying with two of the country's most renowned violin teachers in the picturesque setting of a midlevel New England ski resort.

My progress over the past several years had been rapid. And my parents, eager to support my musical growth, had opted to throw me in the deep end. If my playing was strong enough for a program designed for college students, they reasoned, then a program designed for college students was where my playing should be. And so a few weeks after completing the sixth grade, I was whisked away to Vermont and deposited in the mountains, along with my violin and a loaf of sesame semolina, my favorite bread at the time, for comfort. (It had already been decided that New England Conservatory's Preparatory School and a new violin teacher would follow in the fall.)

I learned a lot that summer. I heard a lot of great players and I was exposed to a lot of great music. I was also exposed to *other things*.

The students—most of whom were between the ages of nineteen and twenty-six—lived in groups of four or five, in various condos spread out over the mountain. Apart from mandatory concert attendance and biweekly lessons, the time was largely unstructured. It was, in fact, a very questionable parenting decision—in the sense that I have questioned my parents about it often, and very directly—to send a tween into something that resembled a spring break party hub for two whole months. (The festival no longer exists, in spite of its legendary teachers. I'd offer this as evidence of its unmatched depravity, but in fact, the majority of other music festivals I've attended have been equally debauched—and they're still around. The only real problem with this one was that I was eleven.)

But my parents did at least attempt to preserve my innocence by placing me in a condo with the only other eleven-year-old there: a girl named Caitlin.

She was a sweet girl, but since we were—remember—*eleven*, we were also living with her mother, Irene, who was the second most horrible person I've ever met. (Irene is a pseudonym. My mom is the only one who remembers Irene's real name and she won't tell me what it is.)

Irene's first offense was using my loaf of sesame semolina to make French toast. I told her I didn't eat French toast, but she didn't care. She also made me watch *Lamb Chop's Sing-Along* for half an hour during our afternoon practice breaks, an experience that still haunts me to this day. And then there was the time she took me aside and gave me that deranged stepmothery heart-to-heart in which she said, with no hint of irony, "Now, Ari, you really can't be jealous of *my Caitlin*, because a girl like *my Caitlin* only comes along once in a hundred years."

I remember her saying "my Caitlin" twice in a row like that.

Instead of "her"—or just plain, unclaimed "Caitlin." I also remember being very confused because it had not, in fact, ever occurred to me to be jealous of *my Caitlin*. (And if it had, the thought of *my Caitlin* having to spend her life under the same roof as Irene would have certainly cured me of my envy.)

I lasted about a week before breaking down and calling my parents, begging to be rescued.

They were very sympathetic. My dad, a semolina purist like myself, was particularly moved by the bit about the French toast. He made some calls, and the next day, I was relocated to a new, much less psychologically scarring condo. It was the second-youngest condo at the festival, occupied by sixteen-year-old girls and the joint-rolling, fake-ID-wielding twenty-year-olds they were sleeping with. (For the next few weeks, everything I saw shocked me. By the time I left, nothing did—or ever could.)

I bring all of this up not, as my parents will undoubtedly claim, to throw them under the bus, but because Irene is a classic example of a prevalent classical music archetype: the stage parent.

The Musical Roots of the Stage Parent Archetype

When you think of stage parenting, your mind likely jumps to the Dina Lohans of Hollywood—or the Rose Thompson Hovicks of the theater—or the *Anyone-whose-kid-has-appeared-on-reality-television* of reality television.[1] But Leopold Mozart was parading the pint-sized Wolfgang around the Continent centuries before Wendy Dickey was getting demolished by the internet for dressing up her three-year-old as a prostitute on *Toddlers & Tiaras*.

---

1 Except the *Fixer Upper* family. I love those guys.

Leopold—let's jump to a first-name basis for Papa Mozart to avoid confusion—was a composer, violinist, and teacher, who was well-known, even before the success of his son, for his treatise on the fundamentals of violin playing.[2] A talent like Mozart's may only come along once in a hundred years (to borrow a phrase from Irene), but his interest and education in music were hardly accidental. Any child of Leopold's was always going to be an accomplished musician—*and* get a very early start. (Nannerl, Leopold's daughter and Mozart's older sister, who was also an impressive pianist, is proof of this.) Leopold also functioned as Mozart's manager and publicist (as well as Nannerl's), organizing the family's three-year tour of Europe between the years 1763—when Mozart was seven— and 1766. And there were plenty of other parents like Leopold buzzing about back then because child prodigies, at the time, were as fashionable as wig-boats. (Which is to say: very.)

It could probably be argued, in fact, that classical music *invented* stage parenting.

The size of the classical industry and its level of competition have only increased since Mozart's day, so it's not surprising that the number of stage parents has risen right along with it. I'm not talking about parents like my dad, mind you, who record their kids' lessons and help them practice. In the world of conservatories, that's not a *stage* parent; it's just a parent. What I'm talking about are parents who dress their short twelve-year-olds in tutus and bows to pass them off as tall six-year-olds; parents who choreograph their kids' performances down to the most minute gestures and facial expressions; parents who lock their children in rooms, roping them to pianos or music stands to force them to practice. You can find hordes

---

2   His writings are helpful even today, mainly in revealing performance practices of the era.

of them each Saturday, stalking the halls of America's top conservatories and setting up camp in empty practice rooms.[3]

My sister, Marina—the brilliant cellist I mentioned in chapter 3—had *her* first encounter with a stage parent mere weeks after my initiation with Irene. We'd just joined the prep program at New England Conservatory (marking our official entrance into the classical world) and she'd won a spot as principal cellist of the program's Youth Repertory Orchestra. It was one of the younger orchestras, but most of the students were still quite a bit older than she was, and this was a major triumph. Within weeks, though, the spot was taken away from her and reassigned to a boy named Tristan,[4] who'd placed into the back of the section but had slowly crept up to the front, advancing, one stand at a time, each week. (Marina describes it like a scene from a horror movie; each time she glanced over her shoulder, he was three feet closer.) In the penultimate week, Marina showed up at rehearsal to find that he had replaced her stand partner, and days later my parents got the apologetic call from the administration, explaining that they'd decided to give him *her* spot. My parents found out only later that the decision had come down to the relentless efforts of Tristan's mother.

What made this very stupid, apart from the fact that it was an unpaid orchestra for ten-year-olds whose concerts few people apart from the kids' parents attended, is that Marina and Tristan didn't

---

3 Saturdays are when all the serious musicians who are too young to attend conservatories on a full-time basis stampede through the classrooms and hallways in a condensed regimen of private lessons, chamber music rehearsals, chamber music coachings, music theory classes, and orchestral rehearsals (sending those usual residents who are foolish enough to appear at school that day fleeing back to their apartments and dorm rooms, even if it *does* mean having their practice sessions interrupted by angry neighbors who hate artistic achievement).

4 Tristan is also a pseudonym. My mom (again) will get upset if I use his real name.

give a rat's ass about any of it. Marina even turned around and dated Tristan shortly after. And not in the retaliatory, life-sabotaging way that I suggested, either.[5]

But then, Marina is a cellist.

Cellists Are the GOAT

If you're ever on your way to being stranded on a desert island and you have the opportunity of choosing what sort of a classical musician you want to be stranded *with*, go with a cellist. I'm not sure what it is about the cello that attracts such delightful, easygoing people—the mellow sound, perhaps, or the fact that cello cases make everyone carrying them look like adorable giant turtles—but it's no coincidence that two of my favorite people in the world (my sister and my Andover-*and*-Juilliard-BFF Meta) both found their way to the instrument.

Another benefit to choosing a cellist is that cello practicing isn't nearly as stressful to listen to as that of the other instruments. (I actually enjoy piano practicing even more, but only if the piano is properly tuned, which a piano on a deserted desert island is unlikely to be.)

The cello, as many of you know, is something like a big violin.[6] Its proportions are different, though, and it's played upside down, propped up by a sharp metal spear called an endpin. (If this is the first time you're hearing the word "endpin," by the way, it just proves my point about the nature of cellists. If *singers* had endpins, you would have seen the word, by now, in countless headlines,

---

5   It barely counts as dating, anyway. It was an orchestra for ten-year-olds, remember.

6   As a violinist, I am incapable of seeing it the other way around.

broadcasting tales of passion and revenge.) It's also an instrument of versatile use; often it serves as the harmonic support for the glitzier, higher melodic lines, but just as frequently it puts on a top hat, grabs a silver-tipped cane, and dances out into the spotlight. I'd say it's more Gene Kelly, though, than Fred Astaire.

Bassists Are Chill

Bassists are even more like cellists, in some ways, than cellists themselves. Which is fitting because basses are a lot like cellos, only bigger and deeper. Basses are so big, in fact, that on orchestra tours, they're shipped separately—with the wardrobe trunks and percussion instruments.

Despite the bass's similarities with the cello, there are also several key differences between the two. For instance, basses usually tune in fourths as opposed to fifths, and their shape is slightly longer and more streamlined. You can see this in the middle of the body, where it looks like someone's taken a bite out of each side—and where the body of the instrument meets the fingerboard.

The sound of the bass is rather wide and flat, which is why, in this genre, you rarely hear the instrument on its own;[7] it is more often the lowest component of a thick, multi-instrument texture. This absence of individual pressure—along with the fact that bassists are perpetually enervated from lugging their instruments around—is probably what makes bassists so *chill*—there's no other word for it. It may also be that after years of functioning as the foundation of the orchestra, they've begun to evolve into concrete.

---

7 Jazz is different—in part because the instrument is used differently; it's plucked rather than bowed.

Violinists Are High-Strung

If bassists are the cool, unflappable kids sitting in the back of the class, then violinists are the athletic-field show-offs and the front-row overachievers with the messianic complexes who just want Ms. Fulton to call on *them*, God damn it, because their answers are always way better than Cindy's.[8]

A violinist filling out a job application for a normal job might list, among their positive qualities, their dedication, their attention to detail, and their single-mindedness. For their negative qualities, they *could* list their competitiveness, their egocentricity, and their obsessiveness, but they'd probably just write something annoying like "Sometimes I'm too hard on myself." Which, in fairness, would probably be true.

The violinist personality represents one of those difficult chicken-egg cycles in which it's unclear whether our competitive, perfectionist training is responsible for our competitive, perfectionist tendencies or whether it is our competitive, perfectionist tendencies that are responsible for our competitive, perfectionist training (which is implemented, of course, by the competitive perfectionists who emerged from the previous cycle). Either way, whoever coined the term "high-strung" was likely thinking of a violinist at the time.

We also struggle with arrogance. When I was engaged to Golden Violin Boy, he always insisted on practicing in the middle of our double-story living room, which functioned as a kind of megaphone, sending his sound blasting through every wall in the building, instead of in the closed-off study I had very subtly filled with all his

---

8   This doesn't mean that violinists are athletic or that they sit in the fronts of classrooms outside of this metaphor. Many of them actually mail it in athletically and academically in order to maximize their practice time.

diplomas, press clippings, and music stands. He had simply never considered the possibility that there were people in the world who might not have wanted to listen to his playing for hours and hours every day. People like me. Or our neighbors. Who obviously would have rather listened to *my* playing for hours and hours every day.

It all comes back to the violin sound. Violins have the highest, most brilliant sound of any of the stringed instruments—and as a result we have a huge and magnificent solo repertoire that's equal parts lyricism, exhibitionism, and *transcendence*. We're used to being heard, which leads to expectations—and a lot of pressure.

I should mention that there are two types of violinists whose personalities differ from the standard model. The first type is composed of players like Maxim Vengerov—players who are so genuinely confident in their abilities and so comfortable in their skin that they don't succumb to the self-doubt and anxiety that plagues so many of us. The second is composed of those violinists—and there are many—who will (or should) ultimately become violists.

Violists Are (in a Lot of) Jokes

The first thing you need to know in order to understand violists is that they are the only classical instrumentalists who have their own category of joke. There *are* jokes about other instruments (like: "What did the drummer get on his SAT? Drool.")—but these are few and far between. Viola jokes, on the other hand, outnumber viola *pieces*.

The solo viola repertoire is quite small when compared to the solo repertoire of the violin or the cello. The sound of the viola is neither as brilliant as the violin's nor as deep and rich as the cello's, which means it's easily lost in front of an orchestra. When heard alone, however, it has a lovely, warm sound that you can't help but like.

The majority of the viola repertoire is orchestral or for small ensembles—in contexts where the instrument can act as the glue and the center of the collective sound. But there are a few notable exceptions where the viola *is* featured, like *Harold in Italy* by Hector Berlioz. Which brings me to this:

What's the longest viola joke in the world?
Harold in Italy.

Viola jokes are all like that. Insulting. Belittling. Hilarious.

What's the difference between a viola and an onion?
No one cries when you cut up a viola.

In what way is a violist's finger like lightning?
It never strikes the same place twice.

What's the difference between a viola and a trampoline?
You take your shoes off to jump on a trampoline.

How is a viola like a lawsuit?
Everyone's happy when the case is closed.

Now, is it *fair* to imply that all violists are incompetent, unintelligent, and universally despised? No. None of these generalizations are fair. I hope you know that. And violists are lovely. But I do know one who once embarked on a three-day "juice cleanse" and was unable to grasp that the point of such cleanses is to consume *only* juice—no matter how many people tried to explain it to her—so she continued to consume gallons of maple syrup mixed with lemon and water *in addition to* heaping platefuls of pasta, curry, ice cream, and cake—and she was actually surprised when she struggled to zip up her evening gown before her next concert.

Guitarists Don't Get a Section

Guitarists are also string players, with their own exciting repertoire. But there's no guitar section of the orchestra, which means that there are relatively few guitarists at each conservatory—and those who *are* there tend to operate on the outskirts of the scene. I've always imagined them playing Dungeons & Dragons during practice breaks, but I have no idea whether they really do. (I also have no idea how to play Dungeons & Dragons.) The truth is, I just don't know enough of them to tell you what they're like.

Singers Are Prima Donnas

I should really mention singers next. Singers, like the Australian sugar glider, develop emotional and behavioral problems if they do not receive sufficient amounts of attention. I've already imperiled their well-being by waiting this long.

Opera singers make violinists look like a bunch of demure meerkats who have been terrified of spotlights ever since the day they saw their friend get electrocuted by one. Whereas most violinists I know crave adulation because it's a form of validation—a kind of pat on the back signifying that our hard work has been recognized—singers seem to bask in it the way that old, naked Germans bask in the sun. Whether singers are bowing or curtsying or simply walking into a room, their carriage and mannerisms always seem to be saying, "Yes, aren't I?"

I can't say I blame them for this. I felt the same way when I was pregnant. I couldn't get over how miraculous I was for being able to *grow a person* in my lower abdomen, and I developed this internal third-person commentary that would follow me around all day and say things like "Hold on to your hats, folks, it looks like she's going to attempt to shower *while* constructing a pair of kidneys! Wow. I've seen a lot in my day, but I never thought I'd see a thing like this."

Singers are similarly miraculous multitaskers. They're actors *and* musicians *and*, perhaps most impressively of all, instruments. They're completely self-sufficient. They're productions unto themselves. They can sing whenever, wherever, regardless of what they have or don't have with them. Unless, you know, it's a bit damp. Or they've had milk that day. Or there are people around who aren't looking at them.

Singers have a reputation—which is sometimes fair and sometimes wildly unfair, depending on the singer—for being emotional. They also have a reputation for disregarding factors like rhythm, tempo, and their collaborators.

There's a famous joke—yes, another one—about an opera rehearsal. It goes like this:

After running through an opera's big first-act soprano aria, the conductor turns to the orchestra and says, "I want all of you to add three beats to the second bar of letter A and one beat to the third—and then write in a repeat sign at the end of the fourth and put a fermata on the last beat of the fifth—then change to the key of C-sharp major in the sixth—[blah blah blah]—and if everyone's got all that, we can take it from the top."

The conductor then raises his baton, ignoring the musicians who are still frantically scribbling the changes into their parts, only to be interrupted by the soprano's dainty coughing.

"And what shall I change, maestro?" she asks.

"Oh, don't worry," he says. "You just do what you were doing."

A soprano, in this case, is not a member of the Italian Mafia family based in New Jersey but rather a singer whose voice falls into the highest vocal range: the soprano range. Different types of sopranos have different sounds—some richer and some brighter—but the voices of good sopranos are always very high, very brilliant, and very powerful.[9] There are also mezzo-sopranos (sometimes referred to as "mezzos"), who have the second-highest range. Their voices tend to be mellower, with a bit more of what I would call "body." (Sopranos will disagree.) They'll likely still sound "high" to you, though—because they are. (Here again, sopranos will disagree.) Next come contraltos, who have the lowest female range (and mellower voices still); tenors, who sing in the range that most people think of when they think of male opera singers (think Pavarotti); baritones (lower—getting into very deep, macho territory); and basses (the Hulk low). There's also something called a countertenor—a male singer with the same range as a female contralto—but they are less common and many of them are not considered to be "true" countertenors because of some technical things that aren't generally interesting or important to people who aren't singers. (It makes absolutely no difference to me, for instance, what kind of countertenor I'm listening to, provided that he sounds nice.)

Pianists Know the Score

Sometimes I'll be very proud of myself for having read an article in *The New York Times* or *Süddeutsche Zeitung* and I'll ask Stephan what he thinks about A Development (to show off the fact that I know

---

9   You sometimes hear the term "coloratura," which is a kind of soprano. "Lyric" is another often-discussed kind. Coloratura sopranos tend to have lighter, more facile voices and lyric sopranos focus on sustain.

about it) and his response will be that perfect blend of concision and sagacity and understanding-for-all-the-flawed-mortals-who-created-the-mess-in-the-first-place that makes you wonder why he isn't the Chancellor of Germany. And his total lack of eagerness in delivering it—the fact that he just *had* this thought sitting around in his head, without ever intending to use it—gives you the feeling that there is no conflict in the whole history of politics of which he is unaware, and that there are volumes more of these brilliant reflections just waiting to be mined, if only I knew enough about what was going on in the world to ask the right questions.[10]

I sometimes get a similar feeling when I'm in the presence of pianists. (Also French toddlers.) They are not, generally, outwardly arrogant,[11] but I always have the feeling that they know and understand things that I don't. Important things. Things that would blow my mind if I knew about them.

This feeling is due, in part, to that quiet bookishness—that studiousness—that so many of them exude.[12] And some of it is probably because my father is a pianist, and I'll always feel like he knows more than I do, regardless of how many times he asks me for help logging into his Gmail account. But much of it comes down to the amount of ink that's on any given page of a piano score.

To begin with, pianists have an obscene number of notes to play. This always impresses me, even though I realize that the physics of

---

10 This is why I have to make fun of his singing all the time.

11 Unlike French adults.

12 The pianist in my trio while I was at Juilliard, Henry Kramer, is actually one of the most approachable, hilarious, unconstrained people I've ever met—but he still intimidates me, because he's won top prizes in so many of the world's major piano competitions.

the instrument allow for it in a way that the physics of other instruments do not. But it's more than that, too.

Most instrumentalists play off of parts. When I play a sonata with a pianist, for instance, I see only the notes that I'm personally responsible for playing—all of which fit into one staff (line of music).[13] The pianist, on the other hand, reads off of a score that consists of one grand staff (something like a double staff) *and* the violin part. In other words, while I'm staring at one-*third* of the staves involved in the composition, the pianist is seeing all three. They are literally "seeing the big picture" when they play, which feels (to me) a lot like wisdom.

Technically, if I'm prepared, I should have a firm grasp of the piano part, too, but since pianists, as I said, have an obscene number of notes, and my brain isn't wired to think in stacked harmonies, I tend to latch on to melodies, catchy rhythmic figures, and major changes in the bass line for my cues (the Blinkist edition of the piano part) instead of internalizing the score in its entirety.

Here's a stupid fact: in an orchestra, the piano is considered a member of the percussion section. This is justifiable because pianos have keys and hammers—as do marimbas and xylophones—but it's not particularly helpful as a classification. If someone told you they loved the piano, you wouldn't say to them, "Oh, then you've *got* to hear the snare drum solo in Shostakovich's Symphony No. 10."

The same thing goes for the harp, which is a member of both the percussion section *and* the string section. It's impressive and all, that someone was able to identify it as a thing that is percussed and that has strings, but I'm not really sure *who benefits* from shoving it into two categories that have nothing to do with its essential function.

---

13 Except under very specific circumstances generally involving modern and contemporary compositions.

(Harp players may belong to two sections in the orchestra, but they belong to no sections in this chapter because, as with guitarists, there are too few of them for me to generalize about.)

All of this makes a bit more sense, though, when you consider how many instruments fall under the percussion section—and how many roles fall under the percussionist's duties.

Percussionists Roll with the Punches

Most percussionists—real percussionists, that is[14]—specialize in one particular area, but they all study the same group of instruments in school. Usually: timpani, snare drum, marimba, vibraphone, xylophone, and glockenspiel, along with accessories like: tambourine, cymbals, bass drum, and triangle. (There are more, but we all have things we need to do.)

Percussionists end up taking on a lot of odd jobs. Whenever anyone has a sound that needs to be made, whether it's the splashing of water or the cracking of a whip or the screams of a desperate musician getting chased through the audience by a hungry pack of wolves, the task of creating that sound will fall on a percussionist.[15] I remember a rehearsal being paused once, in Japan, because the piece we were playing called for paper shredding, and the percussionist had exhausted his supply of parchment paper. Normal paper was too quiet.

What this means is that percussionists tend to be good at rolling with the punches—and they all have a bit of that experiment-happy mad scientist in them. They sometimes act very cool, but most of

---

14 I.e., not pianists, whom we've covered, or harpists, whom we'll leave unscathed.

15 Timpanists' duties are limited to the timpani.

them are fidgety and nervous on the inside, like Captain Hook whenever he's near that crocodile with the clock in its belly. Except that they're also like the crocodile, ticking away internally, haunted by their inner metronomes. They're quite intelligent (in spite of that joke I told about the drummer's SATs), if not always intellectual. The two I dated were also lying sociopaths, but I've known other percussionists who were not. As far as I know.

Brass Players Are Frat Boys

Speaking of people I've dated, we should talk about the brass section.

Brass players have always struck me as the rowdy fraternity brothers of the orchestra. (There are a few sisters, too, but even if you scoured all the major symphony orchestras in the world, you'd be hard-pressed to find enough to populate one sorority.) They are often attractive when they're young, but the men tend to go bald early in life. The brass players I know have theorized that this is because of their role in the orchestra: they spend a lot of time waiting for and anticipating their next entrance, which is stressful because they wait with the knowledge that *when* they come in, their instruments, which were built to blast across meadows and mountains in hunts and battles and moments of imminent peril, will be heard by absolutely everyone in the hall.

The standard brass instruments in a symphony are the trumpet, the trombone, the French horn, and the tuba. (There are also several variations and subcategories, but knowing about them won't enrich your quality of life.) The trumpet is the most brilliant of these, the French horn is the noblest and warmest, the trombone is the loudest, and the tuba is the *oompah-pah*-est. Oddly, though, most of the trombonists I've met have been quieter, in social interactions, than their section colleagues.

There are, of course, plenty of intelligent brass players, but this is not a sect of the orchestra that's known for braininess, which is why so many musicians failed to catch that the article, from a few decades back, about the trombonist who lit a firecracker out of the bell of his trombone during the finale of Tchaikovsky's *1812 Overture*, resulting in widespread injury and mayhem, was a joke. And by "so many musicians," I mean me.

Wind Players Are (Probably) Cat People

Generally speaking,[16] there's more homogeny—of sound, of character, of scalp appearance, and of gender—within the brass section than there is within the wind section. Flutists are closer to the violinist/singer end of the diva spectrum, for instance, while bassoonists are closer to violists. Mainly in the sense that they're very good sports about being made fun of. But the winds still feel like a united entity, set apart from the other sections in the orchestra.

I have yet to conduct the survey that will prove this, but if I had to guess, I'd say that the majority of wind players are cat people.[17] I can't explain why I'm so convinced of this correlation, or why every string player I've discussed the theory with has been so quick to agree with me. It certainly has nothing to do with my aversion to cats. There's just something about the sounds of certain wind instruments— and the faces that wind players make while playing—and the way they all seem to conduct themselves independently, spending hours on instrument maintenance, that reminds me of cats. Brass players

---

16 All of this is generally speaking, of course—and a tad hyperbolic.

17 The two harpists I know are also cat people.

remind me of dogs. There's no pretense with dogs or with brass players. Wind players, on the other hand, are shrewder, more subtle. Even if the bassoon *is* known as the "farting bedpost of the orchestra."

There are four primary wind instruments in an orchestra, and they are: the flute, the oboe, the clarinet, and the bassoon.[18] Each of these creates a different color, used by composers to achieve a specific effect. They are very much like the brass section in that they, individually or as a whole section, can either serve to fill a layer of the full symphonic sound *or* pop up in brief solos scattered throughout a composition. Their primary function in classical music *is* symphonic, but they can also appear as proper soloists (in concertos, for instance) or in small chamber ensembles.

> * Note: if any of the musicians listed in the sections above is a full-time participant in one or more ensembles specializing in historical performance or contemporary music, they will display fewer of the characteristics I have described above and behave, instead, like vegans. Not Hollywood vegans, whose activism is displayed in a glossier, trendier way, but the kinds of vegans you find hiking the Appalachian Trail or existing in any place called "Portland."

Conductors Are Assholes

The whole summer camp business with Irene was the first true test of character I encountered in my life. It was the first time I had to decide who I was, where my limits were, and whether or not I wanted to start stuffing my bra. (The condo with the sixteen-year-olds was governed, primarily, by pinup ads.)

---

18 There are also their offshoots: the piccolo is an offshoot of the flute, the English horn is an offshoot of the oboe, the bass clarinet is an offshoot of the clarinet, and the contrabassoon is an offshoot of the bassoon.

The first character test I'm encountering *here* is the subject of conductors—or "maestros," as they insist on being called. There are a lot of things I'd *like* to say about conductors. That they're overpaid figureheads, for instance. Or that they're arrogant pricks. Or that the YouTube video of the three-year-old boy conducting Beethoven's Fifth Symphony is *not* proof that the three-year-old is a musical genius, but rather that the role of conductor is one that can be executed by a three-year-old. I have decades of pent-up grievances just waiting to flow forth and knock the podiums out from under these venerated divas.

But the goal, here, is to provide insight into the music world, not into my issues with authority figures. So I'll attempt to keep my commentary on the subject as unbiased as possible. Or, at least, as unbiased as it's been for the rest of this chapter.

Conductors are certainly impressive figures. The way they emerge from the wings at the start of each concert and sweep up to the podium before turning with furrowed brow and wizard-like arms to the orchestra is a display I would miss if I were ever successful in eradicating the breed in its entirety. But it's just that: a display. It's a parade—a pageant—one that shows few of the realities and none of the complexities of the conductor-orchestra dynamic.

I like to think of conductors as existing on a spectrum. On one end, you have the conductors who truly *are* wizard-like—who transport their players and audiences, taking them on a kind of aural magic-carpet ride through the gorgeous landscape of the music. They're inspiring leaders endowed with vision and diplomacy, who create hierarchy and sublime structure out of the score's clutter of two-dimensional scribbles.

I'll never forget what it was like to play Brahms's Symphony No. 2 under Bernard Haitink, whose twinkly blue eyes looked to contain the wisdom of the galaxy and whose soul seemed to flow directly from his fingertips and wrap us all in a tender but totally appropriate hug of genius. And no one who was lucky enough to be assigned to Juilliard's 2007 production of *La finta giardiniera* will ever forget Gary Thor Wedow, whose artistic vision was rivaled only by the consideration and unprecedented levels of respect he extended to the players.[19]

On the other end of the spectrum, you have characters who are more Wizard of Oz than Gandalf the Grey: bumbling, overblown charlatans who offer little in the way of inspiration or leadership, without whom the orchestra would be far better off. I can't list any of them by name, though, because Stephan is a lawyer and he worries about things like defamation.

The vast majority of conductors fall somewhere in the middle, fulfilling the basics of the role but adding little artistry to the equation. These conductors are like less heroic crossing guards—if crossing guards also dictated whether people sprinted or crawled or tour-jetéd from sidewalk to sidewalk. (Which, incidentally, should totally be a thing that crossing guards do.) This is helpful even when the piece is relatively straightforward, but it's crucial in modern and contemporary music, where the potential for pileups is amplified. In operas and ballets, too, the conductor serves an important function: conductors are the sole visual link between the orchestra, which is buried in the "pit" and therefore cut off from the rest of the world, and whatever it is that's going on aboveground.

But no conductor, however helpful or brilliant, is a Drosselmeyer-esque puppeteer capable of extracting sound from a sea of black-clad

---

19 At the end of the project, the whole orchestra chipped in and bought him a gift to show our gratitude. It was a bassist who organized the effort, so the gift ended up being a bottle of Grey Goose vodka.

minions who would, if left to their own devices, remain silent for the entire two hours you paid to hear them.

In fact, orchestras generally look and sound about the same whether or not there's a conductor standing in front of them—provided that the piece they're playing falls within the standard repertoire and that the orchestra is not the kind my middle school had, where only half the kids could read music and the other half showed up to rehearsal with their instruments in six pieces.[20] Conductors, without orchestras, on the other hand, sound like nothing. Actually, no—they sound like a lot of heavy breathing and panting and grunting. And they *look* like mimes engaged in the simultaneous acts of tossing a salad, painting a fence, and knitting—while doing an interpretive fly-swatting dance.

Many conductors, however, seem unable to grasp the precariousness and inherent dependency of their position, and they go around behaving like petulant authoritarian monarchs who think they poop gold bullion. The majority of orchestral players are too polite (and attached to their jobs) to stand up to these system-empowered bullies.

But not always. I remember hearing about an incident some years back, when the principal horn player of a major symphony orchestra allegedly stood up to a visiting conductor and said, "We're the goddamn [insert name of major US city containing the Empire State Building and Statue of Liberty] Philharmonic. You're here to play with us. We're not here to play with you." (Or something to that effect.) Not everyone approved of the outburst, but his point was made. The conductor was not invited back.

So there you have it. There are good conductors and bad conduc-

---

20 In fact, there are many smaller orchestral ensembles that perform without conductors. In these cases—and in cases where a conductor is abominable—the orchestras rely on their concertmaster to signal the beat and major cues (while also continuing to play).

tors. Just as there are crisp, sweet, tangy blueberries and blueberries that you really wish you could go back in time and un-eat. And as with blueberries, the ratio is not quite what you want it to be.

Here's another joke.

You're driving down a dark, isolated road when you come across a conductor and a violist standing in the middle of it, arguing about a recent performance of Harold in Italy. *Which one do you hit first: the conductor or the violist?*

The conductor. Business before pleasure.

The First Conductor I Ever Knew

I think one of the reasons I'm so hard on conductors is that the first one I ever knew was such a wonderful man. He was also a cellist—a giant from Lexington, Kentucky, with coppery skin, a golden heart, and an Afro that later grew into a skinny ponytail at the back of his head. He liked to wear colorful geometric prints. When I was at Andover, I called him Mr. Thomas. But I knew him, from birth, as William.

He was one of my earliest mentors and possibly my first champion, inviting me to play with Andover's orchestra—"as a ringer," he'd say—years before I matriculated. He was extremely round and he used to mock himself for it, threatening to sit on us and squash us like bugs if we misbehaved in rehearsal. There was nothing, actually, that he didn't make fun of himself for. He once suffered the most spectacular onstage clothing malfunction, when the elasticized trousers he was wearing under his brightly printed tunic slid down to his ankles in the middle of a piano concerto and he had to extricate one of his feet from its pant leg so he wouldn't have to waddle off the stage like a penguin. He shared the story the next day with everyone who wasn't already laughing about it.

I didn't realize, back then, that his humility, his kindness, and the color of his skin made him an exception in the field—nor did I realize that there were plenty of other conductors out there who ended up with their pants around their ankles, surrounded by students, for different reasons entirely.

I've been far luckier than some of my colleagues when it comes to this fouler element. I did have a run-in with one of the industry's ancient and famously creepy (now-canceled) maestros, but I'd been warned in advance that an invitation to "the theater" meant something else when it was coming from him, so I used those words as my exit cue. I was twenty at the time, which is the same age my sister was when a different ancient, creepy maestro pulled her into his limo after a concert and tried to abscond with her to his hotel room. (Thankfully, he was unbelievably drunk, which made it relatively easy for her to escape his clutches.)

Many of them got swept up in the big #MeToo reckoning.[21] The lesser offenders are likely living out a nightmarish waiting game—hopefully on their best behavior. But whether they're in exile, in hell, or in Poland, conductors like these are just manure on the shoes that William Thomas so magnificently filled.

---

21 Rather late, since movements like this always take a while to reach the dustier corners of our world.

Chapter 5

million-dollar baby grands (and violins)

The Literal Price of Excellence

One Saturday I was standing in line at Espresso Royale (which was the place, just across Huntington Avenue, where all the New England Conservatory prep students and horrible stage parents [and regular nice parents] picked up sandwiches and coffee) when the man behind me asked if the thing hanging over my shoulder was a violin.

I told him it was.

"I've heard that violins are really valuable," he said.

It was super awkward.

"You know," he went on, his eyes widening, "sometimes they can even be worth, like, *ten thousand dollars*."

I don't always get to play the role of Informed Sophisticate. I used to think that Elie Saab was a woman—and that the "gulf" in "Gulf War" was the Gulf of Mexico. And once, when my cousins and I were building something top secret, and we got glue all over a bottle of Elmer's, I was the one with the brilliant idea to rinse it off in the fish tank.[1]

---

1 I knew that glue was bad for tables. I *didn't* know—yet—that it was bad for fish. (Very bad.)

So I always feel pretty good about myself when I'm in the know. And what I knew, on that Saturday when I was standing in line, waiting for my turkey on rye, was that while violins *can* be worth ten thousand dollars, ten thousand dollars is not an impressive amount to spend on a violin.

My first real violin—the half-sized model I had when I was seven (after I'd graduated from those tiny orange factory-made rentals I started out with)—was probably around ten thousand dollars. But I upgraded when I was nine—and again when I was twelve or thirteen, to the Jean-Baptiste Vuillaume violin I have now.

It was a thrilling process, finding my violin: a fantastical exploration of history and sound and the very real chemistry that's possible between a player and an inanimate wooden artifact. It's an experience I can only recommend, particularly to anyone who enjoyed the Ollivanders scene in *Harry Potter and the Sorcerer's Stone*.

Ollivanders, in my case, was a shop in Boston's Back Bay, called Reuning & Son. It had its own floor in an old brownstone and its darkly lacquered, wood-paneled elevator carried the smell of wood shavings and varnish right down from the shop to greet you in the lobby. It may be that I was simply addicted to the fumes, but I always loved going there.

The main room was filled with violins and violin parts and violin bows and violin blueprints and fantastic carved wooden music stands inlaid with mother-of-pearl and exotic woods. There were also display cases filled with all types of rosins and strings and the most precious, ornate pegs for tuning.

In the back, through a set of French doors, there was a brighter room with a bay window. I think the walls were light blue. That's where they kept the cellos—and a heavily framed floor-to-ceiling mirror that looked very much like the Mirror of Erised. Back through the French doors and across the main area was a smaller, windowless room, with cozy, old wallpaper and a collection of small, framed musical cartoons. This was where I spent most of my time, trying violins.

It was essentially a glorified closet, and it was far less resonant than the blue room, which was the one I always hoped they'd put me in. I used to wonder why they kept hiding me away, until Peter Jarvis, the Reuning's expert who guided my family through the process, explained that its dry acoustics made it better for trying instruments. Everything sounded good in the blue room.

Peter would always have three or four violins laid out for me, along with several bows for pairing. Each violin had a different tone and personality—a different voice. There was one I'll never forget; it had a gorgeous burl wood back that I found completely mesmerizing for its iridescent, intoxicating swirls. I almost picked it, because I was thirteen and it matched my hair and I couldn't let go of how good we'd look together. But its sound felt so delicate—brittle, almost—and there was something forthright and dauntless about my Vuillaume that made me trust it.

So I made my choice. Peter assured my parents that it was a good investment and my parents, in turn, made me swear that when I eventually found the man of my dreams, one or two decades down the road, we would elope.

Because the violin cost ninety thousand dollars and my parents had to remortgage their house to pay for it.[2]

This was, without question, *insanely* generous of my mom and dad, who were teachers, not oil magnates, remember. But while my violin is an extremely fine specimen—it's still far, *far* from the most expensive violin ever sold.

---

2 They must have found it so hilarious when I quit just a few years into my professional career.

The (Literal) Price of Excellence

Let's look at some numbers. Then we can discuss what they actually *mean* for musicians. First off, instruments outside of the string family don't sell for the same astronomical prices. High-end brass instruments (those that did not once belong to Miles Davis and aren't made out of platinum) do not generally exceed $4,000 to $13,000, depending on the specific instrument and model, with trumpets and French horns topping off at around $4,000 and trombones and tubas falling on the higher end of the scale. Top-tier wind instruments, on the other hand, generally range from around $10,000 to $20,000. These don't appreciate with age, and they deteriorate with frequent use.

Pianos come the closest to stringed instruments in terms of value. Most of the concert pianos you see in the great concert halls of the world are priced in the low six digits. Steinway's largest model, for instance—a "model D"—is just around the $200,000 mark, though the exact price varies depending on its place of origin. (Steinways made in Hamburg are more expensive than those made in New York.) Bösendorfers and Faziolis are in roughly the same bracket. There are also pianos valued in the millions, but these are lent their worth by their historical or anecdotal significance, or by embellishments to the exterior of the piano itself, which have more to do with the furniture-like qualities of a piano than with its function as a musical instrument. They have no impact on the larger "piano market."

Here are a few of them, though, for fun:

- The Steinway Alma-Tadema—a custom model D that looks, with its Greco-Roman–style hand-carving and mother-of-pearl inlay, like something one might have found in the palace of Croesus—sold for $1.2 million at Christie's in 1997.

· John Lennon's old upright—which, in contrast to the Alma-Tadema, has that buttoned-up-librarian look that all uprights share, as if they're compensating for the wildness of their leggy sister, "baby grand," so that their melodramatic, perpetually scandalized mother, the organ, will have *one* daughter she can rely upon—was purchased by George Michael for £1.67 million in 2000. (Because in this case it doesn't really matter what the piano looks like, does it?)

· The Heintzman crystal piano that Lang Lang used to open the 2008 Beijing Olympic Games sold for $3.2 million, which is also the exact amount I would pay to *not* have a crystal piano in my house.

But these uniquely significant pianos, as expensive as they are, are still echelons below the highest violin prices seen on the market today. Here are two violin sales from about a decade ago:

· In 2011, the 1721 Lady Blunt Stradivarius[3] became the most expensive violin in the world, selling for $15.9 million at auction.

· In 2012, the Vieuxtemps del Gesù surpassed that, selling for $16 million in a private sale.

---

3 They all have great names like this. There's the Gibson ex-Huberman; the ex-Liebig; the ex-Berou ex-Thibaud; the Duke of Cambridge ex–Pierre Rode; the Firebird ex–Saint-Exupéry; the ex–Count Vieri . . . I could do this all day, but you may not be enjoying the exercise as much as I am.

Most of the lists touting the "world's most expensive instruments" begin with these two violins and then drop off, sinking to three- or four-million-dollar amounts. But these are mostly outdated—and always incomplete.

We know about the Lady Blunt Strad because it was sold publicly, by Tarisio, a leading auction house and dealer specializing in fine instruments.[4] The Vieuxtemps del Gesù, on the other hand, was sold privately. The only reason we know about that one is that its owner *wants* us to know. (Presumably, the violinist who was granted "lifetime use" of the instrument doesn't mind, either. I certainly wouldn't.) The details of most high-end sales, however—including several that have since broken the Vieuxtemps del Gesù's record—are kept private.

Luckily, I have friends in the business who can tell us—approximately—just how much we all need to be saving for our next Strad purchases. Friends like Florian Leonhard, one of the world's most important instrument authenticators and dealers—and a man who always looks as if he's stepping directly out of a *GQ* editorial.

(When I say that he's one of the world's most important instrument authenticators, I mean that he has the power to issue certificates of authentication and value, and that his word can, in fact, *assign* value to an instrument. Theoretically, he could say that a cucumber was a Strad and it would go down in history as such, provided that no one ever tried to play on it. But he would never do this, of course, because the only things he cares about more than his reputation are his violins and Elly Suh, the incredible violinist [and my former classmate] who also happens to be his wife.)

---

4 Tarisio also keeps a handy online database of makers and auction records in case you want to check it out.

"The very finest of violins," he told me, "with the great history and good condition, are beyond twenty million dollars in value. Sometimes asking prices are as high as twenty-five million, but this is uncommon. Golden-period Strads [Stradivarius violins made between 1700 and 1725] cost from twelve million onwards, unless they are quite damaged or parts are replaced; normal Strads from later periods are ten to twelve million, but they can also drop down to three million when pieces are missing and they are damaged."

Strads and del Gesùs are the two most famous and most expensive kinds of instruments, referred to by the names of their makers, Antonio Stradivari—sometimes rendered "Antonius Stradivarius"—and Giuseppe Guarneri. (Guarneri comes from a whole family of violin makers—and because that family includes another Giuseppe Guarneri, he is referred to as "Guarneri del Gesù" due to the *nomen sacrum* IHS and cross fleury that can be found, after the year 1731, on his instrument labels.) There are other makers, too, whose instruments are very sought-after—and very expensive—but their price tags usually have fewer zeros.

The Number of Zeros

"But why are these instruments so expensive?" some of you may be asking.

This is a question that often comes up in string-playing circles. Normally, though, it's asked rhetorically, while weeping and falling to the knees, with hands upturned to the heavens.

It's a tragedy that Strads and del Gésus cost as much as small but luxurious private jets when most musicians would rather stow away in the baggage hold of a B-level commercial airline than pay for an actual ticket.[5] Only a handful of players (and by "handful," I mean two) will ever be able to afford even the least expensive of these instruments. The rest will either go their lives without playing one or find themselves at the mercy of a sponsor, who can strip them of their prize at any given time.

I know I've spent a lot of time trying to convince you, so far, that this genre is for everyone, but this is a corner of it that's basically for no one.

On the other hand, having played on both Strads and del Gésus in the past—having felt their smooth, worn wood and the history and magic that seems to radiate from them—I can't say they don't deserve the respect and cachet—and, yes, the price tags—they're awarded.

But what are the factors that go into determining those price tags?

When I was a kid, I always assumed that the value of instruments was based purely on sound. The point of a violin, after all, is to play on it. But the matter is far more complex—and sound is subjective.

When Florian appraises a violin, he bases the value on a set of tangible criteria. Sound is *part* of the equation.

"A Strad," he says, "is a ten out of ten. It checks off every box perfectly."

When I questioned him about del Gesùs, he said, "Del Gesùs are not [a perfect ten]—but they are an exception. A del Gesù may not tick all of the boxes in the same way as a Strad—the beauty or

---

5 Even musicians of the highest caliber frequently have to pay for their own concert air-fare, and at the beginning of the pandemic, when concerts were canceled but airlines had yet to develop flexible refund policies, many freelancers ended up absorbing those costs themselves. (And *then* they had to go over a year without income.)

craftsmanship is sometimes less pristine and refined—but the two are still equals because del Gesù creates something equally beautiful that is rough and flowing and fluid: he achieves an amazing result."

He describes the sound of a Strad as having "that golden feel to it"—whereas the sound of a del Gesù he calls a "rough roar." I'm not sure whether I would have chosen the word "rough"—this roughness he refers to is much like the roughness one might see, under a microscope, when examining the apparently smooth, burnished surface of a copper pot—but then, he works so closely with these instruments that the differences *are* likely magnified. I fully agree, in any case, that there is a power and depth of character to del Gesùs—and it's one that I actually prefer to the luster of Strads.[6] One could say, possibly, that a Strad is like a Rolls-Royce, while a del Gesù is more like a Bugatti.[7]

The respective tones of the best-sounding Stradivariuses and del Gesùs are incomparable. But can I say that they're worth millions and millions more than those produced by Giovanni Battista Guadagnini's violins? Or millions and millions and *millions* more than the sound of my Vuillaume? It's difficult to say. Hilary Hahn, a phenomenal celebrity violinist, would say no. She famously prefers her Vuillaume to the old Italian instruments. Which . . . I mean . . . I love my Vuillaume—I call it J.B. for short—but I did not hesitate to lock it up in a closet for half a year when Juilliard loaned me a Strad.

There are also plenty of players who prefer the sound and feel of modern instruments. In fact, Florian once took part in a screened comparison of modern instruments versus a handful of Strads, del

---

6   So now you know what to get me for my birthday.

7   This is another gift I wouldn't mind getting.

Gesùs, and Guadagninis (listeners seated in a hotel ballroom voted on their preferences)—and the modern instruments came out slightly ahead. Florian believes that the acoustics of a ballroom (and the fact that the musicians played into a curtain) favored the more present, immediate sound of the modern makers. But it's an interesting result, nonetheless—one that highlights the impact of the other components of instrument valuation. Such as:

AGE

There is, I gather, a friendly, one-sided war betwixt modern makers and the centuries-deceased Italian ones—which the rest of us indulge, I suppose, because the defenseless (dead) side is still winning.

One reason that the older violins have an advantage is that their age—their history—makes them inherently more valuable. This is why I found it so adorable, a few years back, when a friend of my sister's had the idea of buying her a new cello for Christmas—"because the one she has now is so old." (Her cello was even more expensive than my violin.)

I should mention, though, that while modern instruments are not generally seen as investments—not to the same degree, anyway—there *are* living makers whose work has appreciated significantly within their career spans. Samuel Zygmuntowicz, for instance, charged around $53,000 for a new violin back in 2009, whereas in 2019, a Zygmuntowicz violin went for $132,000 at auction.[8]

---

8 There were, in fact, Zygmuntowicz violins selling for around that price already back in the early 2000s; his wait list is so long, though, that people were willing to pay triple his asking price to own one right away.

CRAFTSMANSHIP

Another factor is craftsmanship, which is inextricable from the instrument's make. There are minuscule discrepancies that make a huge difference to the value and reputation of each maker—discrepancies so minuscule that I, along with most players, probably wouldn't be able to spot them. At least, not without the help of a trained expert.

Which brings me to another escaped *GQ* model: Carlos Tome, the director and head of sales at Tarisio (of Lady Blunt Stradivarius fame). Reader, Carlos. Carlos, reader.

Carlos explains that the criteria of "craftsmanship" here aren't necessarily (or even generally) a matter of aesthetic beauty—that the proportions of an instrument, or the decorative nature of the wood, don't always determine an instrument's worth:

"Del Gesù from Guarneri's later [and most expensive] period are comparatively rough.[9] By this time in his life, he had come to prioritize the efficiency of his creations over their physical beauty. Which is a kind of beauty unto itself."

Carlos went on to explain that Guarneri was more concerned with the outcome than the aesthetics.

"So with these instruments you're not looking for ideally formed beauty. You're looking for uniqueness—but also for the consistency with his production. He wants an instrument that works."

Still, sometimes appearance can be a factor.

Strads, apparently, do tend to be aesthetically perfect—and this perfection is one of the things that heightens their appeal.

---

9 Note that here we have that same word—"rough"—that Florian also used to describe del Gesù.

Carlos also points out that *painted* Amati violins—those featuring original embellishment or decoration—tend to carry a premium. This is partly because the visual artistry is attractive to buyers. But it's also because the extra attention given to these instruments signifies that they are somehow "important."

It's not uncommon, he says, to find Amatis with "fake" paintings—or rather, with embellishments that were added by people from later generations, attempting to boost the instrument's value. Carlos told me about one such Amati that crossed his desk—that *looked*, at first glance, to feature authentic decoration. But a closer inspection revealed that one of the pigments the artist had used wasn't available in the 1600s, when these instruments were being made. The violin was worth less, therefore—even though the quality of the artwork was exemplary. The craftsmanship here had nothing to do with skill, but rather with the materials that were used, which revealed the artwork's inauthenticity.

CONDITION

As with any artifact, condition is also a major consideration: whether the wood has been injured, whether key parts of the instrument have been replaced or damaged, whether major repairs have been made to the body.[10]

In 2003, Eugene Fodor brought his 1727 "Smith" Stradivarius to

---

10 Very few Strad violins and violas are in possession of their original neck (the piece between the scroll and the body of the instrument), but this is considered normal and does not detract from the value. Even those necks that *are* intact have been detached from the instrument on the end closest to the body of the violin and placed at a new, more optimized angle. (As the technical demands of the violin repertoire increased, the angle of the violin neck evolved to suit the players' needs.)

Florian and asked him to repair a crack in the back of the instrument. It wasn't a new crack—it had already been repaired decades earlier—but it was still visible, and Fodor complained that it was "an eyesore." He challenged Florian, who's known for his meticulous repair work, to erase all evidence of it. "I don't even want to know it's there," he said. Florian had no idea, when he accepted the challenge, that Fodor planned to sell the instrument through another dealer—without disclosing the crack.

Fodor succeeded in selling the instrument for twice what it was worth. But the sale backfired several years later, when the violin changed hands again and an expert in Cremonese instruments, who'd seen the violin in a previous auction, remembered the now-invisible crack. He called Florian (few people can repair major damage at this level), who readily told him of the work he had done, and after a trial in which Florian testified, Fodor had to return the money he'd made in the previous sale.

This is all to say that one crack—whether visible or not—can reduce an instrument's value by millions.

SENSATIONALISM

Sometimes, though, instruments are priced without reference to these criteria—or any criteria at all. The "Macdonald" Stradivarius viola was famously offered up at a mind-boggling $45 million and no one seems able to explain why.

Florian suggests that there may have been some flawed logic involved: a computation based on the viola's rarity and its selling history in relation to that of the Lady Blunt.[11] But neither he nor any

---

11 Strad violas are rarer than Strad violins, which makes them generally more valuable.

of his London colleagues who examined the Macdonald could find a justification for such an unprecedentedly high figure.

Carlos agrees.

"An Amati viola is worth twice what an Amati violin is worth," he explained. "That is responsible. But this is not the case with Strads. Even if they did try to apply this formula with the Macdonald, they should have based it on the Lady Blunt's *starting* price, which was much lower."

The viola didn't sell. In spite of a hugely extravagant media campaign involving one of the world's only true (and truly excellent) viola virtuosos.

Carlos went on to speculate that the price was picked for the sake of being sensational—with the hope of thrusting the instrument into a wider, flashier pool of buyers. "I think for the person they wanted . . . violin, viola, it doesn't make a difference. They wanted someone to buy the campaign. Someone who would say, 'You know that expensive thing that was on TV? I bought it.'"

How Not to Steal a Million

In case any of this inspires you to stage an elaborate heist—to pose as a potential buyer with unusually thick facial hair and a very full bladder that simply *cannot wait* to be emptied until after the pegs of the Strad you were inspecting have been untangled from your beard—you should know that you won't make any money out of it. Every expert in the world will recognize your stolen instrument. And you won't be able to sell it *without* an expert because no one wants to pay for an instrument that isn't authenticated. Plus, you'll be on wanted lists. If you're not already.

To demonstrate my point, here are the most successful instrument thefts of the last century:

THE GIBSON EX-HUBERMAN STRADIVARIUS

This violin was stolen twice from violinist Bronisław Huberman—once in 1919, from his hotel in Vienna, and again in 1936, from his dressing room at Carnegie Hall. And before you ask yourself or anyone else what it was that Huberman did to deserve this kind of karma, let me just say that the man was *literally* a hero. His founding in 1936 of what was then the Palestine Symphony—and is now the Israel Philharmonic—provided a means of employment and escape for dozens of Jewish musicians and their families during the Nazi regime, sparing close to a thousand lives in total. He was just very unlucky where violin thefts were concerned. And he had two violins, which made him an easy target.

The first time the violin was stolen, it was returned by the police within days; the thief made the mistake of trying to sell it and was caught as a result. The second time, however, after the violin disappeared from Huberman's dressing room at Carnegie Hall (it was taken while he was performing on his del Gesù), it remained missing for half a century. It was recovered only when the thief revealed to his wife, on his deathbed, that the violin he had been playing publicly for the past fifty years was Huberman's famous stolen Strad.

There are questions as to whether the man who made this confession actually *was* the thief, or whether he bought the stolen violin from a friend in a bar. What is not in question, though, is that he was an absolutely horrific human being who committed all sorts of horrific crimes, which is why his name will not darken the pages of this book. It's also why you should choose not to follow in his footsteps.

THE TOTENBERG-AMES STRADIVARIUS

This story ends, once again, with the wife of the thief uncovering the stolen instrument. But in this case (as it were), the violin had been locked away the entire time.

The instrument was taken in 1980, from Roman Totenberg's office at the Longy School of Music. The thief was the very person Mr. Totenberg had always thought it was—Philip Johnson, the ex-boyfriend of one of Mr. Totenberg's students (who was also "quite sure" of Johnson's guilt). But because, back in 1980, the police were reluctant to move forward without evidence, the violin wasn't discovered until 2015—four years after Johnson's death and three years after Mr. Totenberg's.

ONE THAT'S LESS FAMOUS BUT ALSO WORTH MENTIONING . . .

. . . was the time, in 2010, when a trio of bumbling thugs snatched Min Kym's Strad out from under her seat in a Pret a Manger by London's Euston station. Having absolutely no idea what it was worth, they tried to sell it to a random man in an internet café the following day. *For one hundred pounds.* The man didn't want it, though—because his daughter already had a recorder. (I mean—guys—she had a *recorder.* What could she have possibly wanted with a £1.2 million violin?)

Once the violin appeared in the news, of course, the thieves realized their mistake—and stashed the instrument away. They managed to hide the violin for three years, but they were only able to hide themselves for four weeks before they were arrested.

See what I mean?

Lives ruined in the above thefts: 7+

Money made: $0

But, you know, do what you want.

DURING WWII

I would say that history offers many more examples of violins that have been stolen than of stolen violins that have been sold, but to do so would ignore the dozens of Strads, del Gesùs, Amatis, and other precious instruments stolen by the Nazi regime during the Holocaust that were later sold back into the market before their rightful owners (or heirs) could claim them.

The Sonderstab Musik, a division of Hitler's M-Aktion force, targeted the finest instruments from "Jews, Freemasons, and other similar ideological adversaries of national socialism"[12]—both within Germany and in occupied territories—and brought them to Berlin until after the war, when they were meant to serve the students of Hitler's planned university in Linz, Austria.

There have been concerted efforts, in recent years, to return these instruments—or their monetary equivalents—to the victims of these crimes, but the process is hindered by the incomplete, inexplicit, and sometimes nonexistent documentation that was standard before the war. It wasn't until *after* the war—with the recognition of need and the increase of instrument value—that recording the identities and properties of these instruments became common practice.

---

12 These were the instructions of Alfred Rosenberg, Hitler's "Chefideologe."

The Time I Almost Struck It Rich

I've always wanted to discover a Strad or del Gesù (or any instrument of value) in a dusty old attic or cobweb-covered cellar. Not enough to actually go *into* a dusty old attic or a cobweb-covered cellar, but enough to fantasize about it while zoning out to *Antiques Roadshow.*

So imagine my excitement a few years back, when my father-in-law, who collects all kinds of worthless, questionable-in-origin knickknacks, arrived at my door with the same dream—and three banged-up violins. I still have no idea where he got them. (Stephan and I have found it's better not to ask.) One of the violins, I could see right away, was a waste of our time. It was one of those assembly-line creations that look like they're made out of melted orange-flavored lollipops. A second one looked less flagrantly conveyor-belty, but someone had still punched a hole in one of the ribs—and it bore none of the markers I'd come to associate with concert-level instruments (like variations in the stain—or the patina that comes with six daily hours of practicing). The third violin intrigued me. The label inside the instrument was illegible (which was fine because labels can't always be trusted, anyway), but it had an attractive back, with a lovely, splotchy stain that fluctuated in color from a light gold to a deep red—and a scroll that looked slightly mottled. It was playable, too, if not resplendent in sound. I didn't think it was worth a fortune—but perhaps, I thought, it could be worth a couple thousand. Even, if we were very lucky, ten. And maybe a very small part of me hoped it would make us millionaires.

As it turned out, though, it was entirely worthless. Which is why I turned to Carlos and Florian for help with this chapter.

$\mathbb{C}$hapter 6

welcome to
the jailyard

The Truth About Competition in Classical Music

According to countless Reddit threads, NPR stories, and *New York Times* articles, the act of hiding razor blades between the ivories of the school pianos—to Sweeney-Todd the fingers and career aspirations of the competition—is a time-honored Juilliard tradition. This is partly why the school is referred to, in conservatory circles, as "Jailyard."

It's also why I spent the weeks after matriculation shining flashlights into the cracks of every piano I encountered.

I'd grown up hearing the stories. Everyone had. And just as my kid has spent much of his life, since watching *Home Alone*, brainstorming ways to keep "the bad guys" from breaking into our house—like leaving piles of his brother's used diapers at each point of entry—I spent much of my own striplinghood anticipating and preparing for the various ways in which my future Juilliard classmates might try to sabotage me. (Poison? Easy. I'd drink only sealed bottled water. Sniper hit? I'd walk in a zigzag line. Falling piano? I'd plan to have my chats inside—or very close to the curb.)

My perception that Juilliard was as cutthroat as Paris's Place de la Révolution ca. 1793 was intensified by the fact that when I first auditioned for the school, I didn't get in.

I had no way of knowing, then, how fickle the audition process was—or how close I'd been to making the cut. So what I took away from the rejection was that my efforts—and my own unique musical voice (which was something I still believed in back then)—hadn't been enough.

I wasn't about to give up, of course. I'd always seen Juilliard as a kind of trial by combat, anyway—which made this the first punch in a longer fight rather than the big K.O. Nothing was lost. I just had to up my game.

I spent two years at Northwestern University's School of Music grinding my fingertips down to the bone—honing my skills with the same teachers who'd brought me (and *my Caitlin*) to that picturesque New England mountainside back when we were eleven.[1] I was Rocky Balboa training for his match against Apollo Creed—only without the blushing hesitancy and becoming modesty. And instead of a concise training montage, it was two years of day-in, day-out *slogging*, with occasional bouts of collegiate fun and debilitating strep throat mixed in to keep things interesting. In the fall of my sophomore year, I applied again to Juilliard and this time I got in.

I arrived, armed with my flashlight and steeled against every kind of uppercut and hook I could imagine being thrown my way. But much to my disappointment, no one wanted to fight me. Instead

---

1 They were wonderful teachers and lovely people. Just not very motivated camp counselors.

of a boxing ring and jeering crowd, I found a bunch of perfectly nice, peaceful people who just wanted a room on the fourth floor to open up so that they could practice in solitude for the next five to eight hours. (The amount of time Juilliard kids spend locked up in the school's practice rooms is the other reason for the "Jailyard" moniker.)

The rumors about the razor blades, I concluded, were bullshit.

Of course, I still kept checking the pianos for another five years, until I finished my master's. In the end, I reasoned, checking wasn't going to kill me, whereas hepatitis might—and *not* checking meant staring blankly at the blue velvet curtains that lined those rooms while contemplating *how* sure I was that the rumors were bullshit, which took just as long as checking.

I never found any razor blades.

I found a lot of pencils. And once I found a mouse.[2] And once I found some reed-making tools left behind by a forgetful oboist.

And when I did I thought to myself, *The razor blades! I know what really happened!*

You see: oboists use blades to make their reeds. Half an oboist's life is spent making reeds, and while most conservatories (including Juilliard) have a reed-making room, it's perfectly plausible that an oboist would decide to make or finish a reed in a practice room instead. But plenty of people—whether string players, pianists, stage parents, or school custodians—have never seen the tools they use. The only reason *I* have is that one of my old neighbors was the principal oboist of the New York Phil.

---

2 It was so cute that I threw out the next two mousetraps I passed in the hallway—in spite of the risk of hepatitis. So any nibbles taken out of the school's precious original manuscripts that year were probably thanks to me.

If a blade had fallen from between the pages of a Juilliard oboist's score (for instance) and landed in a crack or on top of the keys, it could have easily sparked a chain of rumors and ultimately evolved into the legend.

Don't like it? Fine. But it's less far-fetched than the original story.

Classical Musicians Are Competitive, but Not (Usually) Vicious

As I said, Juilliard kids don't want to fight. Most of the rivalries there—and in the music world in general—are playful. We have competitions, which are like our Olympics—to measure and compare our skills—and at chamber music sight-reading parties, we sometimes pretend we're seeing pieces for the first time so that our fellow musicians will be awed and amazed when we nail all the tricky bits. I also remember one of my old teachers, Lynn Chang, chuckling about his days as a student at the Meadowmount Festival, when he and his fellow violinists, in the classical music equivalent of a *Pitch Perfect* sing-off, would race one another through particularly fast or treacherous violin passages.

I'm actually more competitive than most of the other people I met at Juilliard. But even during my last few years there, when the brunt of my competitiveness was directed at one easily neutralized target (Golden Violin Boy), it mainly manifested itself in snide remarks about his shifts and attempts to outshine him whenever we played double concertos. *Not* in turning on the in-sink disposal whenever he reached down it to retrieve a fork.

Here's a flowchart:

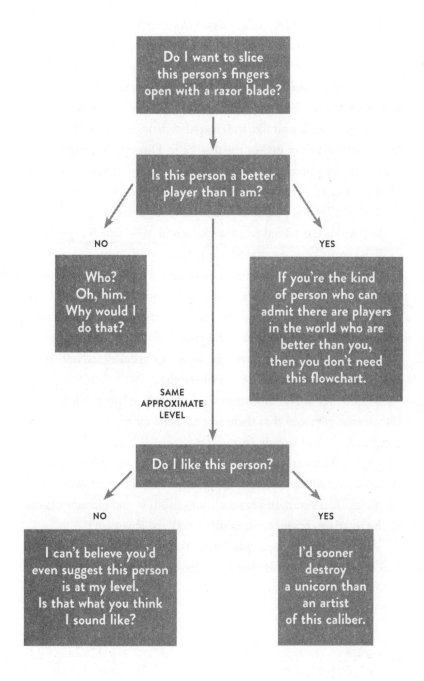

There's also nothing to be gained from torpedoing the competition. There is no line of succession to the top of the industry. This isn't the House of Windsor. Or the waiting room at the DMV.[3] There are just thousands of deserving musicians with varying skills and strengths jumbled together into a weird tier system that would look, if illustrated, a bit like the dilapidated, uncooked birthday cake that Fauna the fairy makes for Aurora in Disney's *Sleeping Beauty*. Except the candles, in this case, can slide up *and* down the broom. (The candles are the musicians.)

The candles don't all come from Juilliard, either.

Juilliard is the school you always hear about—which is great because it means I can go around using its name to intimidate my kids' sing-along instructors—but it doesn't have a monopoly on musical talent. The students at Curtis and Colburn and New England Conservatory are just as strong. And there are also a number of conservatories and universities where the general fields are weaker, but the top players, who usually attend because of a specific teacher, are as excellent as the top players everywhere else.

My teacher at Northwestern tried to explain this to me before I transferred. She said that there was no need for me to leave because great players could come from anywhere—as long as the teachers were good. I just assumed, at the time, that she was lying. (I mean, *surely* she would have said anything to get me to stay.) It wasn't until I took Juilliard's start-of-year orchestra audition and placed in as one of the rotating concertmasters that I realized she wasn't.

What all this means, apart from the fact that Juilliard has one hell of a PR machine, is that you'd have to plant razor blades at all

---

3 Not that I'd know the first thing about the DMV. Remember my parents' Volvo? I still don't drive.

these schools—and risk wiping out your entire pool of colleagues—in order to benefit from it professionally.

Juilliard is one of the more antisocial conservatories, but I still felt supported by my classmates while I was there. You have one main private teacher, who's responsible for your instrumental (or vocal or compositional) progress, and all the students who study with that same teacher meet regularly for something called studio class, where you play for the group and give/accept comments from your peers. It's kind of like an Olympic team, but without that sense of infectious team spirit and affection that leads to those effusive Olympian pile-hugs you see on TV. (Effusive pile-hugs aren't good for instruments. And as I said: Juilliard is one of the more antisocial conservatories.)

There are also other group performance classes—like excerpt class, which is where people go to study the hardest passages of the orchestral repertoire. (Excerpts are required for the final rounds of orchestral auditions.) I never took that one, though—in spite of all the people who tried to tell me I should—because I'd written off the idea of ever playing in an orchestra after hearing a horror story, once, about an orchestra player who had to throw up during a concert and couldn't get offstage in time because of all the stands and chairs and colleagues blocking the exit.[4]

Practicing in the Jailyard

"The way to Carnegie Hall is practice, practice, practice." So goes the punch line of the famous joke. It's really the only path to the top, short of sleeping with a famous conductor on a regular basis. (And even that wouldn't exempt you from practicing. It would probably just mean you had to be really good at *two* things.)

---

4 I'm pretty sure it was made up. Fairly certain. Probably.

My fingertips eventually became so thoroughly calloused that they would have been impervious to even the sharpest of razor blades. There was a period of several years—which began as I neared the end of my bachelor's program and continued until a year after I graduated from my master's—when I practiced six to eight solid hours per day.

It was in those practice sessions—when I was alone in a room, striving for perfection, pitted not against my classmates but against my own physical limitations—that the darker side of my competitiveness came out.

While some people will tell you that practicing is a meaningful exploration of your innermost soul—a whole *Eat, Pray, Love* ablution without the hassle of airports—it can also be a psychological thriller about an escape room experience gone wrong, where your only way out is the attainment of absolute musical perfection, but your hands are refusing, in HAL-like fashion, to obey the commands you're giving them. (It can also be an innocuous, mindless chore, like doing the dishes.)

At some point, all the top string players and pianists have to lock themselves away in this obsessive, solitary hell, where the police officers are metronomes and the cooks are vending machines and the lovers are imaginary and absolutely no one keeps things running on time because practicing doesn't bend to things like opening hours or sleep schedules.

I know people who have spent entire nights on the fourth floor of Juilliard. I know people who have practiced through fire drills and medical emergencies in those rooms. I once drank a whole liter of unsweetened, undiluted cranberry juice because I was peeing blood and I would have had to give up my practice room—and several hours of practicing—to seek medical attention. I also broke a toe once, I think (I can't be sure because I never had that checked out, either), when I became so frustrated with my progress that I kicked one of the surprisingly dense cubes that serve as the piano benches.[5]

Without this kind of fanaticism, you might still become a good player—even, with powerful connections, a successful one—but you won't become the high-performing machine that wins major international competitions.

The World of Major International Competitions

I know I said that competitions are playful. And they are—kind of—once you're *at* them. There's always an opening ceremony, and whether it's a black-tie gala in a gorgeous ballroom or a fluorescent-lit start-of-the-SATs kind of deal, the occasion offers a chance for all the competitors to hang out and feel good about themselves for having been accepted into the competition in the first place.[6] Usually you get to stay with lovely host families, too. Although once, at a competition in Switzerland, I had to stay in a haunted prison-like convent filled with strange guests who kept showing up at my door with offerings like crumpled flowers and half-eaten loaves of bread. (I also had bars on my window and a toilet next to my bed.)

What's not playful is what goes *into* competitions. You have to prepare hours of technically and mentally exhausting repertoire—including, if you're a violinist, two Paganini caprices. (I guess I don't have to remind you of how I feel about those.) You have to drill and scrub and polish every note until you can execute them all flawlessly and consistently. And it's not enough, of course, if you can do all

---

5 People kept breaking and stealing the real ones.

6 There's always a speech about how everyone who's gotten there is already a winner. Which is nice, but if that were true, we *wouldn't* be there.

that in your practice room. You have to be able to do it in front of an audience, in any acoustic, whether the temperature in the hall is a perfect seventy-two degrees and your fingers are loose and nimble or it's a full twenty degrees colder than that and it feels like your fingers are just a bunch of skinny half chubs that are too stiff to bend but simultaneously too flubbery to be effective.

As I was preparing for the Indianapolis Violin Competition, one of the top five[7] violin competitions in the world, my teacher at the time frequently impressed upon me the importance of being bulletproof. It wasn't that *he* demanded it; in fact, he often expressed sympathy for my generation, which suffered more than his, he said, because of digital, edited recordings (which have reset the expectations for live performance) and because of the high level of competition that dominates the field.[8] But his charge, as my teacher, was to help me succeed as a violinist—and without this bulletproofing, that success wasn't likely to come for me.

He was the first teacher who'd used the word "bulletproof," but terms like it had been floating around my lessons for over a decade.

I remember a master class I played in at NEC when I was thirteen. The teacher giving the class was a well-known, pleasant but pompous pedagogue who always reminded me of Toad from *Frog and Toad*. (Only in appearance.) I can't remember anything he said to me, but I'll never forget what he told the girl who played after: that if she ever wanted to fix her bad intonation, she'd first have to become disgusted by it.

The difference between "in tune" and "out of tune," on a violin,

---

7   It's probably one of the top three.

8   There are far more worthy players than the industry's current allotment of money and adulation can support.

is a fraction of a millimeter. Without disgust, the teacher argued, she'd never be able to summon the focus, the patience, or the tenacity she'd need to grapple with an issue of such physical subtlety.

His logic spoke to me. As did the implication that he himself found her—or her playing (which felt like the same thing)—disgusting. I've never been able to let go of the fear that I, too, might elicit disgust from a teacher or colleague or audience member, and I still, to this day, experience physical revulsion whenever I hear (or worse, play) anything that's out of tune. Except for my husband's singing—because I love him, and because there's no real pitch involved.

It was another one of my teachers, though, who took me off real music for a year, assigning me instead a daily regimen of scales, etudes, and exercises until I'd repaired the gaps she'd spotted in my technique.

At the time, I supported this undertaking. I, too, wanted to iron out the kinks in my playing, and the idea of removing the "distraction" of real music—and of breaking down the act of music-making into scientific components—seemed like a logical problem-solving measure. But I somehow missed that by *practicing* without feeling, I was, in fact, practicing how to *play* without feeling.

Which is a shame. Because feelings were the whole reason I decided to become a violinist in the first place.

The Whole Reason I Decided to Become a Violinist in the First Place

You may remember, from the introduction, that story my parents like to tell about how I decided to become a violinist at the age of two. And if you do, you will also remember that it's a lie: that while I did, indeed, begin violin lessons—and possess a deep love of music—at the age of two and a half, it wasn't until I was seven that I truly *decided* to become a violinist.

Here's how it happened:

I was sitting in Andover's Cochran Chapel between my dad and Mark, one of my dad's colleagues in the music department and my violin teacher at the time. Mark was a wonderful teacher. He fostered my early love of music—and indulged my (sometimes frustratingly specific) musical whims, letting me find and follow my own inspiration whenever possible. If I told him I'd fallen in love with the film score of an old movie, he'd find me the music for it; if I wanted desperately to play Bach's D-Minor Chaconne, one of the most infamously challenging pieces in the violin repertoire (far too demanding for the musculature of a seven-year-old), he'd section off a playable passage and send me home feeling like I'd won the lottery.

On that night in the chapel, we were attending a concert: the "senior concerto" (or final, graduating performance) of a handsome, popular high school boy named Rex. The piece he was playing was Mendelssohn's Violin Concerto in E Minor.

I'll never forget how it felt to sit there in the semidarkness, under the skyscraping, barrel-vaulted ceiling—at the foot of one of those tall wooden columns with the fat, naked cherubs on top—watching Rex stand, poised and confident, in his tux. I still remember hearing his shining sound soaring over the pulsing orchestral accompaniment—listening to that haunting opening for the first time.

I now know the Mendelssohn as one of the most popular pieces in the classical repertoire—one that finds its way into the annual programming of most symphony orchestras. But at that time in my life, it was entirely new to me, and nothing had ever struck quite so close to my core. I'd encountered plenty of pieces I loved: pieces that promised me all kinds of future adventures and spoke to the things I'd feel while having them. But the Mendelssohn was the first piece that spoke to the adventures and feelings I already *knew*. It conjured up dark, lantern-lit streets—the gleefulness of a game of hide-and-seek—the delight of a snow day—my fear of that giant, scrolled tombstone in the graveyard: the one with the door that led into the ground so that all the undead corpses could come and go as they pleased. And the slow second theme in the first movement seemed to me to be the perfect expression of all the love and tenderness I felt for my family.

That night was also the first time I experienced the way that silence, the silence of the rests and around each note, could slow the passing of time; it was the first time that I was transported.

I have no idea where I was transported *to*. But by the time the applause brought me back, I'd already decided I wanted to be a violinist just like Rex.

After the concert, I begged Mark to let me play the Mendelssohn. *Of course* I could, he said.

Those months that followed—when I shut myself in my room and simply *played* through that favorite of all pieces—when I felt my bow and fingers gliding over the strings—freely, almost effortlessly, as if I were a marionette with Mendelssohn as my puppet master—were the most joyful months of playing I can remember. And Rex, who was patient and kind enough to take me under his wing, quickly became my hero.

Mastery

You often hear spirit-guide types (whether in bad music movies or soapy Netflix holiday specials) saying things like "Play it from the heart." The expression, now, makes me gag almost instantaneously. Even though I suppose that in the months following Rex's Mendelssohn, "playing from the heart" was exactly what I was doing.

The problem was, I didn't sound very good while I was doing it. Having read all my chapter 2 rants about the fallacy of "natural players," you already know that there's no direct path from the source of your emotions through your fingertips and into/out of your instrument of choice. It takes mechanical know-how and physical conditioning to produce music that stirs and transports, that successfully conveys feelings.

It also takes creative discipline. You can't just *play* the music the way you want to. The musicians of previous generations could get away with that, maybe, but these days we're limited by the interpretive principles of "taste."

Of course, the way one should play Mozart or Bach changes depending on whom you consult—which means that you spend much of your education getting scolded for your artistic ideas and feeling generally constrained and suffocated.

There are very few people who can juggle the myriad technical standards and demands, along with the rules of interpretation, that world-class musicians face while *also* playing in a way that feels organic, spontaneous, and emotionally authentic. This is partly because the path to achieving this kind of technical mastery is damaging to things like passion and spontaneity. But it's also because *feeling* things—particularly powerful things—makes it harder to meet these technical standards during performances.

Powerful emotions, if you can harness them, are the fuel for powerful interpretations. But if you can't harness them, they can unravel everything you worked toward in your practice room.

I learned this when I was nine, at Rex's memorial service.

The service took place in Cochran Chapel, on the very stage where Rex had played his Mendelssohn two years earlier. I'd been asked to play Bach's "Air on the G-string"—the same "Air on the G-string" that's used so hilariously in *The Spy Who Loved Me*. It was chosen for its quiet, solemn beauty. There's something consoling about the way the bass line unfolds, the constancy with which each note drops steadily into place. It seems to chart a way forward—a way through the listener's suffering—while also promising a kind of endlessness of memory, and of spirit, if you believe in such things.

I knew, as I stood waiting offstage, that I had to play well. My performance was my only offering. It was my only chance to express my gratitude, to demonstrate that I'd been worthy of the inspiration and guidance Rex had given me. And in order to play well, I knew I needed my fingers to glide smoothly to their places. I needed to save enough bow for that long, plaintive whole note that started the piece and held on for what felt like an eternity.

But I couldn't stop shaking.

Bach's "Air" is a piece that still brings comfort to me when I hear it, but its serenity was miles from how I felt at that stage of my grief. I wasn't ready, yet, to be comforted, or to provide that comfort for others.

If my knowledge of the repertoire had been as broad, then, as it is now—and if I hadn't been limited by what I, accompanied by my father, could play at the time—I might have programmed the more anguished Mozart's Requiem or Beethoven's Piano Sonata No. 17 ("The Tempest"), or even Penderecki's *Threnody for the Victims of Hiroshima*. Then, after I had raged and writhed and run through my vengeful thoughts, I would have withdrawn into the darkness and melancholy of the Shostakovich Piano Trio No. 2 or the slow movement of Beethoven's "Eroica" Symphony, which would have been fitting for a boy who was my hero. *Then*, with my fury sapped and my insides hollowed out—with nothing left that could object to its serenity—I might have turned to Bach's "Air." Or Handel's "Lascia ch'io pianga." Or Brahms's "O Tod, wie bitter bist du."

Rex had been murdered. He'd been walking across campus with

his girlfriend one night—after having won some big university election—when someone had shot him. Twice. His killer, who'd been drawn to Rex for all the same reasons everyone else was, had called himself a *friend*. The violence of it—the unfairness—the sadness—the sickening thought that the person who'd done this was still living and breathing—was overpowering. I had never felt so much anger in my life. It was the anger that made my hands shake.

I couldn't feel everything I was feeling and also play well. So I detached. I shut myself off.

I got through the performance, feeling nothing. I can still see the audience as I saw them that day, over my bridge and strings and the scroll of my violin. And I can still feel that numbness that I felt as I looked out at them. They looked so strange to me, just sitting there in their rows. I made it off the stage, to the skirt of the school cello teacher, and I buried my face in it to hide the fact that I wasn't crying. And then, suddenly, I was.

Over my years of performing, I came to utilize this numbness with more and more frequency. The shaking was never as bad or uncontrollable again, but as my standards of precision and cleanliness grew more stringent, and my definition of what constituted a "miss" grew smaller, the mechanism of my playing became so finely tuned that even the slightest of tremors was disruptive. The cleaner I got, the less bulletproof I felt. There were so many things I couldn't miss—so many things I wasn't allowed to do. It was as if each piece I played was crafted out of eggshell—as if I spent the entirety of my performances balancing on a razor's edge.

Chapter 7

it's easy to get lost

Navigating a Composition—
and a Career in Classical Music

I was visiting home one summer break—I have no idea which year it was because of the practicing-induced stupor that consumed the first half of my twenties—when my dad took me aside and handed me an old cassette tape. He said he'd gotten it from Kenneth, Andover's recording engineer, sometime earlier. He'd waited to give it to me because he hadn't been sure, at first, that I'd want to hear what was on it. But he'd concluded, ultimately, that it didn't matter because I *needed* to. That's when I knew we were building up to one of his beloved "teachable moments."

His role in my musical development had changed a lot since my childhood. He'd only practiced with me for those first few years, and he'd stopped sitting through my lessons when I was in middle school. (It would have happened sooner if the Polish wine enthusiast hadn't enjoyed—quite so much—having his good looks beautifying her studio.) When I left for college, he let go of the reins completely. In his words, I was a boat he'd spent the last seventeen years building, and now it was time for him to sit back and see whether or not I could float.

But he was still my dad, of course. He still liked to check in with me about my studies and progress, and offer up wisdoms, periodically, when I let him. It's just that the *gist* of these wisdoms was nothing like the directives of those early practice sessions. He'd watched my work ethic grow into something greedy and insatiable. He'd seen my obsession with perfection choking the joy out of my playing, and he'd begun, accordingly, to advocate for balance.

During my Juilliard years we'd argue, sometimes, about my technique. He'd try to convince me that it didn't need more work, citing reviews of my performances that used words like "immaculate" and "meticulous." My fingers were the fastest in the West, he'd joke. (Of course, according to the industry's ugly racial stereotypes, it was the *East* I needed to worry about.) My focus should be analysis, interpretation. What did I want to *say*? What parts of the music did I want to bring out? What could I do to make playing more fun?

I remember, too, having many (many, many) conversations about the well-known Yo-Yo Ma–ism of the "emotional bank account." Artists and musicians, according to Ma, needed reservoirs of emotions and meaningful experiences to draw from. A *whole* person, with (some of) the memories of a normal human, would supposedly make a deeper artist than one who'd spent their entire life locked away in a practice room, watching the world through a tiny window like the Lady of Shalott. (Or, if it's one of Juilliard's fourth-floor practice rooms—which don't have any windows—staring at those blue velvet curtains.)

Was my reservoir full enough? My dad wanted to know. Was I doing enough listening? Enough soul-searching? Was I meditating? Was I frolicking? Wouldn't it make sense to take a break from practicing so we could all finish *Lost* together before the end of summer break? Kate and Jack had feelings. So did Desmond.

But my dad, who'd gone to the prestigious Eastman School of

Music at a time *before* the number of competitors in the industry had exploded, didn't know what I was up against. Just like he didn't know that *Lost* was going to bring us nothing but dashed hopes and exasperation.

I knew. *I* was the one who got knocked out of competitions whenever I screwed up my Paganini caprices. *I* was the one who'd watched class after ridiculously talented class of Juilliard kids graduate into financial struggles and faceless oblivion. *I* was the one who would be classified as "disgusting" if I played out of tune. And I didn't believe, anymore, in the importance of emotional connectivity while playing, because I could re-create the *effect* of it with the right bow speed, vibrato, finger pressure, and timing.

Half the time I was onstage, I was having existential monologues about the strangeness of performing, and the other half, I was asking myself questions like "Can I put butter on a panettone?" All while my feet hurt.

The recording, as I'd suspected the moment I'd laid eyes on it, was of Rex's Mendelssohn concerto. I knew my dad was going to use it to make a point I didn't want to hear, but the idea of listening to Rex again—and of revisiting such a crucial moment in my life—was irresistible. I was also curious, if a little frightened, to hear how his performance would sound to my older, sharper ears. I waited eagerly as my father popped the tape into my parents' old cassette deck.

Ambient noise, then a few seconds of that pulsing, spellbinding orchestral accompaniment, executed with the expected level of mediocrity—then Rex's entrance.

My dad kept looking at me as we listened, to make sure I was getting the message. And I knew well what it was: *Cleanliness wasn't everything. The most moving performance I'd ever heard was far from perfect.* But he had crucially underestimated how literal and hypercritical—how damaged, really—my listening skills had become. He'd been counting on my ability to hear, through the speakers, what I'd heard more than a decade earlier, in the hall. But I couldn't. My obsession with precision wasn't merely a *dimension* of my musical conscience; it was an invasive, parasitic force that had taken over all the things I used to appreciate and love about music.

All I heard, in Rex's recording, were his sticky shifts, his unrefined sound production, and his intonation, which was, to use a rather telling industry euphemism, "expressive."

I was wholly immune to his passion, his conviction, and his voice. I'd forgotten how to listen.

The Shape of a Composition

If my life were a symphony or a concerto, the part of it I've been describing in these last chapters would have been the *development*— the murky middle where all the themes (and sometimes the listeners) get blown off course.

Let's back up and look at a few of the more common compositional structures so you can better understand what I mean.

Symphonies, concertos, and sonatas—and most of the meatier pieces in the classical repertoire—are composed of multiple movements (or segments). Movements are entities unto themselves, with their own beginnings, middles, and endings—and they're generally followed by a pause (if it's an early movement) or *applause* (if it's the final movement). We'll go over the clapping bit more in chapter 12.

Think of them as episodes in a well-constructed miniseries. Together, they build a larger arc, tell a larger narrative, and convey a larger journey—but individually, they represent smaller stories, which have their own resolutions. This is why they can be separated out, on more casual occasions, and performed alone.

Movements composed between the Renaissance period and the

early half of the twentieth century generally adhere to specific compositional structures, which function as templates or patterns, dictating a movement's shape. The most common—and important—of these compositional structures is the *sonata form*.

Sonata Form

Sonata form is distinct from the *sonata* (which, as a multi-movement piece for one to two instruments, is a whole miniseries). However, the first movements of sonatas generally *use* sonata form—as do the first (at least) movements of symphonies, concertos, and countless works of chamber music.

It's confusing, I know. There's a meme that compares the grid-like streets of New York with the winding, one-way streets of Boston. Under the New York map are the words "because we want you to know where you are and where you're going," while under the Boston map it says, "because fuck you." Classical music is a bit like Boston.[1]

But just as a good map can help you avoid stopping in the middle of the intersection at Huntington Avenue and Mass Ave (so that you can issue a primal scream while honking cars and buses swerve all around you and your two terrified teenage daughters clutch onto one another in the back),[2] a clear understanding of a few key musical layouts can help you navigate this sprawling genre and its sometimes overwhelmingly long pieces.

So let's continue.

---

1 Probably because classical music wasn't designed to be a real genre and Boston wasn't designed to handle cars.

2 And I'm definitely *not* suggesting that my mother actually did this once when my dad couldn't drive us to NEC one Saturday and grades were due and she was pissed because I was dating a Republican.

As I said, sonata form is the most important (and probably most used) compositional form. It's like Alex the Lion in *Madagascar*—or Meryl Streep in any movie with Meryl Streep in it. There *are* other forms—very nice, deserving ones—but everyone knows who's getting the Oscar nomination.

Sonata form is made up of a few basic building blocks: first the *exposition*, then the *development*, and finally the *recapitulation* (or "recap").

The *exposition* is the initial, authoritative statement of the thematic material. It's a bit like the beginning of a story, when the basic situation and the main characters are laid out for you.

Here's my best impression of an exposition, using a vaguely British example (because I watch a lot of *Masterpiece*):

Charles and Winnifred emerge, disheveled, from behind a linden tree. They are in love. They stroll into the garden, where the birds are chirping and the sun is shining beatifically. Charles announces that he has asked Winnifred's parents for her hand and that they have given their blessing. He proposes; she accepts. They join hands. All is well and uncomplicated.

The *development* is the part of the piece where things begin to get complicated and disorienting. It's much like the second act of a three-act play—or like absolutely everything that happens in *Lost* after season 1.

Here the composer uses modulation (shifts to different keys) and fragmentation (the breaking up of previously heard material) to make you feel unsettled and uncertain.

Winnifred's father begins shooting clay pigeons from the terrace, causing the birds to fly off. Archibald shows up, ducking as shards of clay fall around his head. He claims that he has also asked Winnifred's parents for her hand, that they have also given him their blessing, and furthermore, that Winnifred herself accepted his proposal an hour earlier. Charles runs off into the woods, wounded (figuratively) and upset, recounting and analyzing the events of the day in an attempt to understand what has passed. The clouds descend, rain falls. Winnifred turns angrily to Archibald. What does he mean by coming here and spreading these lies? The person he proposed to was Wilhelmine, her twin sister. And it was she, not Winnifred, who accepted his proposal. Archibald gapes, realizing his mistake. He's always been terrible with names. Thunder rumbles. Meanwhile, in the woods, Charles paces by tree after tree until he looks up and realizes he is lost.

The third and final section is the *recapitulation*. In the recap, the world returns to normal—but a slightly altered normal from that of the exposition. The theme comes back, but there are small differences in the way it's treated. This is why recaps are the most dangerous parts of a piece to perform by memory; if you're not paying attention, you might miss a crucial key change and find that your fingers have taken you back to the exposition—without your collaborators.

The thunder has stopped; the rain clouds have cleared. Sunshine has returned. Charles and Wilhelmine emerge from behind the linden tree, disheveled and drenched in rainwater; Wilhelmine found him wandering, distressed, and resolved the misunderstanding. However, in the process, she and Charles have fallen in love. Happily, Winnifred, who has suddenly developed feelings of her own for Archibald, is relieved. Charles and Winnifred commence their stroll—but this time Charles holds hands with Wilhelmine and Winnifred holds hands with Archibald, who can't tell the two sisters apart and therefore has no preference between them. Winnifred's father has gone inside and the birds are chirping once more—but the grounds are now covered in shards of clay, which crunch loudly underfoot.

Another good reason to keep track of things like compositional form is your bladder; if you don't know the *shape* of the piece you're listening to, it's hard to predict whether you can make it until the end of it before you have to get up and pee.

With that in mind, there are several other forms we should cover.

Binary and Ternary Form

Binary form and *ternary form* are the most basic structural forms used in classical music. They are also the forefathers of many of the more complex forms found in the canon. Like sonata form. Neither binary form nor ternary form is particularly exciting (though much of the music written in them *is*), but the flip side of this is that they're also not particularly confusing. *Binary form* is, essentially: AABB. There are two sections, A and B, and each of these generally repeats (hence: AABB).

Ternary form, on the other hand, is ABA. *However*—and I know I said there was nothing confusing about these forms, but I might have been lying depending on how you feel about what's coming next—while in binary form, A and B share thematic material (in other words, they sound related), in ternary form, A and B are entirely distinct.[3]

Ternary form is often used in arias and songs. Binary form had

---

3 So the problem, it seems, is really just B. Using B to delineate the non-A section for both binary form *and* ternary form is a mistake. Unfortunately, though, this use of letters is

its heyday in the Baroque period, but it's used in later periods, as well. Versions of both binary and ternary form can be found in things like *scherzos* and *minuets* (which are both short movements that appear most often as the third movement in four-movement works)—and the principal theme in any *theme and variations* movement is often in binary.

Theme and Variations

In a *theme and variations*, a statement of a short but complete theme is followed by a set of variations that use the theme as a blueprint. If you were paying attention, you already know that said theme is often in binary (AABB) form. The melody is generally simple, leaving room for the variations to become more and more elaborate as they progress.

There are several ways a composer can transform the theme, one of which is by filling out the melodic and rhythmic texture. If we were to apply this technique to the first sentence of this section, for instance, it would look something like this:

In order to better explain the nature of *a theme*—*and* the ways in which its *variations* might expand upon it—I am taking *a statement* and, through a series *of* frustratingly nonsensical augmentations, creating *a* sample variation using words instead of notes. It isn't *short*. Or enjoyable for you to read. *But* I hope you will hate me for it a bit less when I tell you that writing it is *complete*ly maddening and I already regret both my choice of *theme* and my decision to take this on in the first place. There *is*, I'm sure, a much easier and more entertaining way of going about this—and if I'd just *followed* Stephan's advice, I'd be done with the whole section *by* now. But *a*

standard, so it would be unfair of me to change it here. Especially if you're plotting a con that hinges on your ability to pass as a music theorist.

large part of what motivates me in life is making use of the now-unused skill _set_ I developed during my training. And the main skill I developed during my training was, essentially, the ability to grind through all manner _of_ unpleasantness and to tolerate minor _variations_ of torture. _That_ is what practicing through excruciating muscle over_use_—and _the_ even more excruciating mental fatigue that is the _theme_ of these all-day practice sessions—is. Of course, I don't expect you to be _as_ tolerant of this kind of _a_ thing as I am. Which is why I will put an end to this ridiculousness with the word "_blueprint_."

Of course, in a real theme and variations—even a bad one—the effect would be much, _much_ prettier. There would also be more variations,[4] which would use other methods of embellishment. In these other variations a composer might:

- Play with instrumentation/voicing (if multiple instruments are involved in the piece)
- Change the tempo (slow things down, speed things up)
- Change the meter (alter the rhythmic lilt or flow of the music)
- Visit the relative minor/major (i.e., change the key but without leaving the established harmonic realm of the theme)

There's a glossary in the back in case any of this is confusing.

Rondo

Whereas the return of the theme, in sonata or ternary form, indicates that the end of the movement is near, this is not the case in a _rondo_.

---

4 Don't worry, I wouldn't put either of us through that again.

In rondo form, the theme can return many times—without significant alteration and in alternation with contrasting sections. Think: ABACADAEAF . . . and so on and so forth until the composer runs out of creativity. Or patience. Or letters in the alphabet.

It's generally reserved for lilting and upbeat music, and often shows up in final movements. The lack of development is better suited to frivolous celebration than deep, soulful meditation.

I've adapted the following joke (which I found hilarious when I was ten) to illustrate the formula:

A duck walks into a bar.

DUCK:
Do you have any grapes?

BARTENDER:
No.

The duck goes outside, paces a few times on the sidewalk, then comes back in.

DUCK:
Do you have any grapes?

BARTENDER:
I already told you. No.

The duck goes outside, does a jig in the street, then comes back in.

DUCK:
Do you have any grapes?

> **BARTENDER:**
> No! And if you show up here asking that question one more time, I swear I'm going to staple your bill to the bar.

> *The duck goes outside, sings the first three verses of "God Save the Queen," then comes back in.*

> **DUCK:**
> Do you have a stapler?

> **BARTENDER *(CONFUSED)*:**
> No.

> **DUCK:**
> Good. Do you have any grapes?

There are a lot of popular songs that use the rondo form, as well. "Old MacDonald," for example. Regardless of how many animals say "moo" or "bah" or "pffwrhöm,"[5] Old MacDonald always has a farm, *E-I-E-I-O*. It's this unaltered repetition that makes the song so catchy for children and so absolutely infuriating for adults. It's also what makes it a rondo.

Lost in the Shadows (of GVB)

The development in what I promise to never again refer to as "the larger symphony of my life" was at its most convoluted and entangled

---

5   Which, I believe, is how you spell the noise an elephant makes.

immediately following my graduation from Juilliard. Being engaged to another violinist, as I was at the time—especially to one who was more successful than I was, as *he* was at the time[6]—brought out the very worst that my disposition offers. I couldn't hear his playing without comparing our abilities; I couldn't watch his success without fearing my failure. At times I derived a shaky confidence from the knowledge that there were ways in which my technique surpassed his, but just as often I struggled with the suspicion that there was something intangible—something he had that I was missing—that made his playing objectively stronger. And rather than searching within myself to figure out what that something was—or contemplating whether my dad had, perhaps, been right about my misplaced priorities—I became even more committed to the path of technical mastery. I wanted to beat him—and this was where I thought I could do it.

The competitiveness went both ways. Golden Violin Boy was extremely supportive—he often recommended me for concerts and arranged for me to play for important people—but when it came down to it, neither one of us wanted to play second fiddle. That is, he would sometimes choose to play *literal* second fiddle to me (because it made him look good, he always joked), but even then, he was just as determined to show me up as I was him.

My friend Meta and her husband often perform together in the Weiss-Requiro cello duo, and when they do, it's a beautiful, joyful, playful-but-profound outpouring of love and camaraderie: the harmonic embodiment of everything they said and didn't say in their wedding vows. When GVB and I played together, we were more like Zoolander and Hansel walking it off on the runway.

---

6 He might still be. It really depends on how many copies of this book you give to your friends.

A lot of this was simply the fact that we were both stereotypically competitive violinists. We hadn't won the Juilliard concerto competition or led the school orchestra as concertmaster (he did both a few years ahead of me) by being serene and unambitious.[7]

For GVB, though, the competition was entirely playful. In my case, it felt like a matter of survival. Without it, I was destined to become one of the classical world's many plus-ones: musicians whose abilities, however impressive, were subsumed by the careers and reputations of their (literally) better halves. And that wasn't okay with me.

It was while I was in the midst of this all-consuming battle for independence and recognition that I attended the previously mentioned concert in Montréal—the one where that woman told the story about her five-year-old daughter and the first time she'd heard classical music. The girl's response—her declaration that it was "beautiful music"—brought the metaphorical roof crashing down over my head. It was like I'd been staring at this one windowpane for years and years, desperately trying to scrape off some crud from an old sticker because I was convinced that *that* was the biggest problem in my life—and all the while I'd failed to notice that the house I was standing in—the walls, the roof—everything that made it a house—had completely disintegrated. I had, in fact, forgotten that the rest of the house was a thing that existed, or that taking care of it had been the very reason I'd started cleaning the crud off the window in the first place.

But the crashing of the roof had forced me to look around, and once I did, there was no getting away from the fact that I was standing in a pile of wreckage. Wreckage I had no idea what to do with.

---

7 Meta and Dave, by the way, have *also* won numerous competitions—and they're two of the most serene people I've ever met. But then, they're *cellists*.

Was it fixable? Did I even *want* to fix it? Did I still care about the house? Or had I just built it for my dad—and then let it fall apart to give myself a way out?

I was utterly lost. I started to question everything: my future, my values, my relationships. I didn't have any answers. All I knew was that I didn't give a shit about that window anymore.

Chapter 8

sometimes there
are curses

Beethoven's Hair, Mozart's Requiem,
and Other Superstitions of the Classical Universe

I remained lost, kicking aimlessly at the wreckage, for quite some time. I was stuck—in music, career, and relationship—and I didn't know how to unstick myself.

It wasn't a fun phase for anyone. My disillusionment and general feeling of fecklessness meant that I wasn't particularly pleasant to be around. Remember when I said that once upon a time I used to be a snob? *This* was that time.

I still shudder when I think of the horribly embarrassing reply-all incident that took place while Meta and I were brainstorming with a jazz pianist named Max about an upcoming collaboration. Meta was my duo partner at the time (this was several years before she and Dave started the Weiss-Requiro Duo), but Max had been assigned to us by a third-party presenter. And while he was a wonderful jazz pianist, he was still a jazz pianist, and we weren't quite sure what *we*, who had never played jazz, were supposed to do with him.

I emailed the group asking if Max would be up for playing

Mendelssohn's D-Minor Piano Trio, and Max wrote back proposing that he kick it off with a jazz intro of his own—which would then transition directly into the opening of the Mendelssohn. Instead of acknowledging the fact that it wasn't wholly unreasonable for a jazz pianist to want to play jazz—or pausing to consider whether a bit of experimentation might be just what I needed in order to get myself out of the rut I was in—or asking myself whether cross-genre lead-ins might be precisely the sort of innovation classical musicians needed to be embracing in order to ensure the future of the art form—I sent Meta a crotchety knee-jerk-reaction email that read something along the lines of *"Is he kidding me?"* Except the language was more colorful than that and I also (accidentally) sent it to Max.[1]

My mother believes that it was my unhappiness and suppressed anxiety during this time that caused me to not only send this email but also to break out in shingles *in my ear.* It was excruciating for my whole head—and mostly my jaw—and everything tasted like ash and I got a horrible blistery rash all over half my face. I skulked around the house wearing a black veil for weeks, enduring obnoxiously cheerful quips from Golden Violin Boy about how I looked like a fortune-teller—and about how proud he was of himself for enduring the temporary depreciation of his favorite asset.[2]

Then, one very scary night, I lost all the hearing in my right ear. It turned out not to be permanent—it was an accumulation of fluid from an ear infection, caused by the shingles, which resolved itself

---

1 In my defense, this *was Mendelssohn* we were talking about.

2 This makes him sound like an asshole, but actually he isn't one. Our dynamic was just much closer to that of warring siblings than loving partners.

within a week—but I won't soon forget the panic I felt in those moments. On my way to the emergency room, I couldn't help but think of Beethoven, whose hearing deserted him at the peak of his career. I doubted I'd ever be as adept at performing without my hearing as he'd been at composing without his. But I comforted myself with the bitter thought that my soulless musical offerings, unlike Beethoven's godlike ones, would hardly be missed—particularly when the world still had its beloved GVB.

When I performed, I nearly always felt like I was piloting an unmanned aircraft from somewhere very far away. During practice sessions, I binge-watched *Game of Thrones* or *Project Runway* or *Antiques Roadshow*—to lend flavor to the flavorless communion wafer I'd allowed my life to become.

Sometimes, instead of practicing along to Netflix, I went down investigative Google rabbit holes. I'd set up my computer on the dresser next to my music stand and read Wikipedia articles—or anything that had a long page I could scroll through with a quick push of the down key—so that my fingers could continue to work away mindlessly.

One day, my rabbit hole of choice was a deep dive into the subject of Beethoven's hair, which is a surprisingly absorbing topic. Beethoven's much-admired tresses have been clipped, tested, auctioned off, and turned into diamonds. Various locks of it were taken from his deathbed—or bestowed upon friends and acquaintances during his life. Recently, in fact, one of those locks sold for about $64,000. (One of the diamonds, which was created by extracting carbon from ten strands of his hair, went for $200,000.)[3] In 1994, a different lock was purchased by two Americans who tested it for

---

3   I'd like to take this opportunity to state that (*a*) this would make another good present for me and (*b*) I would *also* like to be turned into a diamond after I die.

various substances and ultimately discovered huge amounts of lead in it, explaining many of Beethoven's health problems and possibly his eventual deafness. There's even a book called *Beethoven's Hair* that follows the journey of this same lock—from Beethoven's death-bed through Nazi Germany and all the way through these tests. There's also a defunct computer game called *Beethoven's Hair: The Haunting* that follows a reanimated butterfly corpse through a haunted adventure involving a talking portrait of Beethoven (whose mouth is a portal), as well as plenty of lightning and manuscript paper.

Which brings me to the oddest thing I came across in my googling that day. After combing through all the legitimate articles and sources I could find, I arrived at a very unofficial-looking, basic HTML, made-in-a-basement-type site. It didn't seem to be affili-ated with the video game, which had exhibited a degree of polish that the owners of this website did not seem to value, but it did share the game's interest in the paranormal. The text on the site described, with sincerity if not eloquence, a number of incidents that had taken place in close proximity to various locks of Beethoven's hair: faint but ghostly apparitions, strange noises, moved objects—the usual horror movie stuff.

It also claimed that visitors to that very site had reported para-normal phenomena occurring in their homes.

When I read this, I scoffed shakily and put down my violin (be-cause my hands had started to sweat and that's not great for the wood). I was just climbing into bed to read more when the printer that was sitting on my desk—which was off and hadn't been used in weeks—turned on by itself and began to whir. Naturally, I was ter-rified; I closed the tab immediately, turned the television on to the first reality show I could find, and dispatched a few quick words of prayer and devotion to Beethoven, who surely had the power to protect me from any evil poltergeists connected to his hair or affiliated URLs. I also unplugged the printer before any horrifying messages could come out of it.

By the time I was brave enough to revisit the site, it no longer existed. And I've been unable to find it—or anything like it—since.

Unsolved Mysteries of the Classical Universe

The history of classical music is filled with similarly unsolved mysteries, although most of them don't involve shady websites and wireless printers. Here are a few of the more famous ones:

MOZART'S REQUIEM

That Mozart died, at the age of thirty-five, in the middle of writing his Requiem is one of classical music's scariest facts.[4] And not only because I'm thirty-four as I write this. The story surrounding it, which every article ever written on the subject will tell you is "shrouded in mystery," makes it scarier still.

Here's what I grew up hearing:

The night was dark and full of terrors when an "unknown, gray stranger" appeared at the young—so young—but ailing Mozart's door.[5] The man brought tidings from his employer, a man of undisclosed identity and great importance who wished to commission a requiem.

---

4 Requiems are masses for the dead.

5 It may have also been during the day, but there was definitely an "unknown, gray stranger" involved because this somewhat redundant quote is the only configuration of words that appears more frequently, in writings on this piece, than the words "shrouded in mystery."

Mozart immersed himself in the project, and as he worked, his health declined further—to such an extent that he suspected he'd been poisoned.[6] *And* cursed. Mozart could not rid himself of the idea that this requiem, this mass for the dead, which had been commissioned under such mysterious circumstances, was, in fact, *for him*. Constanze, his wife, convinced him to turn his attentions to other compositions, and upon heeding her advice, his symptoms subsided. With his strength restored and all suspicions of a curse or poisoning assuaged, he returned to the requiem. Immediately, his symptoms returned in full force. He died weeks later.

Unfortunately, I can't tell you if most of the above is true because Mozart's letters, while very helpful for anyone attempting to diagnose his IBS, are not particularly enlightening in this matter. Contemporary accounts, particularly those stemming from Constanze, are also considered unreliable.

So here's what we do know (insofar as anyone can "know" anything that happened two centuries ago):

The identity of the patron who commissioned the requiem may have been unknown to Mozart, but it is not unknown to us. And—spoiler alert—it wasn't the Grim Reaper. Count Franz von Walsegg was our mystery man, and the "gray" stranger who appeared at Mozart's door was probably his valet. The requiem was intended to honor Walsegg's wife, on the first anniversary of her passing. The reason for the secrecy surrounding the commission—if there was, indeed, secrecy—was likely that Count von Walsegg, who was an amateur musician, planned to pass off the composition as his own.

---

6 Those of you who have heard of Salieri may be interested to learn that the composer was, at the time of Mozart's death, rumored to have poisoned Mozart. There was never any evidence to support this, however, and most historians dismiss it as a possible cause of death. If you don't know what I'm talking about, please watch *Amadeus* immediately.

But it's possible that Mozart was well aware of Walsegg's involvement in the commission, and of his plans for the piece.

When Mozart died before he could finish the score, Constanze engaged the services of Franz Xaver Süssmayr to complete it so that she could claim the remaining compensation from Walsegg. (The version most often played today is this one, which is entirely Mozart's through the Offertorium and then Süssmayr's, based on Mozart's sketches and notes, from the Sanctus on.) Some have criticized Süssmayr's choices, but others stand by them. Beethoven is even reputed to have said, "If Mozart did not write [the requiem], then the man who wrote it was a Mozart." I, for one, agree—and I'd like the whole piece performed, with full orchestra and choir (preferably in the reconstructed Notre-Dame Cathedral), at my funeral.[7]

TCHAIKOVSKY'S DEATH

People disagree about the cause and circumstances of Tchaikovsky's death. The "official" explanation is cholera—he died suddenly at the age of fifty-three, in the middle of a cholera pandemic—but the conflicting accounts and timelines offered by those who were with him in his final days, as well as several suspicious facts, have led many to believe that it was suicide.

Multiple witnesses contest that Tchaikovsky drank unboiled water in the days before his death (which would have been a bit like filling your asthma inhaler with a canister of superspreader-event air back in 2020 or 2021), but accounts of when and where this fateful act occurred are at odds. I actually grew up with the understanding that Tchaikovsky had committed suicide *by* drinking

---

7 Unless my father, who hates Paris, is still alive when I die. The only thing that could upset him more than burying his own child would be burying his own child in France.

cholera-contaminated water, but most supporters of the suicide theory suggest that the water-drinking incident, if it even took place, was a cover-up—and that Tchaikovsky's family and friends were accomplices in hiding the truth: that it was arsenic, or some form of slow-acting poison, that really killed him.

One eerie story persists about a "court of honor" made up of Tchaikovsky's former classmates from the College of Law in St. Petersburg. It asserts that this secret society summoned Tchaikovsky to a hearing regarding some "moral transgression" or other that was linked to his then-illegal homosexuality, and convinced him to take his own life. (They may have explicitly threatened to out him or reveal a specific affair if he refused to comply.)

It sounds like a conspiracy theory (and it might very well be one), but established musicologists have lent it credence. Alexandra Orlova, a Russian musicologist and author of *Tchaikovsky: A Self-Portrait*, was the first to suggest it. And in the first edition of the authoritative *New Grove Dictionary of Music and Musicians*, Tchaikovsky expert David Brown wrote: "That he committed suicide cannot be doubted. But what precipitated this suicide has not been conclusively established . . . the story that he died of cholera from drinking un-boiled water is a fabrication." He also states that Tchaikovsky "almost certainly died of arsenic poisoning."

Anthony Holden went even further in his book *Tchaikovsky*, writing:

> The present author's own extensive researches, while adding considerable flesh to the bones of the "court of honor" theory, point all but conclusively to a deliberate cover-up by [Tchaikovsky's brother] Modest and his medical friends, on the wishes of the composer himself, of the truth: that Tchaikovsky did indeed take his own life.

There is, of course, a whole fleet of less conspiratorially minded musicologists who insist that there was nothing clandestine or intentional about Tchaikovsky's passing—and that the conflicting accounts and timelines can be explained away by other factors.

One possible explanation for the confusion is that Russians drink a lot of vodka.

THE CURSE OF THE NINTH

There is a superstition in the classical world that a composer's ninth symphony is destined to be his last. The theory was made popular by Mahler, who noted that the deaths of Beethoven, Bruckner, Schubert, and Dvořák occurred shortly after completing their ninth symphonies (or, in Bruckner's case, during its composition) and went out of his way to avoid composing his own. After his eighth symphony, he wrote a work entitled *Das Lied von der Erde*, which is very *close* to a symphony but isn't one, I guess, because it's called something else. It also features two singers, which is two more than most symphonies have. Convinced that he'd outwitted the curse, Mahler then went on to write a "Symphony No. 9"—and died before he could complete his tenth.

Sibelius and Vaughan Williams (who came after Mahler) are often counted among the victims of the curse, as well. Vaughan Williams's death was particularly creepy; he was reportedly in excellent health and no one's been able to pinpoint a cause of death. Then again, he was also eighty-five.

Unfortunately for people who find this curse as fun as I do, it doesn't hold together all that well when you look at it closely. Schubert's inclusion depends on which of his six complete and seven incomplete symphonies you count, which is the kind of math that could only get by among musicians. And Sibelius only wrote eight symphonies (one of which he destroyed). You only get to nine if you count his tone poem *Kullervo*, but he wrote a bunch of other tone poems, too, so once again the math here feels a bit fuzzy. Plus, Sibelius was ninety-one. Still, there isn't enough money in the world that could induce me to write a ninth symphony (if only because I'd have to write eight others first).

RAVEL'S "BOLÉRO"

This curse isn't famous—in fact, it's something I've never heard anyone outside of my family talk about—but there is, I'm pretty sure, a link between Ravel's "Boléro" and certain emotional imbalances I've noticed in people who are obsessed with it. It's impossible to say whether these people (who are mostly my sister's exes) were attracted to "Boléro" because of preexisting imbalances or whether their imbalances developed *as a result of* listening to "Boléro" repeatedly,[8] but if you're ever in an old, isolated log cabin and the person you're with suddenly puts it on the Victrola, tell them you're going out for some firewood and then dive into the nearest bear cave you can find. You'll be safer there.

Beethoven's Benediction

The third thing most people notice about my parents' music room (the first two being the nine-foot Steinway and the giant, blindingly colorful, somewhat confusing animal tapestry that hangs above it) is a startling black-framed photograph of Beethoven's face.

8　In fact, to listen to it once is to listen to it repeatedly. It consists of exactly one theme, which repeats *eighteen* times, varying only in instrumentation over the relentless *rat-tat-tat-tat*-ing of a snare drum.

What makes it startling is the fact that it's not his *actual* face. It's a *mask* of his face: his death mask, as my parents used to enjoy telling me.

I spent most of my childhood hiding from it—the very idea of a death mask was terrifying—and in my mind I elevated the stony likeness into something almost paranormal. But by the time I reached adolescence, I'd grown to like it. Beethoven's features were, after all, extremely pleasant—and he looked remarkably vibrant for a dead person—and I'd come to see something wise and impassive in his expression—like the face of the magic mirror in *Snow White* or the commendatore in *Don Giovanni*. Plus, it was *Beethoven*.

I got into the habit of staring at him while I practiced (this was before the dawn of Netflix's streaming service), and sometimes I even consulted him regarding various decisions I had to make. Things like whether or not I could justify going to the dance on Saturday even though I was preparing for a competition. Or whether my mom was right that flats were better for performing than the four-inch heels I always wanted to wear.[9] He never answered me, of course, but the process of consulting him helped me sort through my own feelings on these important matters.

It was because of this that I chose to google the mask one day, near the end of my "stuck phase." I'd begun to fantasize about leaving behind my relationship and my inextricably-linked-to-it career, and trading in Golden Violin Boy's beautiful apartment for my parents' unfinished, spider-infested basement—and I wanted to hear Beethoven's thoughts on the matter. (Or look into his blank, staring eyes and watch his stony, frowning mouth for perceived signs of movement in order to feel sure about my decision.)

---

9 She was.

When I set about my googling, though, I was met not with the plump, wide-set features and lovably round face I'd come to know so well—but with photos of a sunken, shriveled head with demonic orbs for eyes that looked as if it had sprung right out of a Wes Craven horror movie.

As it turned out, my parents had spent my childhood traumatizing me without cause: the mask in their music room was *not*, in fact, Beethoven's *death* mask—but rather a "life mask" made from a mold taken by Franz Klein in 1812. (Beethoven's actual death mask—of *Scream 6* fame—was taken by Josef Danhauser.)[10]

I did not end up conferring with either of Beethoven's masks that day—I had to call up my parents and yell at them instead—but that's not to say that Beethoven didn't get a chance to weigh in on my decision.

GVB and I waited until the most public, least convenient moment in our concert schedules—when our relationship was on display for a whole month at La Jolla's illustrious SummerFest—to call it quits. It was fantastic. Super awkward for everyone—particularly the festival volunteer who had graciously agreed to host us during our stay. And we were stuck fielding questions about "the wedding" from audience members and out-of-the-loop colleagues until the end of the season.

Our actual breakup *moment* took place backstage, just minutes before I went on to perform Beethoven's Kakadu Variations with my trio.

It was the kind of thing that could have shattered me. I'd parted ways with someone I loved—who'd been, for all my complaining, my home and my biggest champion for the past four years. He'd

---

10 I'm allowed to make fun of dead Beethoven's appearance because he knows I love him so much.

been my support even when I'd been unable to bring myself to be his—and he'd become my closest friend and confidant. He'd also been my anchor. Without him in my life, I had nowhere I had to be. I had no idea where I was going to go or what I was going to do or whether I'd ever be as safe and comfortable as I'd been under his protection. I certainly wasn't going to be safe *or* comfortable in my parents' basement—because some of those spiders were really big. But I also knew—as did GVB—that without a leap, there was no way forward.

As I walked onto the stage, I felt as calm as I'd ever been in front of an audience. The darkly haunting opening of the piece—which really is far too dark and haunting for anything with the name "Kakadu" in it—seemed to speak to the nadir I'd hit—and to the uncertainty and obscurity of the future. But in the eighth bar, when the tense, unsettling harmonies melted from minor to a healingly serene major, I felt certain that I had Beethoven's benediction.

It was one of the strongest performances I've given—and one of the most enjoyable.

Chapter 9

they're not all symphonies

All the Pretty (Kinds of) Pieces

I'm happy to report that I did not have to move in with my parents' basement spiders. A few of my boxes did, but only the ones with useless, unimportant things in them—like my diplomas. Most of what I took from GVB's apartment fit into my suitcases.

Which was convenient because I had to pack those, anyway; in a confusing and wholly unexpected twist (one that becomes even more confusing and unexpected when you consider my previous interactions with jazz musicians), I'd suddenly found myself as a featured guest on jazz-trumpet legend Chris Botti's tour.

I'm still not sure how it happened. One minute I was getting an email from Chris's manager, Bobby, asking me what I was doing on Friday, and the next minute I was standing backstage at the Kennedy Center next to Helen Mirren and Aretha Franklin, waiting to play a show that would include, among other absurdities, a brief collaboration with Madeleine Albright on the drums.

There were private jets, fog machines, swanky casinos, and huge, sold-out theaters and halls. It was a ridiculous, mind-blowing adventure that still feels more to me like an ad for Rock and Roll Fantasy Camp than an actual experience I lived through.

But what I appreciated most about the tour wasn't the glitziness or even the fact that it rescued me from those basement spiders; it was that it was so different from everything I'd come to associate with the violin and performing.

In my first show with the band, when it came time for Chris to make my introduction, he chuckled into the mic and said, "I just met this girl twenty minutes ago. She's had two days to learn this set." I half expected the audience to jump up and start pelting me with tomatoes. Where I came from, it was taboo to admit to underpreparation. "Never embarrass your audience," one of my teachers used to say. Everything had to be polished, prepared, well executed—and if it wasn't, you had to pretend it was so that no one would feel like a fool for having clapped for you. But no one seemed upset. No one was demanding their money back, citing the fact that they'd paid to hear something professional and rehearsed instead of a high-pressure musical experiment. In fact, they were thrilled about it. They were in on the story—a part of it, even—rooting for me to succeed throughout the show. And when I *didn't* crumple into a ball of nerves and forget everything I'd tried to cram into my brain over the past two days, they erupted like a pack of Bostonians after the 2004 World Series. The uncertainty—and *humanity*—of the situation turned out to be gold.

I felt like Alice, slingshot through the looking glass into a world of larger-than-life characters, bewildering topography, and nonsensical rhetoric.

The band seemed to speak in code—or in telegrams ending with the words "Send money." (Things like: "Ibiza is great. Stop. Lots of girls and strange white powder. Stop. Send money.") Every night, when Jeremy, our tour manager, came to pick me up from my dressing room, he'd intone a somber "Good luck; we're all counting on you," or hand me part of a takeout container with those same words scribbled on it.

I was constantly disoriented. I'd see the same faces cropping up at shows: devoted fans who followed Chris around the country. I'd bounce from airport to unfamiliar airport, then suddenly I'd find myself in the same Hudson News I'd been in three times that week. In December we played twenty-two nearly identical sets over the course of one eleven-day residency at the Blue Note (it was actually twenty-two days and forty-four shows for most of the band, but I switched out after half). And every night we were on the road, regardless of where we were in the world or what had happened earlier in the day, the whole band would run into one another—by accident—in the hotel bar.

The novelty was intoxicating. It felt so good to get away and do something that wasn't so bogged down with personal frustrations— something that was purely *fun*. I loved how the show lighting, instead of simply baking the performers in sterile white light, took its cues from the music; I loved how the audiences, instead of sitting stiffly in their seats, clapped and cheered and sang as they pleased.

I didn't miss my old repertoire, either; in fact, for months I went without listening to a single classical piece. I understood completely why Chris, who'd also come up through the classical world, had chosen to cross over. And I seriously considered following in his footsteps. I thought about moving to L.A., asking Bobby to be my manager, and reinventing myself. I could open Celebrity Fight Nights and dabble in acting, like the violinists who'd preceded me on the tour. It wasn't what I'd planned, but if that was where my life was heading, then why not? I could trade my Vuillaume in for a Fender. My hair could be purple.

I might have done it, too, but something changed my mind.

The Magic Flute

I first met Stephan during a group dinner at a Korean restaurant, while I was visiting my sister in Berlin between shows. He was, by far, the surliest of the eligible bachelors Marina flung at me that week as part of her campaign to convince me to move to Germany. That's probably how I'd remember him, too, if the jackass at the table next to us hadn't stolen my bag halfway through dinner. But the jackass at the table next to us *did* steal my bag, which led to a group excursion to the nearest police station, which allowed me to get to know Stephan a bit better.

There was something about him that made me feel, if this makes any sense, like me. He was entirely devoid of pretense—he was somehow charming without being even remotely insincere—which made it impossible for me to masquerade when I was with him. I soon learned that he was a law student, that he was a devoted Red Sox and Patriots fan, and that he was the loveliest, most surprisingly funny person I'd ever met. I also learned that his quietness in the restaurant had mainly come down to the fact that the tteokbokki he'd ordered had been silently melting his tender German insides for the whole of the dinner. (It's traditional for Germans to recoil from spicy food with the kind of horror that vampires reserve for crucifixes and holy water and the impalings of not-quite-immortal loved ones.)[1] I made sure that Marina arranged another meeting with Stephan before I left, and our first proper date came on my next visit, just a few weeks later.

Stephan made all the arrangements, maintaining, throughout the process, the kind of secrecy he now reserves for hostile takeover offers. It was only after I arrived that he informed me of the plan. He was taking me to see *The Magic Flute*. (What I mean by this, just to be clear, is that he was taking me to the Berlin Staatsoper to see Mozart's last opera, *Die Zauberflöte*—the one with the Queen of the Night aria I broke my larynx on when I was two. I am *not* speaking

---

1 I was nearly burned for witchcraft once for trying to order a burger with spicy mayo *and* jalapeños, but the server saved me by refusing to relay my order to the kitchen.

of any kind of figurative "magic flute" that I may or may not have also seen that night, after the opera was over.)[2]

I wasn't sure, at first, how I felt about the proposed plan. Was I excited? Or was this an unwelcome intrusion into my holiday, an obnoxious reminder of what I was trying to escape? I hadn't listened to classical music in months—months that had felt like years after a lifetime of hearing it practically every hour. And this was *the piece*—wasn't it—that my parents had turned (however dishonestly) into an anthem for my career. Moreover, the last time I'd attended a concert for reasons other than obligation had been in high school, because sitting in the audience brought out all the same scrutiny and anxiety I associated with performing. (Also because as an audience member I had to deal with the claustrophobia of concert hall seating—and the applause at the end was for someone else.)

After a moment, I was relieved and surprised to find that I was thrilled.

The thrill stayed with me throughout the night, bubbling up when the orchestra quieted into silence—and when the curtain lifted to reveal a still life of a bunch of giant pretzels and sausages dangling from the ceiling.[3] Then the overture began, with its regal opening chords, and I felt the same kind of breathlessness and slight loosening of the tear ducts I sometimes feel when I walk into an old church or cathedral.

It was partly the music and the role it had played in my life, but it was also Stephan. His infectious earnestness was in itself disarming, as was the fact that he wasn't a musician—that he had none of my baggage and none of my scrutiny. His ears were untrained,

---

2 According to my editor, Michelle, "This isn't that kind of a book."

3 This was a staging choice. There's nothing, to my knowledge, about pretzels or sausages in the opera.

untarnished. When I imagined what the music might sound like to him, something in my own perception seemed to unlock.

I knew I'd never be able to hear it exactly the way he did, but there were things—beautiful things that had passed me by for years—that I could suddenly appreciate. It was as if a pile of heavy rocks had been building up over the course of my training—on top of some part of me that had long since gone to sleep and atrophied—and now I could feel some phantom sensation, or some blood flow, returning to it.

It was clear to me then, if it hadn't been earlier, that this music, whatever my history with it, was inextricable from who I was.

This reaction would not have been possible with, say, a violin recital. My issues with attending concerts were directly linked to my struggles as a performer, and anything that reminded me of my career (like the sound of the violin) immediately triggered my closed-off, critical mindset.

Operas use violins, too, but in a different, primarily supportive role. The sound of the instrument is drowned out, in part, by the voices of the singers, which tend to be robust. The collective *timbre* of the composition, in other words, is different. Some people react very strongly to timbre, finding the sound of a piano soothing, for instance, or the sound of a brass fanfare grating, and so on and so forth.

But there are other factors, too, that separate operas from violin recitals—and symphonies from piano sonatas—like volume and form and venue.

I've often found the traditional visual monotony of the Big Concert Hall Experience to be something of a mood killer. The sight of an orchestra, dressed all in black, does little to capture the vibrancy, passion, or playfulness of my favorite compositions. It also does little to suggest the various love triangles, rivalries, and affairs that exist, at any given time, in these large, established ensembles. I don't have the same problem in smaller halls, where I can see the performers' facial expressions and movements more clearly (and play the guessing game about who's had sex with whom). But for me, the boring—yeah, I said it—visuals of the average large-venue instrumental concert make the music sound less interesting and exciting than it really is. It's like that episode of *Brain Games* where they show you an actor's mouth saying "la la la"—synced to the *sound* of a recording in which she's saying "ba ba ba"—and it's impossible, until you close your eyes, for your brain to figure out what the consonant is.

This is all to say that, when I go to the symphony and I *don't* want to feel bored, I often close my eyes or fix them on the seat back in front of me.

Operas, on the other hand—as well as ballets—provide sets, costumes, and story lines that I find very helpful when it comes to getting out of my own way and immersing myself in the music.

Not everyone feels this way, of course. Some people (who haven't watched *Black Swan*) are of the opinion that ballet is too delicate, or that operatic singing is too grandiose and dramatic. Plenty of people prefer the symphony for its dynamic extremes and aural focus. And there are more compositional mediums for people to prefer, too, in case the three I've mentioned don't do it for them.

As with compositional periods, the best way to find out what you like is to sample them all.

A Night at the Opera. Or the Symphony.

Technically, *symphonies* are compositions written for a full symphony orchestra that follow a standard three- or four-movement structure.[4] (Remember, movements are like episodes in a miniseries

---

4 In rare cases there can be more movements. Or fewer.

you're binge-watching: shorter stories that work together to tell one longer story, succeeding one another after only a brief pause, ideally without applause unless it's the end.)

A *full symphony orchestra* means, in today's world, an ensemble of roughly one hundred instrumentalists, made up of the string, brass, wind, and percussion sections—led by a conductor. The string players represent the majority of the bodies onstage, with two groups of violins (generally fourteen to sixteen in each), and slightly smaller groups of violas, cellos, and double basses.

As a performer—and specifically a violinist—I've always found this problematic. First of all, it's very hard, when you've been raised to think you're God's gift to the world of music, to take a seat beside thirteen other violinists and not only play but also *wear* the exact same thing as the rest of them. Because if you'd known you were going to be asked to fold your sound into the group, and to cover your arms and décolleté in a modest black sheath,[5] instead of standing center stage in a spotlight wearing a dress that Chanel herself had come back from the dead to beg you to model, you *never* would have practiced through all those birthday parties and playdates and whatever other activities constitute a healthy childhood. (Plus, while players in the top orchestras make a good living, the salary you dreamed about as a kid probably had more zeros in it. Because, again: birthday parties.)

On the other hand, some people seem to enjoy being part of a "team." There is a power to this kind of ensemble that many audience members and less egomaniacal musicians absolutely love. It creates a sound that's sublimely forceful and well-rounded, with a brilliant palette of colors provided by the wind, brass, and percussion sections. Plus, many composers reserved their best material for the medium.

Apart from symphonies, there are also plenty of *symphonic works*

---

5   Okay, so sometimes it's white *and* black, but you're still supposed to blend in.

that a symphony orchestra can perform. There are *tone poems*, which utilize roughly the same instrumentation but follow a more fluid, connected structure; there are programmatic works (sometimes these overlap with tone poems) that derive their structure and inspiration from a story; there are overtures, taken from operas and presented on their own (usually at the start of a program); there are concertos featuring soloists who *do* get to wear those Chanel gowns (concertos usually follow a similar structure to a three-movement symphony); and there are all manner of suites, serenades, waltzes, and rhapsodies.[6]

Then there are all the *orchestral* works that feature smaller, more limited orchestras that do *not* qualify as symphonies, because some aspect or other of their composition disqualifies them.

In the Baroque period, for instance, the symphony orchestra didn't exist, and neither did the written symphony. There were pieces *like* it—pieces that shared many of its structural elements—but they were called concertos. Or "concerti," if you want people to take an instant dislike to you. What's a little confusing about this is that the word "concerto" can also mean a composition written for soloist with orchestral accompaniment—and in later years, the term came to be used to convey this meaning *exclusively*. (This is what we mean when the word is used today.)

I'm a huge fan of the modern concerto. And of soloists.[7] From the audience standpoint, they function as a kind of protagonist or narrator. They offer a point of focus, both aurally and visually, that organizes and directs the listening experience. Because of this, I've always found solo concertos easier to follow than symphonies and other orchestral works. I mentioned that I often close my eyes to

---

6 And so on.

7 As long as I'm not playing in the orchestra that's accompanying them.

escape the visual monotony of these big-venue experiences—but when there's a soloist to look at, I don't need to. You just have make sure you like the given solo instrument, because the timbre of the piece is colored heavily by it; and, of course, it's crucial that the soloist is proficient and compelling.

Solo concertos also existed during the Baroque period. It's just that there was also another kind of concerto that featured the orchestra alone. (Confusingly, these concertos *did* sometimes feature solos from the front stands, but the solos were more collaborative and less virtuosic.) If you want to be specific, you can call a concerto *without* a true soloist a "concerto grosso." But try not to use the plural form, because "concerto grossos" doesn't sound great and, as is the case with the concertos/concerti situation, the people who say "concerti grossi" are usually the ones who consider friendship a burden.[8]

These mid-sized-ensemble pieces faded in popularity with the rise of the symphony but made a comeback in the twentieth century thanks to composers like Bartók and Lutosławski.

SOME MUST-KNOW ORCHESTRAL WORKS:[9]

· Concerto grosso in D Major, Op. 6, no. 4—Arcangelo Corelli

· Brandenburg Concerto No. 5 in D Major, BWV 1050
—Johann Sebastian Bach

· Orchestral Suite No. 3 in D Major, BWV 1068
—Johann Sebastian Bach

---

8   If you do go with "concerti grossi," however, don't forget to make both words plural (with the *i* endings). Otherwise you will sound not only friendless but also stupid.

9   Once again, these are in chronological order. And to spare us future footnotes: all of the lists from here on out are, too.

- Symphony No. 41 in C Major, K. 551, "Jupiter"
  —Wolfgang Amadeus Mozart

- Symphony No. 5 in C Minor, Op. 67—Ludwig van Beethoven

- Symphony No. 9 in D Minor, Op. 125—Ludwig van Beethoven

- *A Midsummer Night's Dream Overture*, Op. 21
  —Felix Mendelssohn

- *Symphonie fantastique*, Op. 14—Hector Berlioz

- Symphony No. 2 in D Major, Op. 73—Johannes Brahms

- Serenade for Strings in C Major, Op. 48
  —Pyotr Ilyich Tchaikovsky

- *Don Juan*, Op. 20—Richard Strauss

- Symphony No. 9 in E Minor, Op. 95, "From the New World"
  —Antonín Dvořák

- Symphony No. 3 in D Minor—Gustav Mahler

- Symphony No. 5 in D Minor, Op. 47—Dmitri Shostakovich

- Divertimento for String Orchestra, Sz. 113—Béla Bartók

- Concerto for Orchestra—Witold Lutosławski

- *Become Ocean*—John Luther Adams

A FEW MUST-KNOW CONCERTOS (OR, IF YOU ENJOY
LONELINESS, "CONCERTI"):

- Concerto No. 4 in F Minor, Op. 8, RV 297, "Winter"
  —Antonio Vivaldi

- Concerto for Two Violins in D Minor, BWV 1043
  —Johann Sebastian Bach

- Piano Concerto No. 23 in A Major, K. 488
  —Wolfgang Amadeus Mozart

- Violin Concerto in D Major, Op. 61—Ludwig van Beethoven

- Piano Concerto No. 5 in E-flat Major, Op. 73, "Emperor"
  —Ludwig van Beethoven

- Violin Concerto in E Minor, Op. 64—Felix Mendelssohn

- Piano Concerto No. 1 in B-flat Minor, Op. 23
  —Pyotr Ilyich Tchaikovsky

- Cello Concerto in B Minor, Op. 104—Antonín Dvořák

- Violin Concerto in D Minor, Op. 47—Jean Sibelius

- Cello Concerto in E Minor, Op. 85—Edward Elgar

- Piano Concerto No. 1 in D-flat Major, Op. 10—Sergei Prokofiev

- Violin Concerto No. 2 in G Minor, Op. 63—Sergei Prokofiev

ENJOYING OPERAS AND BALLETS

Operas and *ballets* are also orchestral in nature. Their orchestras generally feature full instrumentation (as defined by the compositional period) but reduced numbers in the strings, as the whole ensemble has to hide in the relatively cramped pit for the duration of the performance.

The pit is the hole in the ground between the stage and the audience—the one the conductor's head and arms poke out of so that he[10] can direct the singers without blocking the patrons' views. It's an excellent place to be if you're an instrumentalist who likes to drink on the job, but it's less excellent if you have claustrophobia or a precarious sense of self-worth. I was always of two minds about being stuck down there. On the one hand, it's not the most glorious feeling to be shoved into a dark hole and told to stay there for three hours while the stars of the show get to bathe in state-of-the-art lighting and the audience's adulation. But on the other hand, there's a cozy feeling of anonymity down in the pit, which is especially comforting if you're the sort of person who tends to worry about throwing up mid-performance.

When I'm in the *audience*, however, my feelings on these two subgenres are unmixed; operas and ballets offer some of the very best music in the genre, and there's something magical about the combination of music and scenery and costume and plot that, as on that night in the Staatsoper, helps me escape my professional bitterness.[11] As I mentioned in chapter 3, though, people all over the industry have started breaking out of their boxes and rethinking the parameters of the traditional concertgoing experience, so these days you'll often find accompanying (and sometimes thrilling) visual elements at the symphony, too.

The two main differences between operas and other large-scale orchestral works are the singers and the structure. The singers are a major factor, and one that often divides new listeners. In *Pretty Woman*, a movie I genuinely dislike but refer to fairly often, Richard

---

10 I say "he" because, as of this writing, something like 5 percent of big-budget conductors are women. I hope we progress to a place where I can amend this pronoun in future editions.

11 Even the bleak, minimalist productions evoke enough of the story for me to feel immersed.

Gere claims that "people's reactions to opera the first time they see it is very dramatic; they either love it or they hate it." I can't fully agree with this. I've known plenty of people who have fallen asleep the first time they've gone to the opera, or who have come away feeling both confused and stimulated. It really depends on the opera. And the production.

But I will grant Mr. Gere that there *are* those who instantly fall in love with the sound of sopranos and tenors, as well as those who have trouble getting past their timbre, their immense power of projection, and the fact that their sounds are so different from the ones we normally hear coming out of people's mouths.[12] Whichever kind of person you are, though, I would encourage you to give opera singers a real shot; the good ones are some of the most compelling musicians that exist.

Ballet dancers, on the other hand, while gorgeous to watch, contribute only the occasional clopping of pointe shoes to the actual *sound* of the performance, and so the only real difference between a ballet and a symphony (musically speaking) is the structure.

This is similar for both operas and ballets. Traditionally, both begin with an overture, which features the orchestra alone. The music here either provides an overview of the work's musical themes or sets the stage for the story—or both. After this, the music generally comprises shorter arias or dances that link together into longer acts; and the overall arc of the composition follows the theatrical structure of the libretto (text) or narrative. It's a bit like film music, except

---

12 My dad tells a story about a soprano he knew at Eastman, who was also the winner of a major beauty pageant: one night, she was able to incapacitate a would-be attacker by belting out a high C directly into his ear. He blacked out, she got away, and the attention her singing drew to the scene resulted in the man's arrest.

in opera and ballet the music also serves as the dialogue and there-fore plays a much more crucial role.[13]

Actually, in opera there is a separate kind of musical dialogue that takes place, which is called a *recitative*. Recitatives are fluid, less melodic sections that move the story line forward in a way that arias, which adhere to stricter forms, cannot. One of my less musical exes used to complain that, in operas, characters would sometimes get stabbed through the lungs and then sing that they were dying for a full ten minutes before finally collapsing. He was never able to point to an exact example (and I didn't press him because there are any number of operas he could have been referring to), but his gripe was most likely with an aria—not a recitative. Arias are usually frozen moments in time. They provide a chance for meditation on one or two specific events or emotions, but their texts don't develop in the manner of normal theatrical dialogue. Instead, the words repeat so that the *music* can depict the character's state of mind and depth of feeling. Anyone who listens to pop songs should be fairly comfort-able with this concept, but something about the fact that arias ap-pear in the context of a moving plot seems to throw people off. Recitatives, on the other hand, progress at approximately the rate of normal conversation; to facilitate this, the music they're set to is harmonically and structurally less established. In other words, you won't be humming it when you leave the opera house.

Here's what the libretto of a recitative might look like:

A: *Is it done?*
B: *The deed is already in progress.*
A: *How? An assassin?*

---

13 Not to belittle the importance of film music. Try watching *Psycho* on mute with Barry Manilow playing in the background and see if it's the same.

B: *Chili paste.*

A: *Chili paste! Of course! He's German!*

B: *The spice will melt his stomach. And I've added a pinch of arsenic, too, for good measure.*

A: *He won't detect the bitterness?*

B: *He won't taste it for all the spice.*

A: *And this spice of which you speak—it won't put him off?*

B: *His East German parents have trained him too well. They used to tell him, as a child, that the sun would only shine if he finished all the food on his plate. He will force the poison down his own throat.*

A: *Ha! The fool. What, by the way, was the vessel for this chili paste? Currywurst?*

B: *Tteokbokki.*

A: *No!*

B: *My love, what is it? You look pale.*

A: *The tteokbokki! I came across it in the kitchen—*

B: *You didn't—?*

A: *Alas! I was hungry! And I am particularly fond of tteokbokki.*

B: *No! My dearest! This is all my doing!*

Note that, in the above, there is no particular rhythm or rhyme to the lines. This is different in an aria, which might feature text that looks more like this:

> *Oh, to die of tteokbokki—*
> *How bittersweet a thing.*
> *Poisoned by my lover,*
> *Deceived by chili's zing.*[14]

---

14 I never said I was a poet.

Depending on the specific form of the aria, the above might be followed by a *B section* with different words and contrasting music, after which this stanza would come back again, perhaps even more than once, featuring even more repetitions of certain lines to fill out the score. And so it is very possible that the phrase "Oh, to die of tteokbokki" might flash across the opera house's translation screen(s) five or six times before the aria is over.[15]

Ballets are more episodic than sequential. Because they have no need for recitatives, they often jump from one complete scene to the next, without much transition, and often with applause in between. It's a bit like a series of vignettes that work together to tell a story.

Originally, in fact—during the Baroque and Classical periods—a ballet was a *single* vignette within the frame of a longer opera. Ballets, as independent, complete entities, didn't emerge until the Romantic era.

A FEW MUST-KNOW OPERAS:

- *Rinaldo*—George Frideric Handel
  If you have time for only one aria: "Lascia ch'io pianga"

- *Giulio Cesare in Egitto*—George Frideric Handel
  Aria: "Piangerò la sorte mia"

- *Le nozze di Figaro* (*The Marriage of Figaro*)[16]
  —Wolfgang Amadeus Mozart
  Aria: "Non so più, cosa son, cosa faccio"

- *Don Giovanni*—Wolfgang Amadeus Mozart
  Aria: "Or sai chi l'onore"

---

15 If it were up to me, these running translations would display the entire text of an aria at once rather than feeding it to the audience one line at a time.

16 I know this was in a list already, but it has to be here, too.

- *Die Zauberflöte (The Magic Flute)*—Wolfgang Amadeus Mozart
  Aria: "O Isis und Osiris"

- *La Traviata*—Giuseppe Verdi
  Aria: "Sempre libera"

- *Tristan und Isolde*—Richard Wagner[17]
  Excerpt: Overture

- *Carmen*—Georges Bizet
  Aria: "Seguidilla"

- *Der Rosenkavalier*—Richard Strauss
  Aria: The final trio

- *Turandot*—Giacomo Puccini
  Aria: "Nessun dorma"

- *The Turn of the Screw*—Benjamin Britten
  Aria: "Tower Scene"

- *Nixon in China*—John Adams
  Excerpt: "News"

- *L'amour de loin*—Kaija Saariaho
  Aria: "Pelerin's Aria"

A FEW MUST-KNOW BALLETS:

- *Swan Lake*—Pyotr Ilyich Tchaikovsky

- *The Sleeping Beauty*—Pyotr Ilyich Tchaikovsky

- *The Nutcracker*—Pyotr Ilyich Tchaikovsky

---

17 Have I mentioned he's an asshole, though?

- *Daphnis et Chloé*—Maurice Ravel

- *The Firebird* (*L'Oiseau de feu*)—Igor Stravinsky

- *The Rite of Spring* (*Le sacre du printemps*)—Igor Stravinsky

- *Romeo and Juliet*—Sergei Prokofiev

- *Appalachian Spring*—Aaron Copland

Note: Prokofiev, Ravel, and Stravinsky wrote multiple concert suites for *Romeo and Juliet*, *Daphnis et Chloé*, and *The Firebird*, respectively. They're highlight reels, of sorts, for each of these works—ideal for anyone hoping to listen to the music without attending an actual ballet (or sitting through two hours of sometimes-filler-y music). In all of these cases, I would recommend the second suite. So: *Daphnis et Chloé*, Suite No. 2; *Romeo and Juliet*, Suite No. 2—and the 1919 revision of *The Firebird Suite*. (There are suites for the Tchaikovsky ballets, too, but Tchaikovsky may not have had much to do with them; they emerged only after his death.)

Choral Music

Whenever I try to write about choral music, I end up rhapsodizing about Eric Whitacre's face instead. Which is an unfair, belittling objectification of someone whose accomplishments deserve true recognition and credit.[18] But it's also a residual symptom of the shock I felt, a few years back, when I learned that the well-known choral composer was *not* a ninety-year-old man with a debilitating

---

18 And an unfair, belittling dismissal of choral music, which also deserves true recognition and credit.

case of gout, as I'd always pictured him—but a much younger man who looked like a dashing art-collector-by-day/gentleman-cat-burglar-by-night version of Sawyer from *Lost*. It's because of this—together with the fact that the world of choral music is practically its own universe—that I will cover only the category of choral-*orchestral* music. No one wants to read a sixty-page treatise on Eric Whitacre's jawline.[19]

The choral-orchestral works that are most significant in the classical repertoire are masses, cantatas, oratorios, and requiems. They all bear varying degrees of similarity to operas, featuring story lines, operatic soloists, and, in some cases, recitatives. But they're nearly always performed unstaged and their stories are, for the most part, religious (specifically Christian) in nature.

In short, their orchestration is opera-like, but with a lot more of that "heavenly choir" sound—and they're a bit less fun. They are, instead, transporting and cathartic and purifying and so on—and kind to the orchestra, which gets to appear onstage (or in the church) alongside the singers.

I nearly had a life-changing experience with one of these pieces once: in high school, when our orchestra and choir went on tour to Montréal[20] and we played Bach's *St. Matthew Passion* in the Notre-Dame Basilica. It was hugely inspiring to play and hear this kind of music in such a magnificent setting—so much so that for a few moments I began to question my atheism. But then I noticed that my dress was suffocating me and I started to worry that I might throw up, so I had to enlist my emotionally immature stand partner to surreptitiously unzip me, which he did, with much giggling, while I hid

---

19 But seriously, google him.

20 It really seems like Montréal is the place for life-changing moments.

behind a tenor. By the time this was done, the general atmosphere of piety was somewhat diminished.

In any case, this is a category that was most significant to the repertoire during the Baroque era. I've already mentioned Bach—because he composed the vast majority of the masses, cantatas, and oratorios performed today—but the oratorio that is most familiar to the general population is Handel's *Messiah*.

The *Messiah* is, of course, a great and seminal work. Unfortunately, I can't seem to separate the sounds of the Hallelujah Chorus from various holiday commercials that play during football games, advertising Oscar Mayer turkey and seasonal sales on sweaters and cars. Also, one of the most spectacular concert fails in history took place in the last few bars of a *Messiah* performance, when the organist either pulled the wrong stop or passed out on the keys, leading to the most cringeworthy, heinous-sounding cacophony I've ever heard. I must have listened to it a thousand times on YouTube, and now, whenever I hear that gloriously triumphant final cadence, I find myself missing the horrendous dissonance of the fail version.

SOME CHORAL-ORCHESTRAL WORKS THAT ARE NOT HANDEL'S *MESSIAH*:

- *Gottes Zeit ist die allerbeste Zeit*, BWV 106, "Actus tragicus" —Johann Sebastian Bach

- *St. Matthew Passion*, BWV 244—Johann Sebastian Bach

- Mass in B Minor, BWV 232—Johann Sebastian Bach

- Requiem in D Minor, K. 626—Wolfgang Amadeus Mozart

- Missa Solemnis in D Major, Op. 123—Ludwig van Beethoven

- *Ein deutsches Requiem (A German Requiem)*, Op. 45—Johannes Brahms

- *Messa da Requiem*—Giuseppe Verdi

- Requiem, Op. 48—Gabriel Fauré

Note: All of these requiems are generally referred to simply as "Mozart Requiem," "Brahms Requiem," "Verdi Requiem," and "Fauré Requiem," respectively.

THE PARTS OF HANDEL'S *MESSIAH* THAT ARE WAY BETTER (IN MY OPINION) THAN THE HALLELUJAH CHORUS:

- "I Know That My Redeemer Liveth"

- "The Trumpet Shall Sound"

- "Worthy Is the Lamb"

- "All We, Like Sheep, Have Gone Astray" (but mainly to hear a stage full of people singing the words "we like sheep" over and over again)

Chamber Music

Chamber music is a very broad category of composition from which conductors are entirely excluded. It's no wonder, then, that it was always my favorite kind of music to play. I've also always enjoyed listening to and watching it. (The players interact more in chamber music than they do in larger orchestral ensembles, resulting in more active, engaging visuals.)

Chamber music is pretty much what it sounds like: music for small ensembles (one player per part) that's intended to be performed in small salons or chambers where the nuances and individuality of the players can be heard. But the exact size of the ensemble, in the standard repertoire, can range from duets (two players) to octets (eight players). Any instrumentation is actually possible, so if you want to know what to expect, it's important to study up on your Latin roots and read the program notes.

String quartets are the most famous of these configurations. The natural balance and blend of two violins, viola, and cello is difficult to beat. It's because of this blend—this potential for *perfect* synthesis—that the quartet repertoire is so vast.[21] And it's because of this vastness of repertoire that there are so many pre-formed, professional string quartets.[22]

These quartets—the kind who play together exclusively, travel as a pack, and spend hours rehearsing every day—are the ones you often see bickering and plotting one another's demise in various movies and television shows. In reality, they're not quite as bloodthirsty or resentful as their on-screen portrayals would suggest (if they were, there would be far fewer first violinists left in the world), but neither are the legends entirely baseless. What *is* true, probably, is that every quartet has its tensions, as does any small group that works together with this sort of intensity and pressure. It's also not uncommon for two or more of the players to become romantically involved. (After all, they spend a *lot* of time together playing passionate and exhilarating music.) What is *not* true, however, is that second violinists are universally bitter, resentful, and technically inferior to their first violin colleagues.

In top-tier quartets, all four players are excellent—and the

---

21 Haydn wrote sixty-eight string quartets, Mozart wrote twenty-three, Beethoven wrote sixteen—and that's just in the Classical period.

22 The Cleveland, Emerson, Juilliard, and Guarneri Quartets stick out as noteworthy examples—and to that list I would add the Calder Quartet, the Escher Quartet, the Kronos Quartet, and Quatuor Ébène. These days, though, there is an extraordinary number of quartets playing at a world-class level.

decision of who plays what is usually based not on ability but on how the two violinists' sounds mesh with the rest of the group. (Or, as in orchestras, on what position is available.) It often happens that I'll hear a quartet and prefer the playing of the second violinist to that of the first. I also know violinists (albeit not many) who enjoy playing second because of the more collaborative nature of the role. Many quartets alternate, ensuring that neither violinist has to exist for too long outside of the spotlight.

After string quartets, the next most popular formats are duo sonatas (for any instrument and piano) and piano trios (piano, violin, cello). For vocalists and pianists, there are also songs, *lieder*, and *chansons*. (Or, if we translate these terms into English, "songs, songs, and songs.")

There are plenty of pre-formed duos and piano trios, though few are as well known as their string quartet counterparts. Pre-formed trios often consist of famous soloists—like Daniel Barenboim, Pinchas Zukerman, and Jacqueline du Pré—or Emanuel Ax, Leonidas Kavakos, and Yo-Yo Ma. This is because trios are naturally more individualistic, which means they require less rehearsal time and are therefore ideal for three people with separate travel and performance schedules.

Actually, it often happens, at festivals and chamber music series, that a group of players who have never met before will fly in for the week of a concert (having prepared separately, of course), rehearse for only a few days, and then perform. Sometimes this yields brilliant, electrifying results and you feel, as an audience member, like you're watching a very stimulating, highbrow orgy. And other times you feel like the universe evidently had very good reasons for not bringing these individuals together in the past, and you wish the festival director had respected these reasons instead of forcing you to witness such awkward chemistry.

SOME EXCELLENT EXAMPLES OF CHAMBER MUSIC:

- Sonata for Piano and Violin No. 21 in E Minor, K. 304
  —Wolfgang Amadeus Mozart

- Sonata for Two Pianos in D Major, K. 448
  —Wolfgang Amadeus Mozart

- Piano Trio in D Major, Op. 70, no. 1, "Ghost"
  —Ludwig van Beethoven

- String Quartet No. 11 in F Minor, Op. 95, "Serioso"
  —Ludwig van Beethoven

- "Erlkönig," Op. 1, D. 328—Franz Schubert

- String Quartet No. 14 in D Minor, D. 810, "Death and the Maiden"—Franz Schubert

- String Octet in E-flat Major, Op. 20—Felix Mendelssohn

- *Dichterliebe*, Op. 48—Robert Schumann

- Piano Quartet in E-flat Major, Op. 47—Robert Schumann

- Piano Quartet No. 1 in G Minor, Op. 25—Johannes Brahms

- Piano Trio in A Minor, Op. 50—Pyotr Ilyich Tchaikovsky

- Violin Sonata No. 2 in A Major, Op. 100—Johannes Brahms

- String Quartet in F Major—Maurice Ravel

- String Quartet No. 8 in C Minor, Op. 110—Dmitri Shostakovich

- Septet for Piano Trio and String Quartet—Ellen Taaffe Zwilich

Solo Music

Solo music is music that's written for one single or one *featured* part. It's usually the most technically challenging music in the repertoire of each instrument, and it's the primary focus of most performers' private lessons.

If you're a pianist, your solo repertoire is divided between concertos and music that's composed for piano alone. The latter can include sonatas, impromptus, intermezzos, nocturnes, and any number of pieces of varying structures and length. Solo piano music—truly solo piano music, that is—is set apart from other solo music by its breadth of repertoire and general fullness of sound.

If you're a string player, you have concertos (which we've covered a bit in the orchestral section), a limited number of works for your instrument alone, and a slew of pieces for your instrument *and* piano accompaniment.

It's confusing, I know, that a combination like violin and piano can be classified as either a chamber ensemble or a solo configuration. But the designation comes down to the differing ways in which these pieces make use of the piano. In a violin and piano *sonata*, for instance, the two instruments are equal partners; they share the melody, take turns playing the role of accompanist, and collaborate when it comes to the interpretation. They're costars. In a violin *showpiece*, however, the pianist is more like the uncredited extra who dies in the background of a movie's opening scene but also comes back as a customer in a barbershop and then as a street philosopher rambling in the background (which I guess could happen in a very low-budget film that was shot in the Pitcairn Islands,[23] or any other place with a population of fifty).

---

23 Moving here would be a great alternative to using the word "concerti," in case you desire solitude.

Because most often, in these "solo" showpieces, the piano is actually standing in for a whole orchestra.

The distinction is perhaps best illustrated by the respective bowing[24] protocols for each of these categories. I was taught, at the end of a violin and piano sonata, to wait for the pianist to stand and join me at the front of the stage; only then would we bow together, exit together, reenter together, bow together, and so on and so forth for as long as the applause lasted. At the end of a *showpiece*, however, I was supposed to bow alone—as many times as the audience demanded—and *then* gesture graciously to the pianist as if acknowledging my late-nineteenth-century valet, the one I always brought along for moral support but kept out of sight unless someone needed an extra footman.

None of this has anything to do with the abilities of the pianist in question. It could be the same pianist for both sonatas and showpieces; the only difference is the way in which the piano is used in the composition.

Truly solo works—in the sense that they are played alone—are less common in instruments other than the piano. As a performer, I always felt unnerved by them—and I wasn't alone. Solo music is like the swimsuit competition of a beauty pageant, except instead of your body, it's your interpretation, your abilities of retention, and your sound that are on display. For string players, there are no thick harmonies to hide behind (except those you also have to worry about creating), no residual resonance left over from the piano's many notes. And there are no external prompts to help you remember what comes next. It's just you and your instrument and whatever unhelpful thoughts your inner critic sees fit to lob at you during the concert.

---

24 *Bowing* (to rhyme with *meowing*) as in bending at the waist in acknowledgment or gratitude—not bowing (to rhyme with *sewing*), as in using a violin bow to extract sound from the string.

Bach's solo violin sonatas and partitas—staples of the violin repertoire—are particularly notorious for their perilousness. They are always performed from memory, and they are laden with mental booby traps. I've heard of people taking wrong turns in one partita and ending up in a different partita entirely, and I once witnessed a somewhat painful performance of the notorious Chaconne in which a very well-known violinist got stuck in an endless loop that kept taking her back to the beginning of the piece. Eventually, after three times through the first half, she put herself out of her misery by improvising an ending—which impressed me far more than if she'd executed the whole thing perfectly. And because of her composure, very few audience members knew that anything had gone wrong.

THE CHACONNE AND ITS DASTARDLY (BUT BEAUTIFUL) SOLO STRING BUDDIES:

- Violin Partita No. 2 in D Minor, BWV 1004[25]
—Johann Sebastian Bach

- Cello Suite No. 2 in D Minor, BWV 1008—Johann Sebastian Bach

- 24 Caprices for Solo Violin—Niccolò Paganini

- Grand Caprice on Schubert's "Erlkönig," Op. 26
—Heinrich Wilhelm Ernst

- Sonata for Solo Viola, Op. 25, no. 1—Paul Hindemith

- Sonata for Solo Violin, Op. 27, no. 2, "Jacques Thibaud"
—Eugène Ysaÿe

---

25 The chaconne is the fifth and final movement.

THERE ARE A LOT MORE SOLO PIANO PIECES WHERE THESE CAME FROM:

- Piano Sonata No. 13 in B-flat Major, K. 333
  —Wolfgang Amadeus Mozart

- Piano Sonata No. 14 in C-sharp Minor, Op. 27, no. 2, "Moonlight"—Ludwig van Beethoven

- Piano Sonata No. 21 in C Major, Op. 53, "Waldstein"
  —Ludwig van Beethoven

- *Kreisleriana*, Op. 16—Robert Schumann

- 24 Preludes, Op. 28—Frédéric Chopin

- *Suite bergamasque*—Claude Debussy

- 24 Negro Melodies, Op. 59—Samuel Coleridge-Taylor

- *Gaspard de la nuit*, M. 55—Maurice Ravel

- *Romanian Folk Dances*, Sz. 56—Béla Bartók

- Piano Sonata No. 2—Pierre Boulez

AND, BECAUSE IT'S SO FUN—AND ORGAN IS ALMOST LIKE THE PIANO:

- Toccata and Fugue in D Minor, BWV 565—Johann Sebastian Bach

SOLO WITH VALET (I.E., ACCOMPANIST):

- *Introduction and Rondo Capriccioso in A Minor*, Op. 28
  —Camille Saint-Saëns

- *Zigeunerweisen*, Op. 20—Pablo de Sarasate

- *Carmen Fantasy*, Op. 25—Pablo de Sarasate

- *Navarra*, Op. 33—Pablo de Sarasate

- *Tzigane*—Maurice Ravel

- *Carmen Fantasie*—Franz Waxman

Note: Both Sarasate's *Carmen Fantasy* and Waxman's *Carmen Fantasie* are based on themes from the opera *Carmen*.

Mimery

I was always bad at improvising, which is partly why that violinist's graceful exit from the Chaconne Loop of Hell impressed me so much.

When I was a kid, I could spontaneously produce mediocre pieces of music in a generic Classical-period style, but (*a*) I could only do this when I was alone, which made what was already a pretty useless skill an even more useless one, and (*b*) on these occasions, I was mimicking more than I was creating.

Improvising isn't a skill that most Classical violinists need—unless you're the violinist mentioned above. But it would have come in handy for the Botti tour. Everyone else could improvise. And they did, constantly. Which threw me off at first—because in my desire to *not* screw up, I had written out all my parts, studied the notes and recordings as I would with any other piece, and then gone onstage expecting—as one does in classical music—that everyone would execute their parts in a reliable and consistent way.

In fairness, the group was pretty nice to me on that first night, when they knew I'd only had a few days to prepare. But once I had an overview of the topography, they quickly set about bulldozing it.

Eventually, my internal map became a bit more flexible, but the fact that I could never actually join *in* with their improvising—that I was the only one replicating the exact same notes night after night, however improvisatory I made them sound—made me feel like a fraud.

When I first started playing with them, I was too freaked out about my lack of preparation to listen to the rest of the show. I'd go on for my numbers, and I'd spend the rest of the time in my dressing room, studying my part and stressing out about what kinds of musical shenanigans people were going to throw my way. But as I found fewer challenges in my own role, I started to spend more and more of my time in the wings, listening to the band. Their virtuosity was astounding, but it was their freedom, their comfort, their creativity, and their commitment that made my head explode. Richie Goods always found the most infectious groove on the bass; Billy Childs created nightly sound worlds I'd never have dreamed of, let alone come up with on the spot; Billy Kilson walked offstage each night dripping with sweat, after having poured every ounce of power and strength into his drum set.

Whatever happened during the performance, they handled it, drew from it. They laughed, they riffed, they messed around. They were better than bulletproof. They were like skyscrapers built with seismic base isolation, endowed with inherent integrity and optimized to withstand the stressors of performance. I was like a stone tower made fragile by its own rigidity.

One night, I was waiting in the parking lot for our hotel shuttle with our sound guy, Mickey. This was late in the tour, after my night at the Staatsoper had reminded me that the music that was most authentic to who I was would always be the music of Mozart and Beethoven and Bach.

I'd always felt that Mickey was the unsung hero of the show. All the players were amplified, and a lot of our shows were in acoustically dry theaters (or outside, where our natural sounds would have fallen dead). It was Mickey's job to add the reverb, the sheen, the projection—to make our individual sounds luscious—and then to balance those sounds so that everything came out pretty. It was a big job and I'd always thought he deserved more recognition for it.

This was why, when an audience member passed by us and stopped to compliment me on my performance, I replied with something like "Oh, no, it was all Mickey. He does our sound."

It didn't occur to me that this was a confusing thing to say until a few seconds later, when the guy mumbled awkwardly, "Well, your *motions* were amazing, then—how in sync you were with the music."

I realized, then, that he thought I was some kind of mime. Or one of those inflatable flailing tube-men outside of car dealerships, only in a sparkly dress and heels. I'd led him to believe that I walked out onstage every night, all smiles and bows, and blithely took credit for playing the violin when all I *actually* did was wiggle around a bit.

It would have been hilarious, except that that was exactly how I felt. Not only on the tour, but with the violin in general.

A few weeks later, I played my last show with the Botti band. I booked an Airbnb in Berlin, directly between Stephan's apartment and my sister's so that no one could accuse me of favoritism. And I plopped my suitcases down for a whole glorious month.

Chapter 10

romantic in the candle-lined-hot-tub sense of the word

Famous (and Not So Famous) Love Stories of Classical Music

In those early days, my relationship with Stephan was a bit like my mother-in-law's driving: an awe-inspiring, unstoppable force hurtling down the autobahn at 200 km/hour. Very fun if you're in the driver's seat, but nauseating for anyone sitting in the back.

It was, in fact, pretty inconvenient for both of us; I was in the middle of the Botti tour, enjoying a newly unencumbered, nomadic lifestyle—and Stephan was juggling classes, work, and all-consuming preparations for his *Staatsexamen* (two sets of seven five-hour legal exams that determine the future employment options of every lawyer in Germany). Plus, in my emotional apathy, I'd promised myself that the next person I got into a relationship with would be older and much richer than I was; not a student two years my junior, whose apartment hadn't felt the touch of a paintbrush (let alone a hammer) in nearly half a century.

Of course, none of that mattered. We were smitten—besotted—and instead of trundling unenthusiastically along a path I'd set for myself at the age of seven, or letting breaks like the Botti tour determine which way I wandered, I'd finally found something I knew I wanted, something I was willing to fight for. Or, at least, *fly* for. A lot.

At one point, I flew from Bangkok to Washington to Berlin to New York in a week—and in the middle of that I recorded a whole album with Meta. I existed in a strange, suspended reality where geography was a trifle and sleeping came in shifts and all my money went directly to United Airlines. But despite my commitment to the Star Alliance loyalty program, Stephan and I often had to go weeks between visits. ("Weeks" was a long time to be apart before 2020.)

We coped with the distance by writing letters to each other, each night before going to sleep. Horribly sincere, excruciatingly sappy love letters that make us simultaneously cringe and sniffle whenever we come across them now.[1] I won't make you read any excerpts from them, but I will make you read excerpts from *other* excruciatingly sappy love letters for the same reason that I sometimes make Stephan watch shows like *Bridgerton*: I enjoy wielding that kind of power over people. It's also nice to remember that the great geniuses of the classical genre weren't always armless, legless busts made of stone—but living, breathing humans with their own sets of desires and extremities.

Love Letters of the Not-So-Rich and Famous

There was a time, of course, when writing excruciatingly sappy love letters was a perfectly normal thing to do. People used to *bathe* less

---

1 Stephan had them printed and bound for our first Christmas together. I told you we were gross.

often than they wrote love letters, which also might explain why they preferred to communicate via post.

Robert and Clara Schumann, however—two of the most significant figures in the history of music, who were kept apart for a period of years—would have definitely taken the face time (bathed or not).

You met Clara in chapter 2. She was the second twelve-year-old prodigy to blow Goethe's mind with her piano chops—the one he dubbed "more powerful than six boys put together." What's funny is that one of those six boys might have easily been Clara's future husband, Robert Schumann, who set off to become a pianist only to bump into Clara and realize that he would never reach her level of artistry or technical virtuosity. Luckily, things worked out for him. He's considered one of the greatest composers of all time.

The TMZ facts about the pair's relationship are these:

· Clara's dad, Friedrich Wieck, hated Robert. He described him as "incompetent, childish, unmanly, socially ill-adjusted" and "lazy, unreliable, and conceited." And also: "a mediocre composer whose music is unclear and almost impossible to perform." (Even though plenty of pianists have performed his works successfully. Clara, for instance.)

· *Before* Clara's dad hated Robert, he liked him. He was, in fact, Robert's piano teacher—and Robert even lived with him (and Clara) for a time. Because of this, Robert and Clara met when Clara (who was nine years Robert's junior) was *very* young. It's important to note, though, that their first kiss didn't take place until she was sixteen. (Which, I realize, is still very young, but . . . different times?) Clara was eighteen when she and Robert got engaged, but the legal age of majority at the time was twenty-one, which left them at Friedrich Wieck's mercy.

- Wieck forbade the match, keeping the pair apart for the next three years. (He'd also separated them for a year and a half before then.)

- Things got messy and lawyers were involved.

- Robert and Clara wrote approximately twenty thousand love letters to each other.

- They did get married eventually.

- They had eight kids.

- They made up with Clara's father.

- If you thought their beginning as a couple was complicated, just wait until you hear what the end was like.

According to Robert's letters to Clara, Friedrich Wieck turned on him shortly after the summer of 1835. Hell-bent on putting an end to Clara and Robert's blossoming romance, he took Clara away on an extended concert tour—and even removed all the inkwells from her rooms on the road. Still, she managed to sneak in the odd midnight missive—and upon her return to Leipzig, she conveyed her enduring love for Robert by adding his four Symphonic Etudes to the program of her homecoming concert in the famous Gewandhaus concert hall. This grand romantic gesture led, immediately, to Robert's proposal—which led, immediately, to Wieck separating them again. Eventually, Clara and Robert filed a legal suit against Wieck—and won—though not until Clara was nearly twenty-one. Their wedding took place exactly one day before they would have been allowed to marry anyway, but good for them for sticking it to Clara's dad for those twenty-four hours.

During the whole of these separations, the pair poured themselves into their work. Clara busied herself primarily with concerts: those letters that she *was* able to send are filled with tales from her various performances before kings and queens. But she also produced several important compositions, including her *Romanzen*, Op. 11. This set of three romances alternates between dark, shadowy lullabies and exquisite moments of light—perhaps reflecting the juxtaposition of the various forces (her music, Robert, and her father) in her daily life.

Robert wrote of the work: "In your *Romanzen*, I've heard once again that we must become husband and wife. You complete me as a composer, as I you. Every one of your thoughts comes from my soul, as I owe all of my music to you."

Robert used this time of separation to produce his famous *Kreisleriana* cycle, which was inspired by E. T. A. Hoffmann's character Johannes Kreisler, an eccentric composer-genius whose personality shared many traits with Schumann's. He originally dedicated the work to Clara (an honor, given that many consider it one of his best), but then Clara's dad threw a tantrum so he dedicated it to Chopin instead. Robert also wrote his *Fantasiestücke*, Op. 12: a set of character pieces that begins with one of the most tender, palpitating configurations of notes I've ever heard.

In 1840, the year before his marriage to Clara, Robert became suddenly and completely obsessed with songs (*lieder*), and wrote over 130 of them. It's referred to as his *Liederjahr*—or "year of song." He poured all of his longing and anticipation and sentiment into these compositions.

My favorite of these songs can be found in his *Dichterliebe*, a song cycle based on love poems from Heinrich Heine's "Lyrisches Intermezzo."[2] For me, the two knockouts are the first song, "Im

---

2 *Dichterliebe* was also listed in the previous chapter's chamber music listening list.

wunderschönen Monat Mai," and the seventh song, "Ich grolle nicht." I'm not saying they're the most beautiful, brilliant pieces ever written, but I've never heard anything that I could definitely classify as *more* beautiful or *more* brilliant than they are.

"Im wunderschönen Monat Mai" begins with a short, disorienting piano introduction that sounds, to me, like a musical question. It's almost as if the piano is asking, "When . . . ?" To which the voice quickly replies, "In the wonderfully beautiful month of May." (That's what *im wunderschönen Monat Mai* means.) With this line, the music melts from its unsettling, tonal ambiguity into a halcyon warmth. Then it starts to build.

There's a line, in the text, about buds (it is a song about spring, after all), and this is followed by the words *da ist in meinem Herzen / die Liebe aufgegangen*—roughly: "the love is risen in my heart" (only I've changed the word order to make it intelligible). Here, the music, too, begins to rise. This technique, of mirroring and reinforcing the meaning of the text in the music, is called word painting. The music rises in a sequence, with two tiers: the first peaking with the word *Herzen*—heart—and the second, which reaches a higher point still, with the word *aufgegangen*—risen. It's so effective that you really don't need to speak German to understand what the song is about.

The magic is that the same melody works for the second stanza, too. As in the first stanza, the second begins with the words *im wunderschönen Monat Mai*. This is followed by a brief mention of birds (again: it's a song about spring), and then it continues: *da hab' ich ihr gestanden / mein Sehnen und Verlangen*. This means, approximately, "I have confessed to her my longing and yearning."

This time, the same rising line that was first applied to the words "the love is risen in my heart" highlights a more figurative level of the text. It peaks first with the word *gestanden*—confessed—and then, after regrouping, builds to the word *Verlangen*—yearning. The listener feels, here, the singer's giddily nervous excitement. The rising two-part sequence depicts the swelling of his courage and of his hopes.[3] But in his state of vulnerability, he's aware of the possibility that he might fall or be let down, which is what necessitates the moment of regrouping—the pause—between the two upward waves. The final word, *Verlangen*, is the peak of the climb. It makes perfect sense that Schumann, whose personal life was basically defined by yearning, would place this word at the highest point in the music. He also embeds a hint of dissonance on the second syllable: one note that desperately wants to resolve down a step—yearning's musical embodiment.

It's one of the most consummate examples of songwriting that exists. But don't take my word for it. Listening to it will take up only a minute and a half of your time.[4]

The seventh song in the cycle, "Ich grolle nicht," uses similar techniques to imbue the text with meaning. Here, though, the most striking aspect at play is Schumann's interpretation of the ambiguous poem. The text is written from the perspective of a man addressing a woman. (It could be any person, really—or a pet, even—but we'll treat the subject as a human woman for now because this is the standard assumption.) He professes that he isn't angry—*ich grolle nicht*—even if his heart is breaking and love is lost to him forever. He goes on to tell her a bit about herself, commenting on the irony

---

3 Both my parents were disappointed, upon reading this, that I failed to note that it could also be seen as sexual. To placate them, I will mention now that his courage and hopes may not be the only things that are swelling here.

4 Keep in mind, though, that because it's part of a song *cycle*, it transitions directly into the next song without pause. And the entire cycle takes half an hour.

that even as she shines with diamond-like splendor, not a single ray of light enters her heart. In the second stanza, he says, "I saw you in a dream; and I saw the night in your heart; and I saw the snake that was devouring it." He concludes with the words "I saw, my love, how wretched you are."

Without Schumann's music, Heine's poem reads to me like the kind of guilt-trippy, sarcastic blessing that's so often bestowed by bitter exes. It's an attempt at generosity—or an attempt at *exhibiting* generosity, at least—but it's pervaded by resentment and accusations of cruelty and coldheartedness. Many of the performances I've heard seem to agree with this reading. But the performances I prefer are those that prioritize the story told by Schumann's scoring choices over the more obvious suggestions of the unscored text.

The fact is, most of this song doesn't sound angry. There's strength, certainly, in the opening statement of *ich grolle nicht*, and there's a circumspect hardness to the music—a detachment and exactitude—during the bit about the woman's joyless, lightless heart at the end of the first stanza. But it's the second stanza where Schumann works his transformative magic.

As the singer describes his dream, Schumann builds a gorgeous sequence that rises in waves until it reaches the song's climax with the final sentence: "I saw, my love, how wretched you are." The music here is heart-melting—far more suggestive of pity and generosity than anger. In *Schumann's* version, the claim *ich grolle nicht* seems to be genuine. The singer truly isn't angry, but filled, rather, with compassion and understanding—and, by the sound of it, an even greater love now that he's beheld her suffering. For him the message of the text is "I see you. I know you. I understand why you are the way that you are. And I forgive you."

First of all, this song is breathtaking. Give it a listen and then tell me you don't feel like forgiving absolutely everyone in your life who's ever wronged you.

Second: it makes sense, I think, that this was Schumann's understanding of the text. The love of his life, Clara, had been unavailable to him for most of the past five years, and because of her father, she'd also been trapped in a metaphorical darkness. (One could argue, even, that Friedrich Wieck was the heart-eating snake.) As you'll read in a minute, Schumann also struggled with mental and emotional instability; this struggle would have likely increased his understanding of (and sympathy for) human imperfection.

After their marriage, the Schumanns were seen as a beacon: a beautiful union of soul and mind, a household steeped in artistry and musicianship. Unfortunately, their marriage was not a happily-ever-after kind of deal. Robert's anxiety and depression worsened with age. He developed a fear of metal; he was haunted by a high A that rang constantly in his ears; and at times he found himself shivering spontaneously and uncontrollably. In later years, he experienced hallucinations, which he described as alternately angelic and demonic visions. He began to fear that he was a danger to those around him, and in 1854 he attempted suicide by jumping into the Rhine. He spent his last two years (1854–56) in an asylum, by choice, and from the time of his commitment up until two days before his death, his relationship with Clara returned to its roots: it was, once again, a matter of distance and letters.

Marriage to Robert wasn't an easy path for Clara, but there seems to be no question that the body of work *he* left behind, at least, would have been far less rich without her support and inspiration. Plus, if Clara hadn't married Robert, we never would have had classical music's most famously puzzling love triangle—or throuple—or whatever kind of deeply intense, three-way friendship was shared by Clara Schumann, Robert Schumann, and Johannes Brahms.

A CONFOUNDING TRIANGLE

Brahms's relationship with Clara Schumann (back when Brahms looked like a young Tom Hiddleston rather than the high-end mall Santa he resembled in later years) is even more storied than Clara Schumann's relationship with her husband. His passionate, heartfelt letters to her—and many musical dedications—have been the source of endless speculation. Were they in love? Was Clara's youngest child, Felix, who was officially Brahms's godson, actually Brahms's *biological* son? Or was Brahms's attraction to the older Clara Schumann the result of an oedipal complex? These are the questions that the Gossip Girls and Lady Whistledowns of the classical music world concern themselves with.

While it seems fairly safe to reject the possibility that Felix Schumann was Brahms's son—and to tack the oedipal complex theory up to society's unenlightened view of attractions between older women and younger men—the question of whether Brahms and Clara Schumann were in love is more challenging to address. We only have letters to go by—Brahms's letters, mostly, since the bulk of Clara's were destroyed—and these are very, very confusing. Some of his phrases seem undeniably romantic, but he also displays such love and admiration for Robert—and for the love shared by Clara *and* Robert—that a betrayal seems hard to imagine.

Here's what I mean.

In a letter from Düsseldorf, written on Sunday, August 12, 1855, Brahms writes to Clara, "I think of you constantly, not for a long time have I thought of anyone so fondly and so incessantly."

And in a letter written on May 31, 1856, he writes, "My beloved

Clara, I wish I could write to you as tenderly as I love you, and give you as much kindness and goodness as I wish for you. You are so infinitely dear to me that I can't begin to tell you. I constantly want to call you darling and all kinds of other things, without becoming tired of adoring you."

I've tried very hard, but I can't imagine sending those things to a friend. Ever.

He also writes, *of* Clara, in a letter to violinist Joseph Joachim on June 19, 1854 (which was relatively early on in Brahms's friendship with the Schumanns):

> I believe I admire and honor her no more highly than I love
> and am in love with her. I often have to restrain myself forcibly
> just from quietly embracing her and even—: I don't know, it
> seems to me so natural, as though she could not take it at all
> amiss. I think I can't love a young girl at all any more, at least I
> have entirely forgotten them; after all, they merely promise the
> Heaven which Clara shows us unlocked.

It's extremely difficult to explain any of this as platonic, and when I try, it makes me feel like a politician.

The thing *is*, we have to consider the rest of what he wrote, as well. Other letters document his visits to Robert in the asylum—visits he made alone, at a time when Clara herself was not allowed to see her husband. These visits took place while Brahms was actually living in the Schumanns' home (with Robert's blessing), looking after the children and keeping track of household finances—even while Clara was away on concert tours. Brahms was the one who spoke with Robert's doctors, relayed the news to Clara, and served as Robert's lifeline to the outside world.

That letter from May 31, 1856 (the one that begins with "My

beloved Clara" and then wins love letter bingo before the end of the first paragraph), is one of my favorites not because of its rhapsodizing but because of Brahms's excitement, later in the letter, over an atlas he'd managed to procure for Robert: "Just this morning in Cologne I bought your Robert the *biggest* atlas. 83 gigantic maps, beautifully bound and new."

Clara often sent presents, through Brahms, to Robert, but Brahms was eager to give this one himself: "[I]f your writing set does arrive, I beg you to let me give him the atlas! But only if it's all right with you and if you don't want to give him a lot of presents . . . The huge atlas is magnificent!"

In a line just under all of this, he explains the reasoning behind the gift: "*N.B.* The doctors told me nothing new about Robert, only that some time ago he wished for the largest atlas."

Despite the tragedy of the situation, there is something adorable about the idea of the ailing Robert Schumann, locked up in an old mansion and quickly losing his grasp, but still intent on studying the largest atlas he can get his hands on. I find, too, the earnestness and enthusiasm with which Brahms adopts the cause (knowing, as he did, that Robert was no longer lucid) equally adorable, and I believe it illustrates the immense respect and fondness they shared.

Brahms's letter to Clara from February 1855 following one of his trips to the asylum is further proof of this fondness:

My most beloved friend,

Just as I thought, this evening I have so much of what is most beautiful to relate to you that I don't know where to begin. I was with your beloved husband from 2 to 6; if only you could see my delighted face, you would know more than after my letter.

He goes on to describe the time they spent together, including the moment when he presented Robert with Clara's portrait: "Oh, if you could have seen how deeply moved he was, how he almost had tears in his eyes and how he held it ever closer and finally said, 'Oh, how long I have wished for this.' As he set it down, his hands were trembling intensely."

In the letter's conclusion, Brahms writes that he was "as if intoxicated, at times, so happy."

This language *also* seems like the kind I would use only in a romantic context, but applied this time to Robert. Which makes me think that either Brahms was in love with *both* the Schumanns[5] or, more probably, that he was simply a very effusive character and his love for Clara was more courtly than sexual in nature: romantic, perhaps, but not physical. His love for Robert may have been similar, or it may have been the love one feels for a very dear friend.

At Robert's funeral, Brahms was given the honor of carrying the wreath and leading the procession, along with Clara and two of the Schumann children. He and Clara remained friends for the rest of their lives, continuing to write letters and championing each other's careers. Their language grew less ardent after Robert's passing, but there is ample proof of love in the works Brahms dedicated to Clara and her family over the course of his lifetime.

His Opus 118, a set of six *Klavierstücke* written near the end of his life, contains one of his most beloved works: his A-Major Intermezzo.

An intermezzo is a short piece or movement that's set apart from

---

5   Interestingly, Robert Schumann once referred to Brahms's birthday as the *"Geburtstag unseres Geliebten"*—"the birthday of our beloved"—in a letter to Clara.

what surrounds it and defined, primarily, by one character or fixation. Kind of like Brahms's affair[6] with the Schumanns. And *this* intermezzo (Intermezzo in A Major, Op. 118, no. 2, to be exact) is filled with nostalgia, tenderness, and patient devotion.[7] It sounds very much like someone reflecting on a memory—swelling, at times, with fervor and intensity and then falling back in wistful meditation.

Following the death of Felix Schumann (Clara's youngest son and Brahms's godson, who was also an accomplished violinist), Brahms wrote the beautiful second movement of his G-Major Violin Sonata in his memory.

This is one of my favorite movements in the violin repertoire. It expresses, with such eloquence, so many of the feelings I associate with loss and mourning: the sadness, the anger, but mainly, the transition of grief into memory. There is a warmth to the main theme, after the violin's first entrance and again at the start of the recapitulation, that feels to me like the healing embrace of a very dear friend, offered up in a moment of utter wretchedness. I can't help but feel that this was Brahms's way of embracing Clara—of holding her close and sharing her sadness while also, somehow, softening her despair.

The third movement of this same sonata also contains the theme from his song "Regenlied," which Clara, in many letters, refers to as "her" theme.

---

6   I think, given its intensity, we can definitely call it that—regardless of whether or not there were romantic feelings involved.

7   I love it so much that its opening bars are the only thing I have ever bothered to learn on the piano. Apart from the theme from A&E's *Pride and Prejudice*, during my Colin Firth phase.

Upon receiving a manuscript of the sonata from Brahms, Clara wrote to him of how she played through it right away, and then "out of joy," was overcome by tears.

We will never know the exact nature of Brahms's relationship with Clara Schumann, but what we can say, with certainty, is that it was beautiful.

A BACHELOR

It's one of history's many cutenesses that Tchaikovsky and Brahms— two of the ten-ish most important classical composers (whose violin concertos represent two of the three most important violin concertos in the repertoire)—share a birthday: May 7th. It's particularly cute because Tchaikovsky went around spouting all kinds of nasty things about Brahms and his music until the two of them went drinking and ended up buddies. In a letter to his patroness Nadezhda von Meck, before their night of partying, Tchaikovsky writes:

> In Vienna Brahms is regarded as the top dog . . . Brahms is a
> celebrity; I'm a nobody. And yet, without false modesty, I tell
> you that I consider myself superior to Brahms . . . If I'm
> an honest and truthful person, then I would have to tell him
> this: "Herr Brahms! I consider you to be a very untalented
> person, full of pretensions but utterly devoid of creative
> inspiration. I rate you very poorly and indeed I simply look
> down upon you."

He never did warm up to Brahms's music. But after their night on the town, he wrote to his publisher and friend Pyotr Jurgenson:

I went on the booze with Brahms—he's awfully fond of
drinking, you know; he's a very nice person and not at all as
proud as I had imagined. He has a very cheerful disposition,
and I must say that the hours I spent in his company have left
me with nothing but the pleasantest memories.

He also wrote that Brahms's "comely head" reminded him of "a
benign, handsome, elderly Russian priest's head."

Tchaikovsky's love letters—or those pertaining to his romantic
interests, I should say (because as a gay man in nineteenth-century
Russia, he wasn't afforded the right to open expressions of romantic
love)—are filled with similarly colorful descriptions. You'll also find,
in them, a poignant mix of humor and pathos.

There are delightful fantasies like this one:

"My God, what an angelic creature, and how I long to be his
slave, his plaything, his property!"

And lighthearted references to clandestine meetings:

"I spent the time between dinner and the theatre walking
around and met a youth of stunning beauty although of a purely
German kind. After our walk, I offered him some money, which
was refused. He does it for the love of art and adores men with
beards."

But in this letter to his brother Modest written on September 28,
1876, he lays bare the conflict between his homosexuality, which he
seems to be at peace with, and the pain caused him by society's view
of it:

You say that I shouldn't give a damn about *qu'en dira-t'on*!
[French: what will people say]. That's only true up to a point.
There are people who can't look down on me for my failings

simply because they grew fond of me before they suspected that I was a man who had as good as lost his reputation. Sasha is a case in point! I know she has guessed the truth and forgives me unreservedly. The same goes for a great many others whom I love and respect. Do you really think that it doesn't weigh heavily on me that I am aware that they pity me and forgive me, when in actual fact I haven't done anything wrong! Can you understand how it kills me to think that people who love me can sometimes feel ashamed of me! It's happened a hundred times, and will happen a hundred times more!

It becomes clear, through reading his letters,[8] that his battle was not against his sexuality but against the forces in society that condemned him for it—and his fate in light of that condemnation. This undoubtedly contributed to his depression—and to his ultimate decision to marry a woman he loved "not in the least." It also informed many of the darker emotions captured in his work.

In his words, the opening of his Symphony No. 4 represents "the fatal force which prevents our hopes of happiness from being realized." The music remains doom-filled for quite some time before shifting to a darkly seductive theme. Tchaikovsky describes this as "a sweet and tender vision. Some bright, gracious human form passes and beckons somewhere . . . Little by little, dreams have completely enveloped the soul. All that was gloomy, joyless is forgotten. It is here, it is here, happiness!"

But the illusion soon fades.

---

8 I'd recommend *The Tchaikovsky Papers: Unlocking the Family Archive*, edited by Marina Kostalevsky.

"No!" he writes. "These were dreams, and Fate awakens us harshly. Thus, life is a perpetual alternation between grim reality and transient dreams and reveries of happiness. There is no haven. Drift upon that sea until it engulfs and submerges you in its depths."

In spite of the darkness that defined much of his life, Tchaikovsky is best known for his sweeping, effusive melodies and waltzes.

The music in his *Sleeping Beauty*, which you may know from the Disney movie, instantly springs to mind. And most people recognize *The Nutcracker*'s hummable "Waltz of the Flowers." But it's actually the moment just *after* this waltz that always gets me—when the Nutcracker and the Sugar Plum Fairy are reunited in a heart-rending pas de deux.

The scene opens with a gentle rippling that suggests both tenderness and nobility. The Nutcracker is a prince, after all, and the Sugar Plum Fairy is . . . no one really knows.

There are harmonic and rhythmic complexities that make this pas de deux brilliant, but the melody, here, is essentially a descending scale. This gives the music a feeling of inevitability. We've all heard so many scales in our lives that our ears not only accept but *anticipate* the progression. Each time the scale repeats, Tchaikovsky uses orchestration to ramp up the level of intensity—and poignance. The first iteration is a graceful descent. There's a sweetness to it, as well as an innocence. But as the scene continues, the iterations become more and more powerful, collecting more and more instruments, until the scale is transformed into a breathtaking eruption—an outpouring of love and ecstasy and something slightly sad.

It feels to me, here, as if Tchaikovsky is living out—and yearning for—and blessing—the kind of declarative love and joyful public acceptance that this couple shares: the kind that was denied and forbidden him in his own life.

BEETHOVEN'S IMMORTAL BELOVED

Speaking of forbidden love, we still have to cover Beethoven's letters to his "Immortal Beloved"—or *unsterbliche Geliebte*—if only because they've served as the inspiration for so many books, movies, and wedding vows. (Not Beethoven's, unfortunately.)

These letters are just about the most famous collection of words in the classical canon. Everyone who knows even a bit about Beethoven knows about them. I'm not sure whether it's the letters themselves or the fact that there's nothing more appealing than a spiky badass with a gooey interior,[9] but they are seen by many as the epitome of romantic expressivity.

A large part of their charm, too, is the mystery that surrounds them.

We don't know who this *unsterbliche Geliebte* was. We don't know whether these letters were ever sent. The dates on the letters are missing the year, which means that experts were only able to deduce that they were written in 1812 through careful detective work. If German grammar wasn't so gender-specific, we wouldn't even know that this mysterious woman *was a woman*. (It is, though, so we do.)

The other thing we don't know—and of all the questions swirling around, this is the one that concerns and upsets me the most—is *why*, in spite of all the forever-and-ever language that we find in them, there are only a total of three letters, written over the course of two days. Were the other letters lost? Or destroyed? Did something happen later that summer to separate the pair for good? Or did this Immortal Beloved woman simply never write back? (Which would raise the question: Who the *hell* did she think she was?)

---

9 Think of sea urchins.

All we can do is speculate—and let our imaginations run rampant (while reading the letters in a hot tub, with some candles and a bottle of wine). For now, here's the most famous passage, which comes at the end of the third and final letter:

> Be calm, only through calm introspection of our existence can we reach our goal of living together—be calm—love me— today—yesterday—what longing with tears for you—you— you—my life—my everything—live well—love me still—never fail to recognize the truest heart of your beloved

Forever yours
Forever mine
Forever ours[10]

I mean.

Theories about the Immortal Beloved's identity abound. Antonie Brentano, a wealthy, married woman whom Beethoven often visited, is one popular candidate. Josephine von Brunswik, a countess who had exchanged intimate letters with Beethoven in the past, is another. But many historians believe that her identity has never been touched upon—that the secrecy implied in these letters, moreover, suggests that it never *will* be touched upon—and until I hear a story that's sensational enough to win me over, I will continue to agree with their position.

But I have often thought, for what it's worth, that Beethoven must have met his Immortal Beloved before writing the slow move-

---

10 The original German actually translates as "forever us," but most English-speaking people seem to prefer it this way.

ment of his "Archduke" trio (aka Piano Trio in B-flat Major, Op. 97) in 1810 or 1811.

The movement, which is the third of four (entitled *Andante cantabile ma però con moto; Poco più adagio*), is one of my favorite moments in all of music, and to my ear, it is the perfect and most beautiful expression of the love that the Immortal Beloved letters describe. There are moments in it that capture the hesitant, time-suspending purity of those early glances; the sensation of blood flushing to the face and neck. And the whole of the movement—its overall structure as well as its harmonic and melodic content—evokes that broadening of the world, that sudden evaporation of the selfishness that had previously defined it, and that onset of pervasive gratitude I remember from those early weeks with Stephan.[11]

The movement is structured as a theme and variations, beginning with a simple, almost prayer-like statement and growing, with occasional setbacks, in warmth and momentum. Toward the end of the movement, the music returns to the simplicity and quiet of the initial statement. This is the nadir. Then a series of breathless, pulsating triplets emerge, hushed at first, but constantly progressing, developing, and awakening until the music opens into a tender euphoria.

Listen to it closely, and try not to smile when the cello part soars from its harmonic depths up to the melody line, where it intertwines with the violin part in the most glorious, sublime duet.

---

11 I'm still grateful—whenever I'm not annoyed that he's working so late.

MOZART'S POTTY MOUTH

As far as love letters go, those of the Schumanns and Brahms and Beethoven fall onto the sentimental, respectful end of the spectrum. Mozart's letters are like the eighteenth-century equivalent of the "Dick in a Box" song.

They're the kinds of things you'd expect to find in the diaries of a six-year-old Howard Stern—but they're shocking to discover in the letters of classical music's favorite poster child.

I've mentioned that Mozart often wrote to his family of his bowel movements, but what may not have been clear was that these writings were not sober descriptions intended to help his parents monitor his digestion or diagnose any conditions he may have suffered from; they were strange poems and creative dialogues that often *personified* his excrement and/or suggested exciting new uses for it.

Many historians believe that Mozart was in love with his cousin Maria Anna Thekla Mozart[12] for a period of several years after their meeting in 1777. Marianne (as she was called) was the lucky recipient of many of Mozart's most inspired scatological writings. Here are a few highlights. I'm including the original German— using Mozart's original spelling—so that you can see the *exact* words and rhymes of this hallowed luminary.

In a letter dated December 23, 1778, Mozart writes the following poem (please note that it rhymes in the original German):

---

12 Not to be confused, under any circumstances, with Maria Anna Mozart—aka "Nannerl"—aka W. A. Mozart's sister. When I first read these letters, I didn't realize that the cousin I'd heard so much about had almost exactly the same name as Nannerl— and for about five minutes I was extremely scandalized.

Also komen sie gewis,	So be sure to come
sonst ist ein schiss;	or else it's a shit;
ich werde alsdan	I will then
in eigner hoherperson	my noble self
ihnen Complimentiren,	compliment you,
ihnen den arsch Petschieren,	stamp your ass,*
ihre hände küssen,	kiss your hands,
mit der hintern büchse schiessen,	shoot with the "buttocks rifle,"
ihnen Embrassiren,	hug you,
sie hinten und vorn kristiren,	douche your front and
ihnen, was ich ihnen etwa	behind, pay you all of
alles schuldig bin, haarklein	what I owe you, to
bezahlen,	the cent,
und einen wackeren furz lassen	and let loose a courageous
erschallen,	fart,
und vielleicht auch etwas lassen	and maybe even let something
fallen—	drop—
Nun adieu—mein Engel	Now adieu—my angel
mein herz	my heart
ich warte auf sie mit schmerz	I wait for you in pain.

* "Stamp" as in a wax seal.

Many people have struggled to reconcile this side of Mozart's personality with his music and reputation as a genius. Margaret Thatcher, for instance. According to Peter Hall, the former director of the National Theatre, she scolded him after a production of *Amadeus* (which later became an excellent movie).

"She was not pleased. In her best headmistress style, she gave me a severe wigging for putting on a play that depicted Mozart as a scatological imp with a love of four-letter words. It was inconceivable, she said, that a man who wrote such exquisite and elegant music could be so foul-mouthed. I said that Mozart's letters proved he was just that: he had an extraordinarily infantile sense of humor. In a sense, he protected himself from maturity by indulging his childishness. 'I don't think you heard what I said,' replied the prime minister. 'He couldn't have been like that.'" But he *was*, apparently.

Jet-Settling Down

Stephan and I continued to write sappy love letters whenever I was away. Which was often, even after I left the Botti show. Meta and I had concerts all over the place—and I had my own solo performances—and just as I was getting ready to move to Berlin on a more permanent basis, I landed a gig on Sir James Galway's monthlong American legacy tour.

Throughout all my trips, I was aware of a constant tugging feeling in my gut, as if my innards were magnetized and the world's entire stockpile of ferromagnetic objects was in Berlin. It wasn't that I was miserable; even as I struggled with the monotony of performing and my troubled relationship with the violin, I could still enjoy a joke told in rehearsal or a night at the bar with friends. But as cool as it was to feel like a globe-trotter, there was no moment, during any of my adventures, when I forgot that there was a specific *place* on the globe where I wanted to be.

One morning, at the end of my longest stay in Berlin, the only way I could force myself to walk out of Stephan's apartment and into the cab that was waiting to take me to the airport was by promising myself that one day—soon—the touring would stop.

Chapter 11

here comes the bride

The I Dos and I Don'ts
of Wedding and Event Music

There's a scene in *The Avengers* where Captain America unleashes all of his anger over the war and Peggy Carter—and being fished out of the Arctic half a century too late for their romantic involvement to be marketable—onto a helpless punching bag. (The punching bag manages to hang in there for a few flashbacks, but ultimately it explodes because Captain America is very strong and very, *very* angry.)

Music was my Peggy Carter. And my wedding was my punching bag.

I made an initially graceful transition to Berlin, trading in my tours with Chris Botti and Sir James Galway for a stint as guest concertmaster of the Deutsches Symphonie-Orchester. But the cost of this victory—which I'd needed as much for my ego as for the money it earned me—was that my audition preparations and time with the orchestra erased any perspective I'd gained in the months before. I was plunged back into a state of competitive, hollow music-making, where my primary aims were achievement and status. At the end of the gig, I auditioned for a permanent concertmaster position but failed to win it. And I was told, moreover, that it was the weakness of my orchestral excerpts—the ones I might have studied in that excerpt class at Juilliard if I'd just been less pigheaded—that had cost me the opportunity.

I lost the will to hustle and make new contacts. My interest in practicing dwindled. I started saying no to more and more concerts, and soon my performing schedule dried up. All that was left of my career were a few decorative accolades.

On a personal level, I was more fulfilled than I'd ever been. I was living with Stephan. I was four blocks over from my sister, Marina. I hadn't spent so many blissfully directionless hours of recreation since early childhood. (*Very* early.) But two decades of achievement-oriented, day-in, day-out productivity had left me with a whole lot of industriousness that needed a home.

Unfortunately, my efforts to find a new objective led me down a path of frustration and failure. At one point, I was passed over for a job as a part-time music teacher at a kindergarten. Another time, a modeling agency sent me to audition for the role of "Female Violinist" in a Samsung commercial, and the casting director, without even pausing to acknowledge the authenticity I could bring to the part, suggested that I might be better suited to the "Girlfriend" role. (But not *much* better suited, it seems, because I didn't get that one, either.)

With Stephan's proposal, a new target presented itself: our wedding. I poured all my determination—along with the self-scrutiny and obsessiveness that came with it—into planning the perfect, fiscally responsible nuptials. Instead of polishing shifts, I was trying to bribe the site manager to cover the bright green exit signs that marred the paneled walls of our venue; instead of tuning fifths, I was chopping up and reconstructing my custom-made silk organza wedding gown in an effort to "fix" the princess seams that had been driving me berserk; instead of centering my bow, I was threatening to disown my mother if she showed up to the ceremony wearing flip-flops (which she did, anyway).

When it came to selecting the music, I was a firm but magnanimous despot. I honored Stephan's requests when I could, and when I couldn't I waved my Juilliard alumni ID in front of his face and reminded him that he'd grown up listening to German schlager music. And then he'd have no choice but to cede to my authority because German schlager music is the absolute worst.[1]

My tyranny in this arena might have been justifiable if I'd exploited my knowledge of the classical repertoire (and my network of extraordinary musicians) to present our guests with a dazzling, soul-nourishing parade of gems from the classical canon. But I didn't. I chose only one piece of classical music for the whole ceremony and reception, and it was performed not by any former classmates but by my cousin Fred and his girlfriend, Francesca, who just happened, randomly, to be a world-class soprano.[2]

One of my reasons for limiting the classical music at our wedding was that I wasn't comfortable asking any of my colleagues to play. I knew we couldn't offer them the kind of money they deserved (which, by the way, is not the same as what they're usually *paid*), and I was acutely aware of how undervalued musicians could feel in these secondary performance situations. The only reason I could bring myself to ask *Francesca* was that she was an extension of Fred, who wrote a short book called *My Cousin the Chicken* when he was in second grade and has owed me for it ever since.

I was also reluctant to reinforce the tired "garden party" associations and stereotypes I'd always railed against. I had too much

---

1   Schlager music is similar to pop music—that is, it's a *kind* of German pop music—but what sets it apart is that it's unapologetically bad. Or, at least, intentionally mediocre. Or, at least, entirely unambitious. It doesn't attempt anything beyond a very simple beat—and the only emotion it seeks to capture, as far as I can tell, is "bouncy."

2   Her full name, in case you want to listen to her dulcet tones, is Francesca Federico.

respect for Mozart's violin and piano sonatas and Beethoven's quartets and Brahms's trios to want to use them as the backdrop for someone's (probably my) hunt for crab cakes.

Of course, if it hadn't been for my strained relationship with the violin and my desire to escape the industry, I would have seen that there were ways around all this. Ways to assure my fellow musicians that I valued them. Ways to show respect to the composers whose works I'd spent my life studying. Ways that I will share with you now.

The I Dos and I Don'ts of Event Music

I still don't like the idea of burying certain pieces of classical music underneath a track of tinkling glassware, popping champagne corks, and ambient chatter. I don't like to mix twenty-one-year-old Balvenie with Coke Zero, either. But just as there *are* whiskeys (if fewer whisk*ies*) I'd use for mixing, there are also pieces that make for appropriate "background music." *Eine kleine Nachtmusik*, for one.

The problem with *Eine kleine Nachtmusik*, of course, is that everyone's heard it a million times, and some musicians will go on strike if you even so much as mention it in their presence. One way to avoid the cliché—and the strike—is to omit the first movement. Few people will recognize the rest of the piece, and your musicians will be far less sick of it. Is it kosher to simply *cut* a quarter of the piece? No. But if you don't cut it, the chances are pretty good that one of your players will walk. So assuming you've hired a quartet, which is what most people do (even though the original piece is scored for string *quin*tet), you'll be down a quarter either way.

If you want to be a bit more original, just go with anything from the earlier compositional periods that's called "serenade" or "divertimento." There's nothing sacrilegious about using these pieces (or

Eine kleine Nachtmusik) for event music because they were, in fact, composed expressly for this purpose.

Really, though, I'll let you have almost any piece you want for your cocktail hour if you also promise to include a musical interlude (a short, featured performance) at some point during your event—to give the music and the musicians a chance to be heard and appreciated on their own. There's nothing like a nod to genius to make a host look gracious and sophisticated. Plus, everyone will want to talk about it once it's over, which will give you a chance to show off all your knowledge.

I mean, if you're going to program world-class music—and hire world-class musicians—they should really be heard.

HOW TO HIRE WORLD-CLASS MUSICIANS

There are a number of ways to hire world-class musicians. How you choose to do it probably depends on your price range and the scale of your event. If you, like the Jordanian oligarch who hired the Botti band to perform at his niece's wedding, have billions of dollars and a fleet of private jets to shuttle in performers from all over the world, you should probably have your people buy out the Met Opera or ring up someone famous like Josh Bell or Yuja Wang.

If you don't have that kind of money, though, there are still plenty of more affordable ways to get world-class performers delivered to your doorstep.

One of these ways is to go through the nearest major conservatory. Juilliard, for one, has a button on its website that says "Hire Juilliard Musicians." It's not like hiring a law student to launch your IPO; in the music world, students are often in better performing shape than older, less hungry professionals, and some of them were already performing in major concert halls at an age when you were still learning to tie your shoelaces. They just happen to cost less.[3]

During my first year at Northwestern, I sometimes played gigs on the weekends with a group of slightly older professionals I knew through that Musicians Gone Wild ski-mountain festival all those summers earlier. Some of them were full-time freelancers, others were teachers, and one of them was a cellist in the Chicago Symphony. Marco, the violist, was the contractor, fielding requests for event music and assembling, from his hordes of talented friends, the best groups he could find. He'd also bring a set of massive binders to each gig—filled with everything from Mozart quartets to Beatles medleys—so we could take requests.

Most cities have plenty of Marcos. They use their network of musicians—a mix of students, recent graduates, and seasoned professionals—to find the best possible group for your event.

Of course, there are also plenty of Marco-pretenders, who aren't great players, who don't have talented friends or binders filled with every kind of music imaginable—but who claim to be able to operate at this level. Luckily, all these musicians have websites and YouTube clips now, so you can check them out before you sign the contract.

NOW THAT I HAVE THEM, HOW DO I MAKE MY WORLD-CLASS MUSICIANS FEEL VALUED?

This is a great question; I'm so glad you asked.

It's not only about the money. It's true that if you pay as well as that oligarch did, you probably don't have to worry about your

---

3   Another reason I felt comfortable asking Francesca to sing for our wedding was that she was still at NYU.

performers walking away feeling undervalued, but don't underestimate the impact of kindness on a hired musician's performance.[4]

Juilliard once sent me to play at a wedding hosted by two board members (who were the parents of the bride). I'm pretty sure they donated a lot to the school because I got quite a few emails from the career development department over the course of those weeks, asking how things were going. My first meeting with the bride, the groom, and the board members took place months before the wedding. They were kind and respectful and I liked them. We went over the music choices together, and when we hit upon the "right" processional, I got to see the mist in the bride's eyes and sense the importance of my contribution to the couple's big day. *This*, in the end—the loyalty their respect and appreciation had inspired in me—was the reason I made sure my quartet rehearsed. Not the pay, which was fair but far from extravagant.

CONVERSELY...

When I was at Northwestern, I played a wedding at a church near campus. A classmate of mine had organized the group. The money was crap, we never met the couple, and the (less than coordinated) wedding coordinator told us close to nothing about the ceremony. All we knew, going into the thing, was that there were three different processionals—one for flower girls, one for bridesmaids, and one for the bride—each of which we ran through, half-heartedly, only once.

When we arrived, the coordinator showed us to our seats and she gave us a cue when it was time to start the first processional, and that

---

4   My sister, Marina, is working on the algorithm that will tell you how nice you need to be for the amount you want to pay.

was the last we saw of her until the bride was at the altar. By then it was too late.

The problems began immediately. First, we didn't know how many flower girls there were, and we couldn't really see them from where we were sitting because they were so short.[5] The next problem was that the bridesmaids started walking before we'd wrapped up the first processional. That meant that we had to keep playing the same music, because you can't jump processionals with one of your charges stranded halfway down the aisle.

After the last bridesmaid reached the altar, we checked the doorway and saw that the woman who was poised to walk next was middle-aged, in a short, sea-foam-green dress. *Oh,* we whispered amongst ourselves. *That first processional must have been for both the flower girls and the bridesmaids. This second processional is for the mother of the bride.* We launched into the second processional. Unfortunately, the cellist came in wrong—repeatedly—and the entire piece was one long, excruciating cacophony. Well, not *that* long, thankfully, because the aisle was pretty short.[6]

As we prepared to play the last of the processionals—the one for the bride—the wedding coordinator gave us the kill signal. It was unclear, at first, how she meant it, but it did make us hesitate for long enough to notice that the officiant was starting the ceremony. As it turned out, the woman in green *was* the bride. I felt horrible when I realized our mistake. So horrible that I almost couldn't take the money. But it was so little that I did.

To be clear, none of this should have happened. We'd committed to

---

5   Not for their respective ages, just for life in general.

6   Which makes one wonder why there needed to be three processionals in the first place.

playing the wedding, and we should have prepared—even if that meant pushing the wedding coordinator for more information. My point is only that it's easier to forget that you're an important part of someone's special day when you're not paid or treated like one.

WHAT IF I HAVE NO MONEY AT ALL BUT I STILL WANT TO HIRE WORLD-CLASS MUSICIANS?

Here's the deal. You cannot, under any circumstances, ask a professional musician who is not a very dear friend of yours, or who does not owe you their life and/or livelihood, to play at your wedding for free. If, at any point during your event-planning process, you feel yourself on the verge of doing this, take a break, build a time machine, go back however many decades you need to in order to get to age five-ish, start playing an instrument, practice every day for twenty years, making sure that any and all degrees you pick up along the way are in music performance, and then take the time machine back to that first moment in the event-planning process so that you can smack yourself on the side of the head.

That being said, it is not written in stone that you have to pay musicians entirely *in money*. Musicians nearly always *need* money, of course, and most will prefer to be paid in it.[7] And if you're planning to pay your DJ or photographer with the stuff, then you have to do the same for your musicians. But musicians are also people with interests, and you never know when you might get lucky.

There's a music festival in Burgundy that pays, in part, in wine. (*Really* good wine.) And I once played at a fashion designer's wedding for clothes. (Gorgeous original pieces.) I was happier about

---

7   Unless gold bullion (or Bitcoin) is an option.

that, in fact, than I would have been about money, which was never going to be a life-changing amount.

If you're an established photographer, you could offer to take free portraits and website shots. If you're a certified accountant, you could offer to do the musicians' taxes in exchange. If you're an influencer (according to more people than just yourself), you could offer to feature their performance videos and clips and help boost their social media accounts. If you're offering any of these services as a money substitute, though, you need to ask *nicely*—and acknowledge that this is a break from convention. This is a hat-in-hand moment, not a you've-just-won-the-deal-of-your-life sales pitch. Be prepared for the fact that they'll probably say no.

The important thing here—whether you're paying in money or a lifetime supply of homemade biscuits—is to give your musicians as much as you possibly can. *And to be nice to them.*

THE PLAYLIST

Our processional—"V'adoro pupille," from Handel's opera *Giulio Cesare*—may have been the only classical piece I picked for our wedding, but I did, at least, do an absolutely masterful job of picking it. The aria is beautiful and reverent, its text is about love, and its rhythmic pulsations, which progress at a comfortable walking speed, are reminiscent of a heartbeat.[8] The length was perfect for our aisle (it's always best if you can use whole pieces rather than awkwardly butchered segments), and it was even *intended* to be a processional of sorts; Cleopatra sings it as she walks into the room on the occasion

---

8 Operatic stagings of it are often grand and theatrical (the singers' gestures have to reach the viewers in the back of the house), but if you close your eyes you'll hear what I mean.

of her first meeting with Julius Caesar. (Which . . . I mean, who hasn't fantasized about being one of them?)

I've never understood, when there are so many lovely pieces like this one, why *so many people* end up walking down the aisle to Wagner's Bridal Chorus (aka "Here Comes the Bride") or Pachelbel's Canon.

It's true that the Wagner comes from an actual wedding scene in the opera *Lohengrin*, but is it inspired? Does it smite you over the head with its beauty? Not really. Plus, as I keep mentioning, Wagner was an *asshole*.

As for Pachelbel's Canon: I will give you that it's pretty, in a nostalgic, wispy sort of way. And its face-pulling repetition and lack of thematic development mean that it reaches a natural stopping point every two bars, which makes it practical for aisles of all sizes. But it's an absolute plague.

First of all, it's *everywhere*: at weddings and at graduations, in pop songs and in elevators, on TV and on hold lines. Second, if it takes you longer than the first three notes to recognize it and shut it off—assuming it's a situation where you *can* shut it off (e.g., probably not a wedding)—it will be stuck in your head for the next three to four weeks. But the worst bit about it is that it's actually dangerous to perform. The cello part consists of exactly eight quarter-notes, which cellists are expected to play over and over and over and over again, without variation, until the piece is over. Often while delicious alcohol and hors d'oeuvres are being passed around at nose level, for the enjoyment of everyone in the room but them (and their colleagues). Cellists, remember, have endpins. Sure, they're a laid-back type, but everyone has their limits.[9]

---

9 I also suspect that some are only *pretending* to be laid-back, and are, in fact, deeply repressed and operating on the verge of combustion.

If you're absolutely determined to use the Pachelbel or the Wagner, that is absolutely your right, but please consider the following replacement suggestions before you make up your mind:

- "V'adoro pupille" from Handel's *Giulio Cesare in Egitto*

- The second movement (*Largo ma non tanto*) from Bach's Concerto for Two Violins in D Minor, BWV 1043

- "Ombra mai fu" from Handel's *Xerxes*

- The third movement (*Adagio*) from Mozart's Serenade No. 10 in B Major, K. 361, "Gran partita"

- "O Isis und Osiris" from Mozart's *The Magic Flute*

- The second movement (*Andante con moto tranquillo*) from Mendelssohn's Piano Trio No. 1 in D Minor, Op. 49

- The third movement (*Andante*) from Brahms's Piano Quartet No. 3 in C Minor, Op. 60

- The Intermezzo from Pietro Mascagni's *Cavalleria rusticana*[10]

- "Friar Laurence" from Prokofiev's *Romeo and Juliet*, Suite No. 2

While we're at it, some suggestions for short interludes:
For reflective occasions like weddings and memorial services:

- The third movement (*Andante*) of Bach's Violin Sonata No. 2 in A Minor, BWV 1003

- Schubert's Impromptu in G-flat Major, Op. 90, no. 3

---

10 The bride should start at about the 1:15 mark.

- Chopin's Nocturne in E-flat Major, Op. 9, no. 2

- The second movement (*Andante espressivo*) of Mendelssohn's Trio No. 2 in C Minor, Op. 66

- The second movement (*Adagio*) of Brahms's Violin Sonata No. 3 in D Minor, Op. 108

- Brahms's Intermezzo in A Major, Op. 118, no. 2

- Brahms's "O Tod, wie bitter bist du," from his cycle *Four Serious Songs*, Op. 121[11]

- Ravel's "Pavane pour une infante défunte" ("Pavane for a Dead Princess")[12]

- Debussy's "La plus que lente"

- Samuel Barber's "Sure on this shining night," Op. 13, no. 3

For flashier or less sentimental affairs, there's no reason not to break out the fireworks:

- "Largo al factotum" from Rossini's *The Barber of Seville*

- Schubert's Rondeau Brilliant in B Minor, D. 895

- Chopin's Polonaise in A Major, Op. 40, no. 1, "Military"

---

11 I would recommend this more for funerals and memorial services than weddings—because the title, in English, means, "O Death, how bitter you are"—but I don't know what your relationship is like.

12 This is another one I'd recommend more for funerals and memorial services, but Marina did suggest it as a processional for her own nuptials one evening when she was mad at her then-fiancé (now-husband), Ryan.

- "Sempre libera" from Verdi's *La Traviata*

- Brahms's Scherzo from the F.A.E. Sonata, WoO 2

- "La campanella" from Liszt's *Grandes études de Paganini*

GENERAL BACKGROUND MUSIC

The musicians you hire (even if they're bad) will be able to help you with all of the above—and they'll probably pick your background music for you. Remember Marco's binder. I won't, therefore, recommend specific music for this category, but here are a few thoughts.

As mentioned, anything with the name "serenade" or "divertimento" is ideal for this type of situation—because these pieces were generally conceived as conversational event music. Waltzes[13] are also an option, but only if your venue looks like the set of the latest Tolstoy epic. The reason I'd stay away from the genre's meatier works is that the range of tempo, mood, and volume—particularly in pieces from the Romantic and 20th-Century periods—isn't always conducive to quiet greetings, polite seat-finding, and machine-gun iterations of "Excuse me." Very sudden dynamic outbursts may startle your guests as they make their way, with your new soup bowls, to the gifts table.

GRADUATIONS

Please consider, as an alternative to Vitamin C's "Graduation" song, which is really Pachelbel's Canon with words, Haydn's "Farewell" Symphony (or Symphony No. 45). Haydn wrote it as a playful way of protesting his patron's overly long country residency, which had

---

13 By Johann Strauss II, for instance.

separated many members of the court orchestra from their families back in the city. The final movement features a gradual, comical exodus: partway through the piece, the last stand (pair) of players gets up and leaves, followed by the next stand up—and so on and so forth until only two violins are left on the stage. Mr. Thomas used to conduct it every year at Andover's graduation concert and it never failed to bring down the house. Back when it was premiered, it also convinced Haydn's patron, Nikolaus I, Prince Esterházy, to return his people to the city the following day.

The only problem with this one is that you need a pretty good school orchestra to pull it off. Otherwise it won't just be the players getting up and walking out in the middle of the piece.

A Way Back into Listening

In the end, ripping all the bones and lining out of my wedding dress and reconstructing the whole thing in the most inexpert, unskilled, labor-intensive possible way turned out to be a not-great idea. The bones, I learned, had served a purpose: holding the dress *up*. Unfortunately, due to the fact that I was sewing frantically right up until the end, I only realized this half an hour before I walked down the aisle, when it was too late to do anything about it.

The realization triggered a cyclone of furious self-loathing. I'd tried to find a use for myself, but instead I'd shown I was even more useless than I'd known. I'd tried to compensate for my failures, but instead I'd delivered one of my most spectacular failures yet. As I made my way to the venue, hoisting up my dress by its neckline, I felt exactly as I'd felt before all the worst performances in my career. Doomed. Underprepared. Hangry.

This toxic negativity could have easily poisoned the whole day.

But for one saving grace. As I waited outside the library, around the corner and out of sight, Francesca's voice carried Handel's music through the open door, and together they brought me back from my misery—transformed me from a hostile, cantankerous porcupine into a human capable of actual perspective.

I went from being Captain America at the Avengers' gym to being Captain von Trapp in *The Sound of Music*, when he hears his children singing to Baroness Schraeder and realizes that dog whistles and intermittent, dismissive dialogues sandwiched between long periods of absence do *not* constitute good parenting. It was suddenly clear to me that the wedding wasn't a runway show or a performance or a career stand-in, but a celebration of my partnership with Stephan, the same person who'd somehow managed to make the last year, even with all my failures and stumbles and professional defeats, the best of my life so far.

The wedding was a veritable parade of my shortcomings as an event planner: I spotted a price tag on one of our palms at the reception, a guest had to lend me her nipple covers, and when it started pouring that night I realized I'd forgotten the umbrellas. But none of it—not even our shivering, rain-drenched guests—could get me down.

It was the kind of happy ending that, if it had appeared in a movie, would make you say, "Aw!" And then, a minute later: "Wait, but what about her career?"

The good news, careerwise, is that after the wedding I wrote a vastly oversimplified essay about the whole dress debacle and it became the first thing I ever published, a step that led me—eventually—to this book.[14] The bad news is that everything with music and the violin was still a mess.

---

14 Yay!

I had, essentially, quit. Not in the dramatic, intentional way that that JetBlue flight attendant had quit *his* job,[15] but in the way that a really immature person who hates confrontation might quit a relationship. I just kind of . . . let it fizzle. The violin and I would hook up sometimes, but not very often, and it was always awkward when we did.

Only it wasn't, in my case, a matter of an over-and-done-with love story that was simply taking forever to die. There were still wounds there. Festering ones. I remember a whole week that was ruined, during that stretch, because my sister came by one day and said, "I bumped into François and he asked if you wanted to read some sonatas with him, so I said you weren't playing much these days and he said what a shame that was because he'd always felt you had so much to say."

Instead of responding in a normal way, with something like "Oh, that was nice of him," I was immediately overwhelmed by the desire to punch François in the face. *What kind of a sociopath,* I wanted to know, *went around spouting these sorts of irresponsible, manipulative, villainously seductive falsehoods?* I had nothing to say. This was a fact. I was an empty vessel. If people wanted interpretive genius, they should talk to Golden Violin Boy.

So there was that. But more importantly, *Music*—this thing I'd once loved enough to devote my whole life to it—was still handcuffed to the violin and all of my issues with it.

I let things lie for a few more months. I wrote a bit, got rejected from a few more modeling gigs, and binge-watched *Game of Thrones* again, this time without the simultaneous practicing. I started

---

15 Remember him? The one who grabbed two beers and then slid down the emergency evacuation chute to freedom?

learning German, but then stopped because it's really hard and the grammar made me angry at the whole country.

Then, late one night while Stephan and I were chatting on the couch, I thought of a piece I wanted him to hear, and I found a version of it on YouTube. A few weeks later, I thought of another piece. And a few weeks after that, another. I'd watch Stephan's face as he listened. I'd ask him to describe to me what he heard. It was the natural continuation of what had started that night in the Staatsoper, when his untarnished appreciation—his musical innocence—had refreshed my perspective and I'd felt that figurative tingling in whatever figurative part of me was trapped under that figurative rock pile. I was still far from rehabilitated, but those late-night couch sessions marked the beginning of my return to listening.

Chapter 12

how to be a listener

How to Hear (and Truly Appreciate)
Classical Music

My wedding dress fiasco was a microcosm of my journey as a musician. Not in the sense that I've spent my career living under constant threat of impending nip slips, but in the sense that during my training, as in the months leading up to the wedding, I became so fixated on the technical minutiae (as well as on myself and my achievements) that I lost sight of my reasons for having set out to do what it was I was doing in the first place. I started playing the violin because I loved music. I started planning the wedding because I loved Stephan. But in both these cases, I allowed my obsessiveness, my ego, my scrutiny, and my rampant, destructive perfectionism to take over like an army of invasive, strangling weeds.

As it turns out, the *cure*, in both cases, was also the same. The Handel aria—a piece of music—freed me from my selfish negativity and allowed me to access, suddenly, all those beautiful feelings I'd spent the earlier part of the day trampling over. And it was music, too, that brought me back from the disillusionment and emotional deafness that had developed during my violin training. *Appreciating* it rather than executing it; *hearing* it rather than dissecting it.

In many ways, I'd understood more about music that first time I'd heard Rex's Mendelssohn, at the age of seven, than I did when I listened to the recording of it all those years later—when my priorities were so broken I failed to recognize the beauty and joy he'd brought to his performance. In learning how to *play* music, it seems, I'd also been *un*learning how to listen to it—how to wonder at it.

Rex's parents had donated his personal collection of classical music CDs to Andover's Clift Music Library shortly after his death. I used to listen to some of them, back in the day. I can still remember pulling out the small drawers in the wooden filing cabinet and combing through the cards to pick out recordings by Yehudi Menuhin and Arthur Grumiaux and David Oistrakh: the great "old masters" of the violin, whose playing I first discovered thanks to Rex. But it wasn't until I started writing this book—when I was going through the library's archives with the help of Carl, the current librarian—that I fully understood the breadth of Rex's collection.

This was not the pile of CDs you'd find under the bed of your average high-school-aged classical music enthusiast. It was a collection of over five hundred albums, many of them rare and obscure. They were specific: recordings you had to seek out—not, as Carl put it, the kind you could have walked into a Tower Records and bought. And they covered far more than the standard (or even extended) violin repertoire. There were operas in there, too, and quartets and piano pieces and orchestral works.

There was also a note Carl found, written by Sally, who'd been the librarian back in Rex's day. In it, she described how Rex had often stopped by her desk to check out the odd CD, or to chat about how best to "fill up the holes" in the school's collection. She also wrote that he'd campaigned, successfully, to fulfill his work-duty requirement there, so that he could immerse himself each week in this shrine to listening.

Rex had entered my life on the occasion of his Mendelssohn concerto. He'd appeared to me—and to so many others that night— as a radiant, shining beacon of violinistic splendor. Which is why I'd always thought of him as a violinist.

As I'd thrown myself into the work of conquering passages and sharpening my technique, I'd believed that it was, among other things, a way of honoring Rex and his love of the instrument. But I'd never stopped to consider why a player with his potential had not, himself, gone down the conservatory path. As I think about it now, an obvious explanation emerges. It's possible that Rex, even more than he was a violinist, was a listener.

How to Listen to Classical Music

The standard classical repertoire is less immediate than other genres. It doesn't usually have that beat that cuts through everything around it—that lets you zone out while still participating. It doesn't have that speech-like quality that triggers your conversational multitasking abilities. It doesn't have those catchy, repetitive, bite-sized hooks and lyrics that allow you to internalize the song's main components in just a few listens. Even the genre's shorter compositions develop over time, featuring dramatic shifts in mood, tempo, and thematic material.

You can certainly have it on in the background while you work or clean or cook or socialize—there's nothing quite like baking bread while listening to Bach—but if you want to experience the whole of what it can offer, you'll want to give it a bit more, in terms of focus, than what you may be used to. You'll also want to listen to it in a relatively quiet place, or with noise-canceling headphones, because whereas pop songs generally maintain a fairly consistent volume, classical music often has a wide dynamic range, which means that its quieter moments are easily swallowed by ambient noise. (Like the humming of a car engine or the chatter of wedding guests.)

This is not to say, however, that you have to remain silent and motionless throughout your listening, provided you're at home, which is my favorite place to enjoy this music.[1] I like to shout and gesticulate when a composer does something awesome—or skip back a few seconds if Stephan misses[2] a crucially beautiful moment in the piece. I also like to drink scotch. (In general. But also while I listen.)

Then again, some of my most memorable listening experiences have been at live performances. The energy of live concerts can't be matched; truly great performances are electrifying in a way that even the best sound systems can't convey.

To close out this book, I want to equip you with everything you need in order to experience this music wherever and in whichever way you'd like. I'll offer suggestions for at-home listening and give you an overview of concert etiquette so you can hold your own against any snobs you might encounter at live performances. I'll go over the various factors you might want to consider—like choice of performer, event type, where to sit, and how to decipher the complicated musical titles you'll come across. There's no one right way of getting started; the goal is simply to figure out how to maximize your enjoyment and appreciation of these amazing works.

Don't like sitting quietly in a chair for two hours? Doesn't matter. I'll bet the first five-ish minutes of Strauss's *Also sprach Zarathus-*

---

1 I'm *really* writing this book to bankroll my dream of outfitting every room in our house with Bang & Olufsen Beolab 28 speakers.

2 Read: does not gasp dramatically enough at.

tra would pair nicely with skydiving. There's a perfect place to jump at around a minute and fifteen seconds. Then it gets a little weird and worried-sounding for a bit—which probably fits with how most people feel just after jumping—but assuming your parachute opens at around the three-minute mark, you'll float down over the world to a gorgeous, soaring melody and land just in time to turn off the music before it gets weird again.

But First: What to Listen *For*

Even people who are well-versed in the genre admit to being daunted by the more complex works in the classical repertoire. This is why Aaron Copland wrote a book called *What to Listen For in Music*, in which he takes a look at these compositions' inner workings, breaking them down into individual musical elements like rhythm, meter, melody, and harmony. There are plenty of other books, too, that explain the mechanics of this music in clear and methodical terms.

This book isn't one of them.

I often think of the time, during one of my violin lessons, when a famously eccentric cello teacher burst into the room in a frenzy and shouted at my teacher, "Stop! Don't tell her anything else! I've just realized that the best thing we can do is to confuse them! Just confuse them—all the time—as much as possible—so they have to spend hours in their practice rooms trying to figure out what we were talking about!"

I feel like he might have been onto something. And the last thing I want is to spoil the magic and mystery of this music by reducing it to its most basic parts. But at the same time, I do want to be helpful. So I'm going to give you some random examples of musical *effects* that I find very cool—effects that will open your mind to the riches of this great and vast collection in the same way that the Little

Mermaid's random hoard of pottery and dining utensils spawned her unhealthy obsession with humans. And in case that's not helpful enough for you, there's always Mr. Copland.[3]

All of these effects tie back into the idea of word painting, which we covered a bit in chapter 10. In case you've forgotten, word painting is the use of music to highlight or mirror the meaning of the text it sets. If the words describe something rising, as in "Im wunderschönen Monat Mai," the music, too, might rise. If anyone's describing darkness or sadness, the music will almost definitely be set to minor. If there's any discussion of pain or longing, you'll likely hear something that pulls at your gut—and twists your heartstrings uncomfortably until it resolves. (It's called dissonance.)

While the term *word painting* applies only to music that involves words, all compositions use music to convey meaning—and that meaning can be pretty specific.

Debussy once wrote to his publisher that his nerves were "in triplets." Because triplets—particularly fast ones—are often used to suggest agitation.[4] A drumroll can (and often does) represent the rumble of thunder. Repeated dotted rhythms[5] are often used to depict the galloping of hooves, but when the same dotted rhythms are presented at a slower tempo, they frequently signify nobility or military strength. Leaps—from low to high or high to low—are used in moments of intense emotion, and if there's a *lot* of leaping in a

---

3   His book is most suitable for people who read music, as he uses score excerpts to illustrate his points.

4   Triplets are groups of three notes, where the emphasis is on the first note—as in a waltz.

5   Dotted rhythms are groupings of two notes in which the first is longer (by three times) than the second. The first two notes of "The Star-Spangled Banner" (the "O" bit of "O say can you see") is a dotted rhythm.

composition for voice, it nearly always denotes anger. There's a wonderful example of this in *Don Giovanni*, when the character Donna Anna swears vengeance on the titular asshole in her aria "Or sai chi l'onore," which catapults from one end of her vocal range to the other as the strings tremble furiously underneath. (This trembling in the strings is another technique that indicates fury or panic or agitation.) The aria is also filled with those dotted rhythms I mentioned—because Donna Anna is both noble *and* formidable.

In this case, there *are* words, but the music is concerned less with mirroring the actual text than with depicting the bigger picture. There's another similar example in *Don Giovanni*, in the aria "Là ci darem la mano." Mozart's melody here is sweet but insincere—and very uncomplicated—reflecting Don Giovanni's casual, sport-like approach to seduction, as well as the intellectual simplicity and socioeconomic position of his target, Zerlina. (Zerlina is "a peasant" and she's literally on her way to the altar when Don Giovanni convinces her to have sex with him.) The aria begins with two complete statements of the theme, one for Giovanni and one for Zerlina, with a break in between. But as the music progresses, the separation between the two singers breaks down. Their entrances (singing entrances, that is) get closer together, and soon they begin to overlap and share stanzas—until finally Zerlina submits and they begin to sing together. And probably, depending on the production, do other things together, too.

Many operas and tone poems make use of leitmotifs: short musical figures that are linked to specific characters, events, or ideas. They can act like very short theme songs, heralding the entrance of a specific character—or they can be used to remind the audience of something or someone from earlier in the work. Verdi's opera *Otello* (yes—that's "Otello" without an *h*) does this with a phrase known as the "kiss" (or "baccio") theme. It first appears after Otello's homecoming, during his emotional reunion with Desdemona. Then various forces of evil (mostly the character Iago) lead him to believe she's betrayed him—and when we hear the theme again, it's when he breaks from his jealous fury to sadly mourn the loss of her love just moments before he kills her. The last time we hear the theme is at the end—after Otello learns of her innocence, as he's dying of a self-inflicted wound. It's manipulative in the best possible way.

Shostakovich's Quartet No. 8 is a wonderful and terrifying example of a piece that paints a thrillingly clear picture without adhering to any kind of text or linear story. It's also one of the greatest, most compelling pieces ever written, and one of my all-time favorites.

Shostakovich composed the work in a three-day fit of inspiration, dedicating it to the victims of fascism and war. He wrote it at a time in his life when he was filled with self-loathing—after he'd capitulated, under duress and against his principles, to joining the Communist Party—and there is significant evidence to suggest that he intended it as a suicide note. One piece of this evidence lies in the music itself; the first movement begins with repeated iterations of his musical signature: the notes D, E-flat, C, B, which are spelled, according to German notation, "D, Es, C, H." D for Dmitri, SCH for the German spelling of his last name ("Schostakowitsch"). This signature comes back in the second movement, screeching furiously in the violins and thundering angrily in the lower parts—and continues to appear throughout the piece in various dark incarnations.

The whole quartet is filled with spine-tingling imagery and breathtaking quotes. It makes use of the "Jewish theme" from Shostakovich's second piano trio, and also the nineteenth-century revolutionary song "Tormented by Grievous Bondage." Early in the piece, a chilling pedal tone emerges: a note that sustains, unfeelingly, for measures on end, without regard to what else is going on in the music. Most people interpret this and the other pedal tones scattered throughout the piece as the droning of wartime planes flying overhead.

There's a blood-curdling moment at the start of the fourth movement, when the residual drone from the final note of the third is interrupted by three deafening knocks: the KGB pounding on the door in the middle of the night. Some people describe the eerie, sarcastic waltz in the third movement as the waltzing of skeletons, while others hear it as the waltzing of Jewish victims who were forced to dance on their own graves before their execution. The waltz once more makes use of Shostakovich's signature, so I suppose it could also represent his own forced waltz, which he'd been made to carry out at the hands of the Party. Whatever his exact meaning, there can be no question as to the significance and symbolism of these figures.

I could go on like this for twelve more books. But I'll stop here because it wouldn't be fair for anything to have to follow the Shostakovich. The last three things I'll say before moving on are these:

1. Don't feel bad if your ears don't catch all of these effects. They're often meant to be subtle—to suggest things to your subconscious without making you aware of them. (I would be surprised, however, if you missed the knocking of the KGB in the Shostakovich.)

2. If, while listening to any of this music, you *do* think you hear something—something that strikes you a certain way or tells you a certain story—trust it. Even if you're totally wrong and it isn't there, allowing yourself this freedom will make listening much more fun.

3. If you haven't already, go listen to the Shostakovich. Right now.

Listening Tips

Now that you're all *so* excited to discover the many wonders this genre offers, you're free to decide how and when and with whom you want to listen. The rest of this chapter will walk you through the various choices you'll have to make as you get started.

CHOICE OF COMPOSITION

Your options in terms of repertoire will be nearly limitless if you're at home. Between YouTube, Apple Music, and Spotify it's easy enough to find whichever composers or pieces you might like to hear.

If you're looking for a musical adventure out in the world, you'll be limited by what the concert series around you are presenting.

(I say you'll be "limited," but if you live in a big city, sorting through the various options and programs at your disposal will likely feel far more overwhelming than sorting through a list of tracks on your phone.)

Hopefully you've taken a few minutes to sample some of the pieces I've listed in chapters 1 and 9 and have started to form a rough idea of your preferences. But if you haven't, *start by taking a few minutes to sample some of the pieces I've listed in chapters 1 and 9 so you can form a rough idea of your preferences.* Don't be rude. Those lists cost me years of my life—and most of my sanity.

Whatever you do, don't get overwhelmed and choose a concert blindly without looking at the program. You don't want to get stuck listening to Gregorian chant for two whole hours.[6]

If you're seeing an opera or a ballet, you might also consider

---

6 Don't worry. No one except perhaps Nathan Lane and Matthew Broderick in *The Producers* would program anything so refund-worthy.

reading up on the story before you go. The first time I saw *The Marriage of Figaro* (when I was a kid), I thought it was about a drag cabaret. And I still can't explain much of what happens in *The Nutcracker*.[7]

There are also things that can be upsetting and triggering and it's better to prepare for these in advance. Suicide and rape are not uncommon themes in opera—and as in any collection of work from a bygone era, there are occasionally characters and situations that were deemed acceptable hundreds of years ago but that we now know enough to wholly reject. *The Magic Flute*, as much as I love it for its music, contains an unforgivably racist depiction of a character described as "a Moor," and makes light of a situation involving contemplated sexual assault. Most companies find ways of omitting the racist sentiment, but others lean into the controversy. I find that I'm able to enjoy the music in spite of this ugliness, but you may not be able to, and that's more than okay.

Offensive depictions are less of an issue in the world of symphonies and chamber compositions, but with those you're likely to encounter another problem: deciphering their obnoxiously confusing and sterile titles. Which brings us to our next section.

HOW TO DECIPHER THE GENRE'S OBNOXIOUSLY CONFUSING AND STERILE COMPOSITION TITLES

Beethoven didn't want to be remembered for "Für Elise." As I mentioned in chapter 1, he probably didn't even like it. I'm not saying *you* can't (in case, for some reason, you do), but it's closer to a drunk text[8] than a crowning, career-defining effort.

---

7 I'm actually even more confused now that I've read the original German text.

8 (One that he was still sober enough to decide not to send—and then revisit later—and then decide not to send again.)

And yet, "Für Elise" is one of the most famous classical pieces of all time. Why? Because it has an actual *name*, as opposed to a cryptic six-part title that's probably necessary but also off-putting to the point of hostility.

Think about it. *Eine kleine Nachtmusik*, *The Four Seasons*, "Moonlight" Sonata. Even Beethoven's Ninth is best known for its "Ode to Joy." All the most famous pieces in the repertoire have names or nicknames you can actually remember.

Unfortunately, I can't change the system for you. What I *can* do, though, is guide you through it and assure you that I share your frustration.

Here's the standard formula for most composition titles:

Symphony No. 5 in C Minor, Op. 67

Sonata No. 21 in E Minor, K. 304

Piano Trio No. 2 in E-flat Major, D. 929

It goes: [*Name of technical compositional classification*] No. [*number*] in [*key*] Major/Minor, [*catalog abbreviation*] [*number*]

Sometimes there are minor variations like Intermezzo in A Major, Op. 118, no. 2—which puts the piece number after the opus number because it's trying to communicate that this isn't the composer's second *overall* intermezzo, but rather the second intermezzo of the Opus 118 *set*.

Let's say you just composed your first piece: a symphony in A major. You would call it Symphony No. 1 in A Major, Op. 1. Now let's say, for your second composition, you've written a sonata in G major. The title would be Sonata No. 1 in G Major, Op. 2. It's your first sonata but your second overall work—or opus.

Your compositions, like the compositions of most composers,

would likely be cataloged using opus numbers. But there are a few other cataloging abbreviations, as well. Some of the more important ones are: "K" or "KV," which stands for "Köchel number"; "BWV," which stands for "Bach-Werke-Verzeichnis"; "HWV," which stands for "Händel-Werke-Verzeichnis"; "Hob," which refers to the Hoboken catalog; and "D," which stands for "Deutsch number." These are composer-specific abbreviations, named after the individual people who cataloged the works of Mozart, Bach, Handel, Haydn, and Schubert, respectively. So basically:

- K/KV/Köchel numbers are for Mozart

- BWV/Bach-Werke-Verzeichnis numbers are for Bach

- HWV/Händel-Werke-Verzeichnis numbers are for Handel

- Hob/Hoboken numbers are for Haydn

- D/Deutsch numbers are for Schubert

- Op/Opus numbers are for *most* everyone else—and also for Haydn and Schubert (and others with their own catalogs like Debussy and Bartók), because otherwise things would be too straightforward.

The catalog number is "important" because it speaks to the work's placement in the overall life of the composer, but it isn't always necessary for identifying pieces. Most often, the composer's name, the type of piece, and the number or key is enough. (E.g., "Beethoven Piano Sonata No. 8" or "Brahms A Major Violin Sonata.") Certain listening platforms are actually confused by things like opus numbers, so it's often better to omit them when you're searching for a piece.

If there's a word in there that isn't the composition type or cataloging system abbreviation—and it's in quotations or italics—then it's a lifeline left for you either by the composer or by those who came after. Use it. It's a way around all the other nonsense. The "Moonlight" Sonata is really Piano Sonata No. 14 in C-sharp Minor, Op. 27, no. 2, "Moonlight." And Vivaldi's "Spring" is more formally Concerto No. 1 in E Major, Op. 8, RV 269, "La Primavera." All you have to say is "Beethoven's 'Pastoral'" and people will know you're talking about his Symphony No. 6 in F Major, Op. 68 (even if they don't know that his Symphony No. 6 is in F major or that its opus number is 68). You can also just call it "Beethoven's Sixth." But this doesn't work as well with Mozart symphonies, since he wrote forty-one of them.

None of this is ideal, I know. But when you think about it, it's not so much worse than remembering batting averages or grocery lists or the birthdays of all your friends.[9]

CHOICE OF PERFORMER

Once you've figured out what piece you want to hear—and done battle with its title—you'll want to think about who should be playing it. This is another decision that varies in complexity depending on whether you're listening at home or in a live venue. Either way, it's a factor that will have a tremendous impact on your reaction to the music. Think of Emma Thompson reading a line of Shakespeare. And then think of whichever drunk nonagenarian uncle was at your last family gathering and imagine *him* reading it. Even the greatest piece in the world sounds like crap when it's played by bad performers.

---

9   None of which I can do—which is why I've spent so many hours of my life googling opus numbers.

This is why you have to be a little careful on YouTube and in unknown concert series without websites or accolades, where there's less guarantee of the level. There are certainly wonderful performances to be found in both, but there are also performances that give you migraines. I don't want to discourage you from supporting local or up-and-coming talent, but it's "safer" to start with the more established series and performing arts institutions, or the YouTube videos with hundreds of thousands of views. (What I'm saying, basically, is that if you decide to go with a small, unknown series or a video with three views and you *hate* what you hear, you owe me another listen—of the same piece—performed by a tried-and-true performer.)

Even within the highest level of playing, performers' interpretations will have a profound impact on your reaction to the music, and I encourage you to find those artists whose aesthetics you find most compelling.

Although, even *one* artist's interpretations can differ from performance to performance. Glenn Gould's 1955 recording of Bach's Goldberg Variations is around thirty-nine minutes long. His 1982 recording clocks in at over fifty. Same music, same tempo markings, totally different feel to the music. Both recordings are treasured for their artistry and genius; they simply highlight different aspects of the score.

(Once, I was inspired by Gould to make a bold tempo decision of my own—in a Mozart sonata, at a competition in Switzerland. I should have known, of course, that a competition was the wrong place to experiment, and that a competition in Switzerland, a place known for its timekeeping, was the wrong place to experiment *with time.* But I didn't think of this until after I'd played the piece at nearly half-tempo and the judges all but laughed me off the stage.

Still, there were certain figures and harmonic shifts that I could bring out only at that tempo, and for these reasons I, if no one else, can still respect myself for having made the decision.)

There's also something called a *period performance*. Period performers (aka historically accurate performers), whom I angered by likening them to Portland vegans in chapter 4,[10] use instruments and bows that were native to the era, many of which have fallen out of use in mainstream music (e.g., the viola da gamba, a fretted cello-like instrument with five to seven strings). They strive to re-create what a performance from the Baroque or Classical period might have sounded like. They also play on catgut strings (rather than synthetic-cored).[11] So they're probably *not* vegans, actually. They use minimal to no vibrato or sustain, creating a pulsing and waning effect that's almost incomparably pure. It sounds incredible in chapels and churches. But it's on the sparse side—and the tuning of their instruments is approximately a half-step lower than what we're now used to—which feels, to the ears, like what wearing the prescription glasses of a particularly shortsighted mole might feel like to the eyes.

So again: the choice of performer makes a big difference.

Attending Concerts

It's certainly easier to start your listening journey at home. But let's say, hypothetically, that you still have nightmares about a time, from

---

10 The Portland vegans are likely also angry.

11 "Catgut" is not made out of *cat* guts but rather the guts of other animals, like sheep, which somehow feels better. I was pretty horrified the first time I heard the term—and I don't even like cats.

the not-too-long-ago, when you were cooped up for ages and ages, desperately wanting to get out, suffering from all kinds of anxiety about dying alone and being discovered, without makeup or pants, in an unattractive state of decomposition, by strangers who never knew your beauty. Or maybe you'd just like to see for yourself what a night at the opera—or the symphony, or the ballet—is all about.

Whatever your reasons, I support you.

So does Google.

The internet can tell you about whatever big, grandish concerts your local Lincoln or Kennedy Center is offering, and also about those more casual, intimate concert series that offer comparable musical standards but smaller crowds.

There are, in fact, an overwhelming number of options to choose from. Unless you live in the Arctic Circle, in which case you'll take whatever cultural nourishment the Canadian government sees fit to send you once a year, even if it's me and all I want to do is whine about how cold it is. (Did you know that −40° Fahrenheit is the same as −40° Celsius? Guess how I know that.)[12]

There are big-money music festivals like Tanglewood and Aspen that offer symphony and chamber performances, plus a range of lectures and events. Another one of those is Switzerland's Verbier Festival, where you can start your day paragliding over a veritable who's who of classical music, then attend a tented Verbier Festival Orchestra concert at night, and end the day by shelling out sixty Swiss francs for two ounces of Macallan 12 at a local bar.

But there are also smaller festivals designed with accessibility

---

12 In spite of my (justified) complaints regarding the temperatures there, the audiences in the Arctic Circle and Northwest Territories were some of the best and most engaged I've ever encountered.

in mind. Of all the festivals I've played—including Aspen and Verbier—I have the fondest and clearest memories of a festival called Music and Beyond, which, for a period of a few weeks every summer, fills the streets and halls of Ottawa with affordable (and sometimes even free) music. (Because it's Canada, where the government supports the arts.) There are musicians floating over the canal playing Handel's *Water Music*; there are museum takeovers where each exhibit features a different small-scale, interactive performance; there are "music and circus" nights, where trapeze artists fly overhead to the strains of Mozart and Dvořák. One summer, I played at a multicourse dinner where each dish was created to pair with a specific piece of music; and another time, in one unforgettable evening that fulfilled all kinds of childhood fantasies, I got to perform a series of carefully selected musical excerpts alongside Christopher Plummer, whose masterful interwoven Shakespeare recitations were some of the most moving I will ever witness.[13]

The major symphonies and opera companies generally offer, in addition to their usual fare, things like kids' matinee concerts, open rehearsals, young audience receptions, and free parks concerts, which allow people to sit down with a picnic and get boozed up in a classy, socially celebrated manner. It's not the optimal setting for taking in every *single* note of the music, but who doesn't like a good picnic?[14]

And there are thousands of first-rate concert series with less conventional venues and formats scattered throughout the country and around the world, many of which allow the audience to mingle with the musicians.

---

13 His Captain von Trapp was my very first crush.

14 Stephan, actually.

Again: Google knows. Now it's time for the things Google doesn't know.

WHERE TO SIT

I know plenty of people who'd cut off a finger to avoid a middle seat on an airplane—even for a very short flight—but who happily plop themselves ten seats away from the nearest aisle at a concert. Which makes absolutely no sense to me.

I'm inviting a lot of criticism here by telling you this, but whenever I want to go to a big hall or theater, I actually *start* by checking the seat maps before considering other factors like the program or performers. Is this backward? Yes. But it's the only way to ensure that I won't spend the whole time worrying about what will happen if I have to pee or if the person next to me looks like he's about to manifest symptoms of Ebola.[15]

I don't recommend that you follow my example unless you, too, are terrified of Ebola.

If I have the choice, and particularly if someone else is paying, I'll always sit in a box. Not a corrugated one, but the kind that's found in the balconies of the big halls and theaters.[16] If those are unavailable, I'll look at aisle seats in the balcony. After that, my preference is the cheap standing section in the back of the hall, assuming the hall has one. The boxes are the most expensive seats in the house because they're absolutely awesome, providing superb sound (usually) and far more privacy than the other

---

15 Ebola scares me not because of the dying but because of the throwing up.

16 Now all I can think about is how the ushers and audience members would react if I brought a cardboard box to the opera and insisted on sitting in it for the duration of the performance.

sections. But the standing room section is great, too, because you're not locked into one position for the whole performance and the people there tend to be relatively laid-back and unfussy (and also passionate enough about music to want to stand there for two hours). Plus, space there costs a tenth of what you pay for those box seats.

If you *don't* have my claustrophobia and anxiety about social doomsday scenarios, though, you should sit in the orchestra section. Unless you're very short and you want to be able to see the stage, in which case you'll want a seat in the balcony, where the incline tends to be steeper.

GENERAL ETIQUETTE

We should cover some concert etiquette guidelines. Not because I'm worried you'll answer your cell phone in the hall (which an audience member did during a concert I played in Chicago) or eat a sandwich wrapped in cellophane in the first row (which an audience member did during a concert I played in Beijing), but because I want you to feel comfortable and at ease knowing that you're on top of the relevant conventions.

First off: don't answer your cell phone in the hall or eat sandwiches, noisy or otherwise, in the first row. Or any row. Unless it's an outdoor concert and you're sitting on a picnic blanket. Going to a concert in an actual hall or theater is like going to a wedding where the couple has a strict no-photos, no-babies-or-toddlers-or-pets policy.[17] Nothing that rings or beeps or flashes or poops uncontrollably.

---

17 You can bring kids of any age and behavioral profile to concerts if they're kids' concerts. Otherwise you should probably only bring well-behaved children. And most venues have a suggested age minimum.

Always double-check that your devices are off. It is *very easy* to make a mistake. Don't forget Mahlergate. And speaking of Mahler: I once called a friend—accidentally—while he was onstage finishing up a performance of Mahler's Third Symphony, and his phone was in his pocket, set to loud, and it went off right in the middle of the stunning moment of silence just before the final few bars, where all the world seems to fall suddenly still, as if dumbstruck by the beauty of the universe. (Or, in this case, all the world save one boisterous cell phone.) He's still recovering from the psychological effects of the incident.

The only time you really *should* be making noise is when you're clapping and shouting "Bravo."[18]

WHEN TO CLAP

When it comes to applause, the safest course of action is to wait until you hear everyone else doing it and jump in only after.

You *can* do this—just as you *can* watch the Super Bowl without knowing what a first down is—but if you go this route, you're going to feel like an outsider.

And I don't want that.

At the opera, applause is expected when the conductor comes out, as well as at the end of each act. You're also allowed to clap spontaneously after particularly spectacular arias or ensemble performances. (So in other words: when you feel moved, by the music and the performance, to do so.) Don't wear yourself out, though; you will also be called upon to clap for about an hour after the opera is over while the various singers take their many bows and curtain

---

18 See the glossary for other things you can shout during the applause.

calls.[19] Of course, if it's a truly inspiring performance, you'll feel so invigorated that strength won't be an issue.

There's a similar protocol for ballets: you clap for the conductor, after each act, and after all the big, moving numbers. But you're also invited to clap—frequently—during the "pas de deux/trois/quatre/ etc." sets, even though it doesn't always feel natural to do so. (Basically, these sets are broken up into short segments, and you can clap at the end of each one. But the clapping doesn't make sense on a *musical* level; it's simply an acknowledgment of the technical prowess of the dancers.)

The symphony and solo/chamber music recitals have more rigid rules. At the symphony, you clap the first time the concertmaster appears onstage. (This is only in the States, when the other musicians of the orchestra often settle into their seats before the performance.)[20] Then there's another round for the conductor. And a third round if there's a soloist.

After this initial wave of acknowledgments, you get a break; for the rest of the concert, you clap only at the end of each piece. (There's never any clapping during the music unless it's a holiday or pops concert and someone who's involved in the performance invites you to clap along.)

What makes this a bit confusing is the movements (segments) I told you about in chapter 7.

Because movements are separate entities—like episodes, as we discussed—they sometimes seem like they want applause. And some-

---

19 Don't skimp on the applause, either. These are singers, remember; there was a reason that I said applause was "expected."

20 This is not the case in Europe, where the orchestra files onstage all at once and you clap for all of them.

times you can give it to them. For instance, no one could blame you for jumping out of your seat after the first movement of Tchaikovsky's Violin Concerto (which has one of the coolest, most rousing endings of all time). If the performance is good, they'll probably all be jumping out of their seats *with* you.

The No Clapping rules are relatively new to the genre. It's well documented that audiences of the Baroque and Classical eras applauded freely, between and even during movements. Then again, there were also certain courts where applause wasn't allowed at all.

I'm torn about it. I don't want anyone to feel constricted. But I also don't want anyone to miss out on a gorgeous moment of music because someone *I* enabled starts shouting "Bravo" in the middle of a slow movement.

I suppose it's a bit like following the lights at pedestrian crosswalks; theoretically, you're not supposed to cross when the light is red. Likewise, you're not supposed to clap until the piece is over. But if you're *absolutely sure* there's no traffic, it seems ridiculous to wait.

NEVER BE A DICK ABOUT OTHER PEOPLE NOT KNOWING WHEN TO CLAP

Do you remember the story I told you in chapter 3, about the woman at the Berlin Philharmonic who was screaming at everyone for clapping between movements? Don't be like her.

If a movement ends and there's one guy whooping and cheering all alone with a hall full of eyes staring at him, just chuckle into your hand and silently congratulate yourself on your superior class and culture.

Listening at Home

Whether or not you decide to attend any live concerts, you should also try doing one or more of the following at home:

1. *Start your day with Bach's Goldberg Variations.* Put it on as soon as you wake up, or better yet, set it up as your alarm (unless you watched *The Silence of the Lambs* the night before).[21] The music transforms even mundane acts like flossing your teeth into meditative exercises in mental clarity; it elevates the morning light from something caustic and irritating to something profound and cleansing; it transmutes your coffee into a calming, steeling elixir that will send you into your day poised and battle-ready.

2. *Dance with your kids or intoxicated, childlike roommates to Mendelssohn's "A Midsummer Night's Dream Overture."* This overture is a fantastical, evocative musical depiction of everything that happens in Shakespeare's play. The magic in it is irresistible. It will transform you into a pixie, scurrying around in the woods, and then into a braying donkey, and then into Oberon and Titania sweeping through the air—all in the span of twelve minutes.

3. *Host a house concert.* House concerts are some of my favorite kinds of performances, but you can't usually attend them without an invitation (without getting arrested). The solution, then, is to host one yourself. It doesn't have to be expensive, depending on where you live. There was a famous "run-through" series when I

---

21 My mom made my dad wake Marina up like this the morning after her first viewing of the film in high school. Marina was less than appreciative.

was at Juilliard, hosted by a woman who lived in one of the towers near school, that provided students a chance to test their repertoire before their big performances—and instead of a performer's fee, the host would just pass a hat for donations around at the end of the night. Alternately, you can also host a viewing party of a live-stream concert.

4. *Go on YouTube and find the recording of Florence Foster Jenkins singing the Queen of the Night aria.* It is both the best and worst thing you will ever hear.

5. *Listen on your couch with a drink or an ice cream* (or any food that doesn't crunch loudly when you bite into it) and a partner or pet or friend so that you can look at each other in all the cool moments.

6. *Make up a story to go along with a piece of music,* where the plot twists line up with the changes in the music. (This is another great one for kids or drunk roommates.)

7. *Watch one of the following music movies:*

UNFAITHFULLY YOURS (1948)

This is one of my favorite movies ever. It's a hilarious dark comedy about a resolutely trusting husband (a conductor, played by Rex Harrison) who's forced to confront the possibility that his gorgeous wife (Linda Darnell) might be having an affair with his manager. Much of the movie takes place during a performance; as Rex Harrison conducts, he imagines different ways of handling his wife's betrayal, with responses ranging from generous resignation to murder, as triggered by the music.

It does contain some dreadful fake conducting, but the musicians of the orchestra are really playing, and the movie combats many of the stigmas associated with the industry.

AMADEUS (1984)

Don't let its three-hour running time put you off. Yes, it's a period epic, which I realize may be a turnoff. But it's fascinating, hilarious, stirring, and beautifully scored—and it captures many truths, even if it *is* based on fantasy rather than fact.

It begins with the confession of the successful but less remembered composer Antonio Salieri, who claims to have killed Mozart. (You should be aware that the opening scene, which depicts Salieri's attempted suicide, is unexpectedly gory. The rest of the movie is quite different.) The movie follows Salieri's encounters with Mozart in Vienna, and his ongoing struggle to reconcile the beauty of Mozart's music with his impish, offensive, scatalogically fixated character. It also makes stunning use of several of Mozart's pieces, even if they *are* cut for brevity. So clear your evening, break out the popcorn, and just wait to start eating it until after the first scene—because it really is gross.

A NIGHT AT THE OPERA (1935)

I'm really into B&W films, by the way. So much so that I told Stephan, on our first walk (to the police station), that I wished I could live in the 1930s, without realizing what a statement like that would sound like to a German. It was very nearly the end of both the relationship and Stephan's life, but thankfully I noticed that he was having a heart attack and explained myself before all was lost.[22]

It follows naturally, from my love of old movies, that I also love the Marx Brothers.

A Night at the Opera is essentially a battle between the snobs and the salt-of-the-earth music lovers. In the very first scene, we learn that Groucho Marx has been hired to pave the way for wealthy widow Mrs. Claypool (Margaret Dumont) to enter high society—a feat he plans to accomplish by having her donate lots of money to the stuffy Mr. Gottlieb's opera company. On the opposing side is Riccardo Baroni, a young and extremely charismatic tenor who's only a member of the chorus but whose voice is (supposedly) far better than the famous leading asshole, Rodolfo Lassparri. They're both in love with the opera company's prima donna, who represents, in this somewhat flawed battle metaphor, either the whole of classical music or all the world's undecided listeners.

It's utterly ridiculous—as all Marx Brothers movies are—so nothing in it should be taken literally. But it's a wildly fun and silly way to spend an hour and a half and you'll be exposed, a bit, to Verdi's opera *Il trovatore*.

RHAPSODY (1954)

This one stars Elizabeth Taylor as a romantic, spoiled socialite who follows her impoverished but delightfully arrogant violinist-boyfriend,

---

22 To be clear: I don't wish I could live in the 1930s. I sometimes wish I could live in the glamorized version of the 1930s that my favorite black-and-white movies depict. But that's really only because of the gorgeous clothes and the gorgeous jazz clubs and the gorgeous film sets.

played by Vittorio Gassman, to a conservatory in Zurich. It contains some of the least realistic music scenes of all time (in one of them, Gassman takes out his violin in the middle of a café and everyone else in the café, including a bassist and a harpist, produces instruments in order to accompany him). But if you can get over that (which I can), it's actually one of the best music movies of all time. In many ways, it's the opposite of my parents' Queen of the Night story, which features details that are mostly true to serve a story that is not. *Rhapsody*, meanwhile, gets many of the details wrong, but does a wonderful job of capturing the intensity and spirit of conservatory life, and it builds toward a climactic performance of Rachmaninoff's Piano Concerto No. 2, providing the perfect emotional context for the piece.[23]

Gassman's faking is heinous, but it's fun to watch Elizabeth Taylor's face for signs of physical anguish as he inches closer and closer to her with his scroll, blasting her eardrums with what must have been, by the looks of it, an absolute cacophony.[24]

THE SHAWSHANK REDEMPTION (1994)

This one's not really a music movie. It's more of a needle drop. But it has an unforgettable scene when Tim Robbins hijacks the prison loudspeaker system and plays the arching, soaring "Sull'aria . . . che soave zeffiretto" from Mozart's *The Marriage of Figaro* for all the inmates and guards to hear. The aria is simple, relative to Mozart's more intricate compositions, but it's simple in a pristine, luminous kind of way that contrasts stunningly with the harshness of the concrete yard and barbed fences. It's a breathtaking moment and an

---

23 They trim the music, but it's remarkable how much of it they do feature.

24 A "scroll" is the end of a violin, not a euphemism for anything anatomical.

exceptional use of music, aided also by the fact that Morgan Freeman's voice is a music of its own.

Here are some other needle drops you might want to check out:

2001: A Space Odyssey	Also sprach Zarathustra, Op. 30 —Richard Strauss
The Big Lebowski	The Lacrimosa from Mozart's Requiem in D Minor, K. 626
The King's Speech	The second movement (Allegretto) of Beethoven's Symphony No. 7 in A Major, Op. 92
Melancholia	The Overture from Wagner's Tristan und Isolde
Platoon	Adagio for Strings—Samuel Barber
Pretty Woman	Excerpts from La Traviata —Giuseppe Verdi
Raging Bull	The Intermezzo from Pietro Mascagni's Cavalleria rusticana
The Silence of the Lambs	Goldberg Variations, BWV 988 —Johann Sebastian Bach
There Will Be Blood	The third movement (Allegro giocoso, ma non troppo vivace) of Brahms's Violin Concerto in D Major, Op. 77

How to Be a Listener

The Mendelssohn Violin Concerto set me down the path of becoming a serious violinist—a path that would ultimately take me away from my early love of music and into a prison-like labyrinth of technical pressures and demands.

It also closed out my career as a performer two decades later.

Shortly after Stephan and I moved to Frankfurt, I started playing, as a guest, with the hr-Sinfonieorchester. By this time, the violin and I were in a better place. Practicing was far from the best part of my life, but I was at a point where I could receive a compliment about my playing without wanting to punch its bearer in the face. I'd started to look at the violin in the way that most people look at a nine-to-five job: as a means to an end. It might not be something I loved to do, but I didn't *mind* doing it, either.

Remember how I auditioned for that concertmaster spot in Berlin, made it to the finals, and was told that I might have won if my excerpts hadn't been so bad? The same thing happened again with the orchestra in Frankfurt. But they were nice and they invited me to play with them for several months, anyway. I liked them very much. So much, in fact, that I was thinking of lifting my (totally ludicrous) concertmaster-position-only rule and taking their upcoming audition for principal second.

One of the projects they asked me to play was a tour to Budapest, Monte Carlo, and various other European cities. This was ironic because half the reason I'd let my violin career slide into oblivion in the first place—and the main reason I'd started considering orchestra jobs—was that I wanted to *stop* touring.

The night before I left, I found out I was pregnant. The news came as a shock. A terrifying one. I'd only taken the test to assure myself, after a late period, that I could drink on the trip.

Suddenly, I was faced with a tornado-like future of diapers and purées and fresh anxieties. I had no idea whether I saw myself working or staying at home or spontaneously imploding under the weight of this news. Worries about the tour were stampeding through my head like a herd of vertigo-afflicted wildebeests. What if the daily traveling was bad for the baby? What if the brass section was too loud? What if I got to Ljubljana and couldn't decipher the menus and accidentally ate something raw or uncooked that would make the baby come out with seven eyes and a beak instead of a mouth? I was also convinced, after realizing my recent queasiness was no coincidence, that I was finally going to have to live out my nightmare of vomiting onstage.

The next morning, I forced myself to say goodbye to Stephan—yet again—even though all I wanted was to tuck myself under his chin and slump there listlessly until I could grasp what was happening. I was also slightly worried he'd be in jail by the time I got back. The night before, in his state of bleary astonishment, he'd opened a bottle of wine without a corkscrew and exploded Barolo all over the twenty-foot-tall white wall between our kitchen and hallway—and now he had to convince our landlords that this suspicious red spatter had nothing whatsoever to do with his wife's sudden disappearance.

I spent much of the tour feeling anxious about all of this. But come concert time, I always felt oddly calm. I had this deluded sense, while I was playing, that the baby was responding to the music.

I'd never liked Mahler, and I'd always been particularly disparaging of his Fifth Symphony because everyone else adores it. But each night, as I played the opening phrase of the Adagietto—a phrase that had generally inspired in me no more than a reflexive eye roll—I felt a kind of bodily elation radiating from my uterus, as if the small life inside me was surrounded by a halo of joy and hope.

The other big piece on the program was the Mendelssohn.

I'd heard and played it hundreds of times since the night of Rex's senior concerto. It had long since fallen from the top of my favorites list. In fact, it was a piece I couldn't really enjoy anymore because I always felt pressure to *react*—to feel something profound—whenever

I encountered it. Which usually meant that I rebelled and felt nothing at all. But now, imbued as I was with all my future child's
wonderment—I could once again access that electricity and en-
chantment and delight that had mesmerized me all those years
earlier.

As the tour continued, something interesting began to happen.
I went beyond imagining what the music might sound like to the
baby—or Stephan—or to any set of ears less tired than mine. And I
stopped trying to relive or recapture the way it had sounded to me
when I was young. Perhaps my state of terror had shorted my
wiring—or perhaps, with all the unfathomable changes that were
upon me, I was simply grasping at the nearest form of spiritual support I could find. Whatever the cause, I was suddenly listening—
and *hearing*—in a way that I hadn't known I still could. I found
layers in the music, darker than what I'd heard before: pain, anger,
fear, and sadness. But at the heart of them, there was comfort. A
kind of comfort I sorely needed as I grappled with the terrifying idea
of becoming a mother: in that slow second theme of the first
movement—the one that had seemed to me earlier to capture the
love I felt for my family—I could hear and envision a whole childhood full of bedtime stories.

I felt my chest swelling. I found myself smiling. Tears pooled in
my eyes, but none fell; there was no scrutiny, no resentment, no
anxiety about my career. I was simply a listener, who happened also
to be playing.

Strangely, it was my enjoyment of these concerts that convinced
me to stop performing.

They reminded me of what it had been like to lie under my father's piano—to feel so *full* of a Mozart aria that I couldn't help but
screech it out on the spot, terrible though the sound was. I felt as if
that part of me that was trapped under the rock pile—the one I'd

felt tingling in the Staatsoper and during my late-night listening sessions with Stephan—was now pounding furiously—sending up flares and letting me know it was very much alive and wanting to be let out.

I didn't want to prepare for another audition—to put myself back into that stifling, critical mindset. I didn't want to pit music *against* my life anymore—to worry, with each hour I spent not practicing, about my fingers' conditioning; I wanted to live out the next chapter with music as a part of it.

When I got back from the tour, I put my violin away. I began making lists of all the pieces I wanted my child to hear—listening, as I compiled them, with newfound joy.

I've been listening joyfully ever since.

ACKNOWLEDGMENTS

I wish I could start this off with some kind of quip or another viola joke instead of a heartfelt cliché like "this book is a dream come true for me." But this book *is* a dream come true for me and I'm too grateful to too many people to be coy about it.

It was a dream for me to delve into this music with new purpose and perspective. It was a dream for me to get to discover, in my research, that I live only a few blocks away from the home where Clara Schumann spent her last twenty years. It was a dream for me to comb through dozens of Mozart's letters in the original German, even if they *are* mostly about poop. It's thanks to everyone mentioned here, and their belief in this book, that I've gotten to do all these things—and that I can finally stop feeling like such an asshole for having quit the violin just a few years after graduating from one of the most expensive conservatories in the world on my parents' dollar.

Becky Sweren, who is both the best agent ever and a fierce crusader against the invasion of em dashes that threatens to engulf everything I write, is really The Person Who Made This Book Happen.

Her encouragement, guidance, and crazy agent skills are certainly why I have such an amazing publisher—but they're probably also why this book exists at all. It was through my conversations with her that the idea for this book came into being, and it was her interest in and support for the idea that gave me the confidence to say, "Oh good, I'm not crazy" and move forward. I learned so much from her in the weeks we spent developing our proposal, as I do whenever she comments on anything I've written. Also: she closed our deal with Putnam *the day she gave birth*. So when I say she's the best agent ever, I really mean it. She's also just generally awesome.

I also want to thank Becky's colleagues at Aevitas, particularly Erin Files and Arlie Johansen for their expert handling of the book's foreign rights and Allison Warren and Shenel Ekici-Moling for their fantastic work in the film/TV department.

As for that wonderful publisher I mentioned:

From our very first Zoom meeting back in August 2020, I've felt a festive kind of warmth and enthusiasm from everyone over at Putnam.

My editor, Michelle Howry, brought vision to this project, always with the utmost kindness and consideration for me and my perspective. She encouraged me to put more of myself onto the page—to invest in a way that I now realize I should have done more with the violin—and her masterful assessment of my early drafts spared everyone who's reading this from *pages* of senseless rants and dream summaries (and more rhapsodies about Eric Whitacre's jawline). This book owes its shape—and so much of its soul—to Michelle.

Ashley Di Dio is the patient and very organized shepherd who kept us on track and guided me through the process. She's full of wisdom—like an oracle—and my pilgrimages to her have always yielded the answers I was looking for. She's kind and considerate and efficient—and she has a way of assigning paperwork that makes it impossible for me to resent her for it. (Normally, when people give me forms to fill out, I'm consumed by the desire to incinerate both form and bearer with one of those cartoon incinerators you see in old Looney Tunes sketches.)

I'll also be forever indebted to:

- Sally Kim and Ivan Held, for giving me the opportunity to write this and for making me feel so at home in their imprint.

- My copy editor, Sheila Moody, for grappling with my rambling sentences and playlists filled with annoying catalog numbers and all the em dashes Becky couldn't talk me out of.

- Rob Sternitzky and John McGhee for fixing all the bugs that would have driven me crazy for years to come.

- Emily Mileham, Erin Byrne, Leah Marsh, and Maija Baldauf for taking my manuscript and turning it into an actual *book*.

- Kristin del Rosario, Anthony Ramondo, Vi-An Nguyen, and Tiffany Estreicher for making said book look gorgeous, inside and out. (It really is everything I could have dreamed of.)

- Alexis Welby, Elora Weil, Ellie Schaffer, Shina Patel, Nishtha Patel, and Ashley McClay for their amazing work getting the book to actually sell. Some (less enlightened) imprints won't even touch books about classical music, but you warriors are fearless.

Thank you also to everyone in the legal department (getting sued doesn't sound like very much fun to me)—and to the countless others who were involved in the physical manufacturing and printing of this book.

I am also so very grateful to the brilliant and wonderful Shara

Alexander for joining my team and helping to make my first book launch so magical.

Now for my parents.

Ada Fan and Peter Warsaw gave up half of every weekend and a huge percentage of every paycheck—on top of enduring *hours* of student recitals—so that I could have a career in music. Their sacrifices over the years have been mind-boggling. And when I decided, ultimately, to stop performing, they weren't even mad. Never once did they bring up the cost of my lessons, my instruments, or my multiple tuitions; never once did they complain about the time they'd spent shuttling me around to various appointments and festivals; never once did they ask, as I did myself on so many occasions, *What kind of spoiled, entitled brat* does *that?* Their only concern was my happiness. I poke fun at them a lot in these pages, but I hope they can see that this whole book is really a very long love letter—and homage—to the both of them. It's a tribute to my mother's passion for words and my father's passion for music, as well as physical proof that I was listening to them in their Words and Music course at Andover.

My sister, Marina Warsaw-Fan Bishop, was also a huge inspiration here—as she has been, in general, from the moment she came into this world. Marina and I experienced much of this music together, as kids, and we've spent hours discussing both it and the industry that surrounds it: the good things and the bad things and the beautiful things and the things that aren't necessarily bad but that we nevertheless find difficult or puzzling or frustrating. So many of my thoughts and opinions have been influenced by hers, and so many of my memories of this music are inextricable from the experiences we've shared together.

And of course there are my kids. And Stephan.

Over the past two years, my kids have served as my biggest inspiration and my biggest adversaries. There were times when I was sure they were tiny goblin-agents whose hellish mission was the thwarting of all human productivity. But it was the joy and delight they take in this music—the way their little heads bop along when they hear Mozart—the way their arms wave in the air to Beethoven and Mendelssohn—that fueled me as I wrote, that kept me going through the same fog of sleep deprivation they'd brought upon me.

Anyone who's read this far knows that Stephan Rauch is the absolute light of my life—and also that he was a catalyst for my return to music appreciation. But he was also the first person who supported me in my professional writing endeavors, who saw the possibilities and took them seriously before even I did.

Long before there was interest or money from the world of publishing, he helped me to find regular writing time. He treated it like a proper job when it definitely wasn't one, according it all kinds of respect and status it had yet to earn. I often complain about his lawyer hours, but even in the midst of his weeks and months with a million billable hours, he still made time to read my drafts and provide me with reassurance. Plus, it's really *thanks* to his billable hours that I was able to finish this book at all; if I'd been able to actually *spend time with him*, instead of just sneaking admiring glances at his forehead over our laptops, I might not have had the discipline to work through all those long evenings and nights after the kids were asleep. So thank you, Sullivan & Cromwell, for removing the distraction of my charming and delightful husband.

I also want to thank my aunt and uncle, Linda Fan and Will Schaefer, as well as my cousins Ralph, Fred, and George Schaefer, who have supported me so much over the years and have played such a huge role in shaping my general outlook and perspective on the world. And Francesca Federico, who (luckily for me) married into our family, has served to inspire and advise me—over the years as well as over the course of writing this book. I owe so much to my grandparents, Brynne and Bob Warsaw and Mook-Lan and C. T. Fan, for their encouragement and support and belief. My aunts Wendy Bourland and Robin Warsaw, as well as my uncle John, and my cousins Raina, Caley, Catherine, and Jamie were also hugely influential during my early years of study. And my parents-in-law, Beatrice and Andreas Rauch, whom I know I can always count on, stepped up so many times to babysit and help me meet my deadlines.

There are also my friends.

I grew up with the idea that friends were a distraction: that the time I spent with them was detrimental to my career. But without friends, this book wouldn't exist.

I've said that Becky Sweren was the one who made this book happen—and that's true. But I never would have met Becky if Nicole Clarke, in her infinite and bizarrely effortless kindness, hadn't introduced me to her. It was in the striplinghood of our friendship, when she had no obligation to offer her help—but she did, anyway, brushing aside my "Please don't go to any trouble" with a breezy "No, it really is *that* easy." Her help turned out to be transformative. I'd call her my fairy godmother (she could definitely whip me up a jaw-dropping ball gown in a matter of minutes) if that didn't make her sound kind of old and bland and like an extension of me rather than the brilliant, gorgeous, hilarious, craft-happy, mad-but-meticulous-science-genius that she is. I will never be able to thank her enough for her automatic, entirely uncalculating generosity—in this and all things. Nor can I ever repay the hours of support and nerve-calming she's provided—or that emergency lifeline to her German teacher, Violetta Krok, one afternoon when I encountered a bizarre and archaic phrase in one of Mozart's letters.

I'd also like to thank Jordan Weissmann, whose sudden and unexpected enthusiasm for Brahms back in January 2020 was one of the inspirations that drove me during my earliest brainstorming sessions.

And I really can't go any further before I extend a big thank-you (and an IOU) to Golden Violin Boy. I never planned to throw him under the bus, but I know I kind of did and I'm extremely grateful to him for his support and understanding. You're a good sport, GVB, and I'm glad we've remained friends.

Meta Weiss has been a major influence and constant source of inspiration from our first meeting at Andover to our days at Juilliard and throughout our many concert tours. She was responsible for an extremely high percentage of the laughter and joy I experienced during my performing career—and also during my life so far. I owe her parents, Juli and Larry, almost as much as I owe my own parents—and Aliya has rescued me from at least two major catastrophes, either of which could have easily put me in therapy for life.

The Wong-Changs and Chang-Gordons—Lisa and Lynn, Jenn and Solon and Chris—were also like long-lost and uniquely helpful family members—as were Peter, Susan, Pippa, and Gordon Jarvis. The Hornor-Mas were also a source of support and (this probably goes without saying) inspiration, and their graduation gift to me—that beautiful pen—showed remarkable prescience.

Now for Sol Jin. Between the book and the kids and the various lockdowns and having a husband I only time-share with S&C, I often felt, over the past two years, like I was drowning. During her visits to Frankfurt, Sol used her precious free time between high-powered finance-y calls (and whatever other impressive things investment bankers do) to watch my kids while I escaped to write. She also did my dishes (despite my protestations) and folded my family's laundry, which . . . I still can't really talk about without crying.

Rachelle Hunt was an incredible resource and help, serving as reference, fact-checker, and one of my only readers during the writing process. She also gave me Lorene To, the wonderful photographer who took my author photo.

I have to extend a particular thanks to both Florian Leonhard and Carlos Tome, who allowed me to pick their brains, quote them, and generally benefit from their expertise. I'm likewise grateful to my other friends and former colleagues who were there for me for help and consults: Moky Gibson-Lane, Jenn Chang, Arthur Moeller, Jennifer Christen, Mike Martin, and Simon Gonzalez, to name only a few.

Henry Kramer, Daniel Harding, Elena Urioste, and Gity Razaz, along with David Requiro and the aforementioned Meta Weiss, not only provided valuable insight but also compelled me, through their general awesomeness, to fight for our industry.

Carl Johnson, whose help has been the most unexpected and angelic gift, has provided me with crucial and meaningful research—and spared me (and my dad) from years of self-doubt and what-ifs.

I was unbelievably fortunate, in my formative years, to have a steady stream of wonderful teachers and mentors to guide me. All of my violin teachers—even those I sometimes whine about—were responsible for the perseverance and drive I've needed so much, so often in my life. Nancy Miller, Mark Smith, Magdalena Richter, Lynn Chang, Almita and Roland Vamos, Masao Kawasaki, and Cho-Liang Lin: I am grateful to and terribly fond of all of you.

My earliest music mentors were William Thomas, Chris Walter, Peter Lorenzo, Hilary and Duncan Cumming, Elizabeth Aureden, Holly Barnes, Tess Remy-Shumacher, Judy Lee, and the rest of the Phillips Academy music department, as well as Jean and David Layzer and Mimi Bravar. I will be forever beholden to Rex and his family.

At Juilliard, I was fortunate enough to receive guidance from Barli Nugent and Bill Baker, as well as a series of incredible coaches, including Joseph Kalichstein and Ronald Copes. These wonderful people, along with many others, helped safeguard my love of music from the unstoppable march of my ego, ensuring that it was intact when I rediscovered it all those years later. In Paul Gridley, who was introduced to me through the school, I found not only a generous benefactor but a kindred spirit and an inspiring example of genuine musical appreciation. I also owe Juilliard for connecting me with Elizabeth Caitlin Ward and Roderick Hill, whom I will always cherish.

This book is also the direct result of those mentors and spirit guides who influenced and recognized my passion for writing at various crucial times in my life. My fourth-grade teacher Mrs. Wu sowed the first seeds of confidence in my metaphorical literary garden when she arranged to have one of my poems published in a collection of children's poetry. Mary Fulton's writing assignments at Andover showed me how fun this line of work could be—and I'm still trying to validate the encouragement and belief she extended to me then. Music management legends Jasper Parrott and Charles Letourneau fostered my grown-up writing efforts, taking time, in the midst of their impossibly busy schedules, to read my earliest experiments.

Even with all of this support, I likely would have given up on the idea of writing had it not been for certain editors and writers, who encouraged and put their faith in me as I took my first professional writing steps: Annie Lowrey, Faran Krentcil, Elizabeth Bruenig, Rachel Krantz, Ej Dickson, Nicholas Litchfield, Dan Geddes, Sam Adams, and whichever *New Yorker* staff editor responded to my 2013 "Shouts & Murmurs" submission, explaining that they would not be accepting my piece about a pile of croissants I found in Berlin one morning "despite its evident merit." All I took away from that email was that my piece had merit.

There are also a few more general mentors and guides I have to mention here—because without them I likely would have perished in the wild long ago. Ann Williams, among her many acts of support and generosity, flew to Chicago and moved me into my dorm room at Northwestern when my parents couldn't get away for the start of term. Carol Israel, my Andover adviser, coached me through countless challenges and dilemmas, and showed me a new level of self-reflection and analysis. Rebecca and Elwin Sykes have been the most wonderful and inspiring exemplars and have influenced me in countless ways. And in fact, Phillips Academy's entire faculty and staff—and student body—played a crucial role in my upbringing and evolution.

Lorraine Ferguson and Adam Weinberg's support began at Andover but carried on through my adult years, culminating in the unbelievably magnanimous gift of sharing their home and mailing address with me when I had no base of operations. (I think I still have your spare key, but I really do promise to give it back one day.)

Brian Dawe certainly deserves a thank-you for his general presence, influence, and challenging charades clues. Also for his cakes. (Though it's been a long time since I got one of those.)

I feel the need to apologize to and acknowledge the understanding of several people mentioned in this book. Eric Whitacre, for one. (I respect you as a composer—not just as a source of physical beauty.) And conductors in general. (You're not all bad.) And a few of my exes. (Neither are you.)

Caitlin's mother is also likely less evil than my memory of her suggests.

I also owe a debt of gratitude to the great minds and characters who have inspired me: writers like P. G. Wodehouse and Phoebe Waller-Bridge and Steve Kluger; musical comedians like Victor Borge, Jack Benny, and Igudesman & Joo; innovative artists like Karim Sulayman, J'Nai Bridges, Yuja Wang, Sheku Kanneh-Mason, Tom Poster, and Elena Urioste (again), who have shown us all the way classical music *should* be. And to those authors, like Dan Brown and Henry James, who kept me company on so many a solo tour or competition trip, easing my loneliness and the sting of elimination.

I'll never forget Michael Parloff's rousing and inspiring 2019 talk at the University Club—or the student who gave that lecture on Shostakovich's String Quartet No. 8 at Weathersfield back when I was thirteen. I don't remember your name, but your talk showed me the power of historical and stylistic knowledge in the context of musical performance and listening.

I, personally, will always be grateful to all of these people. But this book would still be nothing more than a very fancy fire starter (or broth base, if you're *Game of Thrones*'s Stannis Baratheon) if it weren't for two final, crucial groups:

- The generations of composers who spent their lives in the service of music—who passed on so many hours of transporting beauty and eloquence to the rest of us.

- And you—the person reading this. Thank you for this dream.

ONE MORE VIOLA JOKE

This is my favorite viola joke. It was told to me by Philip Setzer, founding member of the renowned Emerson String Quartet:

An orchestra found themselves in need of a new principal violist. They advertised the position and were flooded with applications from all around the country. After sorting through the various résumés, they invited a handful of players to their audition—and after four grueling rounds, they emerged with a winner.

The orchestral manager brought him into the hall, where the entire viola section was waiting to greet him.

"We'd like to offer you the job," the manager explained delicately. "But because of a few things that have happened in the past, we have to administer a brief intelligence test before we can make it official. It's very easy."

"Go ahead," said the violist.

The manager looked down at her clipboard.

"What's three times six?" she asked.

The violist looked anxious.

"Take your time," the manager said and smiled.

The violist looked down at his fingers, twisting his mouth.

"Is it . . ." He paused, recalculating. "Is it sixteen?"

The manager frowned and shook her head.

"I'm sorry. We really liked you for the position, but unfortunately—"

"GIVE HIM ANOTHER CHANCE!" cheered the viola section.

The manager nodded reluctantly.

"All right," she agreed. "We'll try another. What's seven plus eight?"

The violist looked down at his hands again. He curled his fingers, counting.

"Is it . . . thirteen?" he asked.

The manager frowned again.

"I really am sorry," she said. "Again, we would have loved to have you, but—"

"GIVE HIM ANOTHER CHANCE!" cheered the viola section.

The manager hesitated, then took a deep breath.

"Fine," she said. "Last chance. What's two plus two?"

The violist looked down at his hands for the last time, his brow furrowed.

Several minutes elapsed.

"Is it . . . four?" he asked finally.

The manager looked up in surprise.

"GIVE HIM ANOTHER CHANCE!" cheered the viola section.

GLOSSARY

ATONAL: Atonal music is music that is not considered "tonal." Generally, it sounds more discordant and less centered than tonal music. There are different types of atonality—some where all the notes flourish equally in a hippie commune of dissonance and chromaticism and others where the notes adhere to a different method of organization—but all you really need to know for now is that your ears are likely to perceive atonal music as less harmonious and hummable than anything we define as "tonal."

CADENCE: A cadence is the harmonic resolution at the end of a phrase or movement or work. And in case that was confusing, you can leave out the words "the harmonic resolution at" from the last sentence. There are different types of cadences. A "perfect authentic cadence" is the one you'll hear at the end of most classical pieces and a "plagal cadence" is the one that scores the "Amen" at the end of hymns and a "deceptive cadence" (which is one of my very favorite things in the world) is one that *sounds* like it's going to end but then takes you somewhere else instead. There are more types of cadences, but these are the most interesting ones.

CANTATA: A work composed for voice (generally soloists and choir) *and* orchestral or instrumental accompaniment. Most of the cantatas you'll hear today were composed by Bach.

CAPRICE: Most commonly, caprices are short, virtuosic pieces filled with party tricks that range in difficulty from "Hey, look, I found this coin behind your ear" to "Watch closely as I get sawed in half—literally, by a surgeon, because this piece is so hard I'm having a heart attack."

CHANSON: "Song," in French. (And also a song in French.)

CHARACTER PIECE: A short composition that tends to prioritize mood or character over structural complexity or ambition. Types of character pieces include intermezzos, impromptus, rhapsodies, berceuses, nocturnes, waltzes, and so on. The ones that are performed now are almost universally pleasant—and they're often used as encores. Chopin wrote a lot of them.

CHROMATIC: A chromatic scale is one that moves stepwise through all twelve semitones (or half-steps) rather than the seven-note scales (that mostly ascend or descend by whole step) used in tonal and modal music. When we speak of "chromatic" music—and keep in mind that there are degrees of chromaticism—what we mean is that the music is flush with semitones that do not adhere to a seven-note diatonic scale. (I'll explain what that is later, but basically it's what you think of automatically when you hear the word "scale.") Chromaticism is relative. Arnold Schoenberg's 20th-Century twelve-tone music is chromatic, but Mozart's music was also considered chromatic for his time.

CODA: The metaphorical "tail" of a piece, when it's (*a*) recognizably separate from what came before and (*b*) clearly in the process of ending. This glossary is a bit like a coda.

CONSONANT: Think "Taps." Taps is an entirely consonant piece. There is generally little to no tension in a consonant piece or chord or moment of music. And when there *is* passing dissonance, it always *wants* to resolve to consonance.

COUNTERPOINT: The combining of two distinct voices that complement and complete each other harmonically while maintaining rhythmic independence. It's like a super busy but also completely fulfilled and in sync modern power couple.

DIATONIC: It's pronounced the way you'd say "diet tonic" if you were ordering one really quickly in a bar, which is funny because a diatonic scale, with its trimmed-down note-count, is a bit like a chromatic scale that's gone on a diet. It consists of seven notes (instead of the chromatic scale's twelve notes), and it forms the basis for tonal harmonies. (Diatonic music refers to tonality, and diatonic scales, as mentioned in our discussion of chromaticism, are the ones you're most accustomed to hearing.)

DISSONANT: Clashing, in a harmonic sense. If you were to sit on the keyboard of a piano, you'd create something dissonant. Unless you happened to have a very uniquely shaped butt and you set it down in exactly the right spot. Dissonance can be used in different ways. It's true that playing the piano with your butt would create a very dissonant sound. But generally, dissonance is used sparingly, in passing; it's a necessary part of nearly every piece of music ever written. (Even "Row, Row, Row Your Boat" and "Three Blind Mice" have passing tones, which are a form of dissonance.)

DIVERTIMENTO: A diverting ("amusing") piece constructed of multiple movements, created (generally) to entertain and accompany rather than to captivate or inspire.

DYNAMICS/DYNAMIC RANGE: It's more subtle than this, but in its most basic definition, dynamics determine how loud or soft the music is. Forte (f), fortissimo (ff), and fortississimo (fff) are the standard terms used to direct musicians to play loudly (or "with force," if you're one of those players who prefers not to use the word "loud"), and piano (*p*), pianissimo (*pp*), and pianississimo (*ppp*) are the most common shushing commands. There are also mezzo-fortes (*mf*) and mezzo-pianos (*mp*), which are moderately forte and piano, respectively. A crescendo, which is another dynamic marking, indicates an increase in volume and intensity, and a diminuendo indicates a *decrease* in volume and intensity. You don't really need to know those, but . . . now you do.

EMBELLISHMENT/ORNAMENT: Decorative notes added to the music, generally at the performer's discretion. Ornamentation can be as simple as a short grace note or as complicated as a rewritten phrase in the repeated A section of an aria.

ETUDE: A piece of music designed to teach or target a specific aspect of technique (either compositional or instrumental). If "exercises" are the musical equivalents of push-ups and squats, etudes, which tend to be prettier and more musical, are closer to a dance workout routine. Generally, etudes are not performed publicly, but Chopin's etudes are an exception, as are Debussy's.

FUGUE: Musical fugues have nothing to do with dissociative fugues—except, perhaps, that the thought of performing one from memory is enough to send me into a fugue state. Fugues are intricately structured, contrapuntal compositions that weave a single theme throughout multiple voices of a work. The theme can appear at both the micro and the macro level, in various incarnations (though usually recognizably). They're very cool on an intellectual level, and they tend to *sound* very cool, too. They're very hard to memorize.

INTERVAL: The distance between two notes, as measured by notes in a scale. A second is an interval in which the two notes involved are next to each other; a third is an interval in which you skip one note in between; and so on and so forth all the way up to an octave (which returns us to the same frequency, only a higher or lower version of it).

KEY: In a piece entitled "Sonata No. 2 in Blah Major," "Blah Major" is the key and "blah" is the note the piece will probably end on and begin with. This is because "blah" is the tonic—the note we can't wait to get home to whenever we stray from it. The scale that's built on the tonic (it can be major or minor, which is usually specified) provides the language—or alphabet—of the composition. Have you ever designed a website using Wix or any similarly user-friendly design platform that gives you color themes so that regardless of which individual shades you pick, your site will come out looking (relatively) cohesive? A key is kind of like that except with notes.

LARGO: This is a tempo marking, so it really belongs with the *other* tempo markings (below, where it says "tempo markings"), but we're here today because I really wanted to put the word *Largo* after the word *Key*. And while we're at it, *largo* means "broad," which musicians usually interpret as "slow."

LIBRETTO: The script of an opera, often written by a librettist rather than the composer.

LIED: *Lied* (pronounced "leed") is the German word for "song." *Lieder* (the plural form, pronounced "leeder"—or, if you want to sound German: "leedair" with a British accent) often appear as part of a song cycle (set of songs).

MAJOR/MINOR: The accepted description is that "major" sounds happy or placid and "minor" sounds sad or angry. This is an oversimplification, but it's also true. The difference between major and minor lies in the third note of a scale, which is a half-step higher in a major scale than it is in a minor one. This also means that in major, the tonic ("home") chord features a major third on the bottom, while in minor, the tonic chord is built on a minor third. This difference of a half-step, small though it is, defines the mood—the sound world—of the composition. Cole Porter aptly alludes to this difference in his song "Ev'ry Time We Say Goodbye." It's important to note that minor pieces (in the classical repertoire) do not stay in minor for the duration—nor do major pieces stay in major. There are frequent shifts and visits (sometimes for whole movements) to other keys, which is one of the things that makes classical music so complex and fulfilling. There's nothing quite like a shift from minor to major to get the goose bumps going.

MASS: Generally, a mass is a composition for vocalists (soloists and choir) and orchestra that follows the traditional Catholic or Eucharistic liturgy, containing a Kyrie, Gloria, Credo, Sanctus, Agnus Dei, and so forth. Bach wrote a lot of them.

MINUET: Originally a dance, a minuet takes the time signature $(\frac{3}{4})$ and feel of the dance and turns it into a movement. Generally, minuets (which are very simple in form) are accompanied by contrasting middle sections called trios, which serve as the pastrami (or buffalo mozzarella and veggies) between the bread that is the minuet part.

MODAL: Technically, modal music falls under the umbrella of tonal music—because it has a tonal center—and tonal music, because of the misshapenly broad, multilevel definitions of both terms, also falls under the umbrella of modal music. But when we in the industry say that something is "modal," we are generally *distinguishing* it from tonal music. Modal, in this sense, refers to the fact that it makes use of one of the established "modes"—or scales—which are different from the scales used in tonal music because they sound super creepy. (By the way, when I, as an individual, say that something is "modal," I'm also distinguishing it from music that I like.)

MODULATION: The act of shifting to a new key.

MOTIF: A figure, usually shorter than a theme; a musical idea.

ORATORIO: Oratorios are similar to masses, only longer and less prescribed in structure. Think of them as operas based on biblical stories without costumes or staging.

OVERTURE: An overture is the opening of an opera, which is performed by the orchestra alone (generally before the singers even appear onstage). Their function is to give an overview of the opera's thematic material, which means they're a bit like medleys in form. They're often performed alone to kick off symphony programs.

PHRASE: A musical sentence, ending in some kind of a cadence.

PRELUDE: Any kind of musical introduction.

REQUIEM: A mass for the dead.

SCHERZO: Literally translated as "joke," a scherzo is a light, quick-paced, playful movement that falls in the middle of a longer work (generally third in a four-movement piece). It's in the same category as a minuet (you wouldn't expect to find both a minuet and a scherzo in the same piece—it would likely be one or the other) and it shares the same sandwich form, incorporating a contrasting trio and returning to the scherzo to finish.

SERENADE: When we speak of "serenading" a person, it's a reference to the form's origins as a courtship song, but it became synonymous with the divertimento or suite: a piece for entertainment value (probably to be played in the background).

SONATA: A piece that's generally written for one or two instruments (the piano is a usual suspect) comprising multiple (two to four) movements. No vocalists allowed.

SONG CYCLE: A set of songs intended to be performed together to paint a larger musical and thematic picture. It should also be an exercise bike—like a Peloton—that serenades you while you exercise.

SUITE: A piece made up of shorter movements. In the Baroque period, each of these was generally inspired by a dance, with movements like *allemande*, *courante*, *gigue*, and so on. In later years, however, the dance associations were dropped. A suite can also be a shortened, symphonic version of a ballet. For instance, Tchaikovsky's

Nutcracker Suite and Ravel's *Daphnis et Chloé*, Suite No. 2, are like best-ofs of the original ballets.

SYMPHONY: Definition 1—a multi-movement work for full symphony orchestra, one or more of which is generally in sonata form.

Definition 2—a "full" orchestral ensemble, as defined by the period of the music being performed.

TEMPO: The speed and sometimes correlating character of a piece. Here's a list of common tempos (or tempi—but the same rules of friendlessness apply), with descriptions, at the end of which you will basically speak Italian.

Grave—heavy, serious

Largo—broad

Lento—slow

Adagio—slowly, gently

Andante—flowing, walking

Moderato—moderate, tempered

Allegro—bright, cheerful (we generally accept that it also means "fast," but there are people who will hate me for saying it)

Vivace—lively, vivacious

Presto—quickly

The words *assai* and *molto* are often used as modifiers to mean "very" (so *Allegro assai* is "very bright and cheerful") and you also see *moderato* used in a similar way, to achieve the opposite (moderating) effect. (So *Allegro moderato*, then, is like if you're happy about something but you also only got three hours of sleep the night before.) The suffixes "-etto" and "-ino" also have a moderating effect—while the suffix "-issimo" is much like *assai* and *molto*, intensifying the marking to which it's applied. (*Larghetto* is less slow than *Largo*, while *Larghissimo* is slower.)

With most movements, their names and tempo markings are one and the same.

THEME: A theme, in music, is a complete thought, generally composed of one or more phrases. (My dad says it's two or more, but he can write his own book.)

TIME SIGNATURE: The symbol, in a score, that shows you how many beats there are per measure. This affects the lilt and feel of the entire piece. Waltzes, for instance, are always in $\frac{3}{4}$ time, and marches in $\frac{2}{4}$, and the theme from *Mission Impossible* is in $\frac{5}{4}$.

TONAL: Tonality is what most people naturally associate with classical music—and most pop music, as well. It's what our ears (in the year 2022) are most accustomed to hearing. What "tonal" *means*, though, is: adhering to an organized system of scales and chords in which every sonority, on every harmonic level, is defined by its relationship to the tonic—the notes in the scale, the harmonies they create, the shape of each phrase and the piece as a whole. Everything pulls toward or away from it, and everything will find a way to return to it in the end.

WORDS TO SHOUT AT A CONCERT

BRAVO: "Woohoo!" (for a man)

BRAVA: "Woohoo!" (for a woman)

BRAVI: "Woohoo!" (for multiple people—or a person whose preferred pronoun is "they")

BRAVI TUTTI: "Woohoo to all"

ENCORE: "Again!"

WOOHOO!: What I (and most musicians I know) say instead of Bravo/Brava/Bravi/Bravi tutti

WORDS TO SHOW OFF WITH

CONTRAPUNTAL: Utilizing counterpoint (which, as you already know, is the combining of two distinct voices that complement and complete one another harmonically while maintaining rhythmic independence).

CYCLIC: A work is "cyclic" if it uses a theme to unify multiple sections or segments. Most often, the theme will occur at the beginning of a piece and then return at the end in order to make you cry.

IDÉE FIXE: A motif or pattern of notes that appears repeatedly throughout a piece, sometimes serving as the source material for the entire work. Hector Berlioz is generally cited for having used the term, early on, in his *Symphonie fantastique*, although Honoré de Balzac also refers to the idée fixe (as a haunting thought or obsession) in *Gobseck*, which was written in the same year (1830).

LEITMOTIF: This is similar to an idée fixe in the sense that it's a theme (or theme fragment) that returns throughout a larger work, but in this case it's always linked to a specific character or event or feeling. It appears most often in opera, but there are plenty of examples of it in other compositions—like video game and film scores.

POTENTIAL MISUNDERSTANDINGS

FAGOTT/FAGOTTO: "bassoon" in German and Italian, respectively
RITARDANDO: a slowing of pace or gradual halting of momentum

BIBLIOGRAPHY

Avins, Styra, comp. *Johannes Brahms: Life and Letters.* Translated by Josef Eisinger and Styra Avins. New York: Oxford, 1997.

Conway, David. *Jewry in Music: Entry to the Profession from the Enlightenment to Richard Wagner.* New York: Cambridge University Press, 2012.

Debussy, Claude. *Lettres de Claude Debussy à son éditeur.* Compiled by Jacques Durand. Paris: Durand, 1927.

Holden, Anthony. *Tchaikovsky: A Biography.* New York: Random House, 1995.

Klassen, Janina. *Clara Wieck-Schumann: Die Virtuosin als Komponistin.* Kassel; New York: Bärenreiter, 1990.

Kostalevsky, Marina, ed. *The Tchaikovsky Papers: Unlocking the Family Archive.* Translated by Stephen Pearl. Adapted from the Russian edition, compiled, and edited by Polina E. Vaidman. New Haven, CT: Yale University Press, 2018.

Krausnick, Michail. *Du bist mir so unendlich lieb* [You are so infinitely dear to me]. 3rd ed. Mannheim: Wellhöfer, 2017.

Ostwald, Peter. *Schumann: The Inner Voices of a Musical Genius.* Boston: Northeastern University Press, 1985.

Poznansky, Alexander. *Tchaikovsky: The Quest for the Inner Man.* New York: Schirmer Books, 1991.

Rimsky-Korsakov, Nikolay. *My Musical Life.* 3rd ed. Translated by Judah Joffe. New York: Knopf, 1942.

Shaffer, Peter. Preface to *Amadeus: A Play.* Harmondsworth, UK: Penguin, 1985.

Stiftung Mozarteum Salzburg und Packard Humanities Institute, ed. "Mozart Briefe und Dokumente—Online-Edition." 2006 ff. https://dme.mozarteum.at/DME/briefe/doclist.php.

Tchaikovsky Research Project, ed. Works, letters, and diaries. 2006 ff. https://en.tchaikovsky-research.net/pages/Project:Tchaikovsky_Research.

Warrack, John. *Tchaikovsky.* London: Hamish Hamilton, 1973.

INDEX